CONTEMPORARY INDIA

Contemporary India: The Basics provides readers with a clear and accessible guide through the richness, diversity, and complexity of twenty-first century India. It explores the reality of the country's cultural diversity which creates both harmony and tension. Covering issues the country faces both domestically and on the global stage, this book analyzes the political, social, cultural, and economic landscape of India and investigates how the future might look for India. The book addresses key questions such as:

- How has India risen to be a major economic power?
- What role does sectarianism play in the world's largest democracy?
- How do caste and gender affect the structure of Indian society?
- What is the domestic and international impact of Bollywood?

Featuring maps, discussion questions, and suggestions for further reading, this is the ideal introduction to India for those who are new to the study of this most fascinating and complex of countries.

Rekha Datta is Professor of Political Science at Monmouth University in New Jersey, USA. She is a Fulbright U.S. Scholar, the recipient of a Fulbright-Nehru Academic and Professional Excellence Award in Teaching and Research.

The Basics

For a full list of titles in this series, please visit www.routledge.com/
The-Basics/book-series/B

Research Methods
Nigel Edley

Semiotics
Daniel Chandler

Special Educational Needs and Disability (second edition)
Janice Wearmouth

Sport Management
Robert Wilson and Mark Piekarz

Sports Coaching
Laura Purdy

Translation
Juliane House

Contemporary India
Rekha Datta

CONTEMPORARY INDIA

The Basics

Rekha Datta

Routledge
Taylor & Francis Group

LONDON AND NEW YORK

First published 2018
by Routledge
2 Park Square, Milton Park, Abingdon, Oxon OX14 4RN

and by Routledge
711 Third Avenue, New York, NY 10017

Routledge is an imprint of the Taylor & Francis Group, an informa business

Cover image: The River Ganga (Ganges) flows through several states in India, covering India's past, present, and future. Between religious significance, commerce, politics, and pollution, the Ganga is a reminder of change and continuity in contemporary India. The Namami Ganga Project of 2014 is a national initiative to restore the Ganga to its purity and beauty. Pictured here is the banks of the Ganga near the Dakshinweswar Temple in Kolkata. Photo: Amrita Mazumdar

British Library Cataloguing-in-Publication Data
A catalogue record for this book is available from the British Library

Library of Congress Cataloging-in-Publication Data
Names: Datta, Rekha, author.
Title: Contemporary India / Rekha Datta.
Description: Abingdon, Oxon; New York, NY: Routledge is an
    imprint of the Taylor & Francis Group, an Informa Business,
    [2018] | Series: The basics | Includes bibliographical references
    and index.
Identifiers: LCCN 2017030973 | ISBN 9780415841559 (hbk) |
    ISBN 9780415841566 (pbk) | ISBN 9780203705254 (ebk)
Subjects: LCSH: India—History—21st century.
Classification: LCC DS480.853.D3827 2018 |
    DDC 954.05/3—dc23
LC record available at https://lccn.loc.gov/2017030973

ISBN: 978-0-415-84155-9 (hbk)
ISBN: 978-0-415-84156-6 (pbk)
ISBN: 978-0-203-70525-4 (ebk)

Typeset in Bembo
by Apex CoVantage, LLC

For:

The 1.3 billion people of India, especially the youth
of the country, who are the torchbearers of the largest
democracy in the world.

My students, who taught me to look at contemporary
India from a whole new perspective.

The loving memory of my eldest brother, Asok Datta,
the dawn's child, who breathed for the first time as
the day broke on India's freedom in 1948, and for the
last time this month, as democratic India prepares
to turn 70, embodying the challenges and hopes of a
generation and others to follow.

Rekha Datta

June 2017

CONTENTS

ILLUSTRATIONS

Figures

Tables

Photographs

PREFACE AND
ACKNOWLEDGMENTS

Writing about India is both exciting and challenging. The prospect of writing a Basic Book on contemporary India was both of these and more. As I undertook the project, I encountered some usual, and some unusual, challenges. Indeed, I was excited about the project. The excitement of writing about one of the most fascinating countries of the world – a country that I was born and raised in, and have maintained close contact with since I moved to the United States – can hardly be expressed in words. I was also filled with apprehension. The understandable apprehension came with the thought of writing about a country, the scholarship on which is as rich and deep as its historical and contemporary reality. It was also about trying to encapsulate a fascinating, complex, often paradoxical reality that is India, with its contemporary society and politics deeply rooted in its mixed historical past, and yearning to break free into a new world of economic prosperity and attain a major power status. Most of all, I felt that the story of India never ends. Hence, what is captured in the book is merely an attempt to tell a story that is filled with complexity, paradoxical puzzles, and remarkable resilience, and which does not have an ending.

The enormity of the task was also deeply humbling. There are few things in this world as awe-inspiring, fascinating, and humbling as India's cultural and socio-political history. Coupled with the complexities surrounding the genesis and impact of India's rising economic and military capability on the country and its neighbors, the task of capturing all this in a short volume seeking to offer a basic understanding of contemporary India became even more daunting. While attempting to understand India's multifaceted prospects and challenges as a rising power, the realization that one comes to is that India is 'rising' on many scores, including economic well-being of millions, increasing literacy levels, and women's empowerment. These are coupled with growing class divisions, millions of children still dropping out of school beyond the primary levels, and a disturbing rise in rates and forms of sex- and gender-based violence – so much so that one realizes that there are not one or two but indeed many Indias, and it is more than a truism. Perhaps this is what makes India so fascinating and perplexing. Presenting this complex reality as a Basic Book, which would open the gates to understanding India for the first timer, and capturing the complexities and the rich contribution of scholarship on India was also a challenge. I chose to keep the book more as a narrative and an overview, and I hope that the curious reader will venture into the more nuanced analyses of the facets of India that make it so intriguing.

Alongside such realization, it is also humbling to experience the resilience of more than 1.2 billion people, many of whom are welcoming and rejoicing the country's economic boom and enjoying a lifestyle that includes visits to newly spurred shopping malls and restaurant chains such as McDonald's and Kentucky Fried Chicken, supplanted with employment in information-technology-related sectors. Yet others continue their lives in slums and streets, or in modest housing. Scenes of everyday life in India capture the coexistence of these different Indias. Some of the remnants of deep discrimination embedded in the caste system raise their ugly head from time to time, as with the cow protection vigilantes and the violence they have sown on people suspected of consuming beef. However, the country is also seeing people rise up recently against such atrocities. In the state of Gujarat, for example, which has seen Hindu-Muslim violence in recent years, in response to such atrocities, lower castes, some considered 'Untouchables' or *Dalits* (oppressed) have been refusing to remove carcasses of dead cows, which, according to the caste system, only those from the *Chamar* caste (*Dalits*) are expected to undertake. They are beginning to demonstrate how their protest can bring things to a halt, and also forcing the government to investigate such actions. But at a deeper level, this must come as a sobering message to those who are challenging India's secular identity by attempting to perpetuate identity politics fomented by the rise in popularity of a rightist Hindu party. Such sentiments are also spilling over to hostilities with Pakistan. However, as events in the fall of 2016 have shown, even as Pakistan has challenged with incursions into the Uri region causing casualties on the Indian side, the Indian government responded with a limited, targeted surgical strike. Such an action by the government is based perhaps on the dual reality that India does not want to escalate conflict with Pakistan, but neither does it want to send the message that it is not willing to act, if pushed. Furthermore, such action on the part of the Indian government will undoubtedly calm the nerves of those in India who are resorting to jingoistic rhetoric against Pakistan with possible spillover onto Hindu-Muslim relations within the country.

They say it takes a village to raise a child. It is no different when it comes to writing a book. I have benefitted from numerous people who helped me in the process of taking the project from conceptualization to fruition. The editorial staff at Routledge has shown patience and understanding, and has guided me through the numerous questions I had, ranging from data, copyright, formatting, and others. Andrew Humprheys, Dorothea Schaeffer, Lily Brown, and many others have provided prompt and supportive assistance throughout the process. Their professionalism, expertise, and courtesy have given me hope for the completion of the project. The anonymous reviewers who took the time and provided detailed suggestions to improve the manuscript will always have my utmost gratitude. I was fortunate to have the opportunity to take their critique to help address various shortcomings of the book. Heather Mistretta – with her experience, keen eye, and patience – has helped me with editing and friendly advice on stylistic improvement of the manuscript. I humbly acknowledge that many weaknesses persist, and, for all errors and omissions, my effort will be to address and improve upon them in the future.

I thank Monmouth University for a summer faculty fellowship and time to devote to the project. The Monmouth University Library remains a steadfast pillar, and I owe much debt to my colleagues at the library. Sherry Xie of the Interlibrary Loan office secured promptly numerous books and articles that were not available in the library holdings and worked with me so I could use these resources effectively. Dena Massa of Circulation always greeted me with encouraging words and offered support whenever I needed it, as did Susan Bucks, working with me to retrieve print sources of rare journal articles. Eleonora Dubicki worked with me on data sources and provided valuable assistance on reference materials. The library also offered me dedicated and secluded space to work, an invaluable resource when I needed to go into hiding away from my office in order to write.

Gregory Woolston's creative cartographical skills in the creation of the maps have enriched the book. I am also indebted to him for assistance with diagrams and charts. Jessica Moise and Benjamin Smith, graduate assistants from the Master of Arts program in Public Policy (MAPP) program at Monmouth University, helped me with census figures and datasets for various chapters. I thank Professors Betty Hanson, Rakhahari Chatterji, Bandana Chatterji, and Manabi Majumdar for reviewing draft chapters. I have benefitted from the input and discussions about India's persistent development and democratic challenges from my friends, colleagues, professors, and mentors. In addition, I have learned much from the insights of scholars and teachers about India, the developing world, and international relations in general – I thank them all. While I have learned much from many, I am still a curious student, aspiring to hone my skills as a researcher and writer. My students have provided me with keen and interesting insights, which have helped me to look at India from different perspectives. My colleagues in the Department of Political Science and Sociology give me intellectual and collegial support to flourish and survive the challenges, setbacks, and vagaries in the political and professional worlds with friendship, perspective, and humor. To reiterate, for all the limitations, errors, and inadvertent omissions in the book, including those in my acknowledgements, I take sole responsibility.

I thank Amrita Mazumdar, Gregory Woolston, and Dr. Richard Veit for permitting me to use some of the pictures from their recent trips to India. Asani Sarkar was generous with his attempts to help me secure media footage. The pictures provide a visual sampling of contemporary India that has kept the democratic vivacity of its people, amidst the colorful chaos of a diverse culture, desperately trying to shine and rise, but also survive, under the shadow of the splendor of its past, and highways to the future.

Finally, I am fortunate and blessed to have numerous supportive friends and family in India and abroad, and their inspiration. My daughter Amrita and my husband Subrata continue to be my steadfast rocks to anchor me during calm and bumpy rides of work and life. I am also fortunate and blessed to have this opportunity to reflect on India, combining the perspectives of an insider and an outsider, attempting to capture and rejoice in its color, complexity, cadence, and chaos. Professor Betty Hanson captured the essence of India beautifully when she said during a recent visit, "Compared to India, every other place in the world is boring."

1
INTRODUCTION

Prologue

"India is a country where women wear beautiful, long-flowing colorful clothes. . . . I don't know what they are called, but they are very pretty." This is how a little girl described India to me during a recent discussion session I had with a group of elementary school children on Gandhi, as part of a summer enrichment program for children in an urban area that faces widespread street and domestic violence. In addition, snakes and tigers still dominate their image of India, they said. Their evening sessions always begin with a half-hour devoted to yoga and meditation, an effort on the part of the organizers to use the power of mind-body connection to help the children focus and calm their minds.

Having been born and raised in India, as an educator who has championed global understanding as a fundamental aspect of peace and respect for diverse cultures and for people around the world, I could not but feel proud of how far the contributions of India have come and continue to grow in the contemporary world – yoga and Gandhi still made a lot of sense! As I drove home after the session, a host of questions that I have fielded over the three decades while living in the United States – ranging from whether people still worship cows, why there are so many poor people in India, if I had left India to escape dowry, why women are discriminated against despite the fact that the country has had a female president and prime minister, how has India made such strides in information technology, will India use its nuclear weapons, and many similar ones – flooded my mind. The pride of India and its beauty and color in the little girl's imagination were, however, tarnished by rewinding to a day after September 11, 2001, when as I was walking in New York City, a visibly angry passer-by hissed, "Go back to your country, the land of Mohammed Gandhi."

Since that day, and to this day, the challenge to present India with all its beauty, history, culture, politics, and economics has captured my imagination. It is indeed a challenge – no matter how much I pore over the vast body of works on various aspects of this culturally and historically rich and fascinating country, it still becomes an impossible task to capture the entire gamut within the scope of a single comprehensive book. No matter how much I try to root myself in presenting a portrait of contemporary India, its historical landscape and the culture of continuity maintain a stubborn and indelible imprint. This book thus represents an opportunity and a struggle. It is an opportunity to reflect and analyze contemporary India in its historical backdrop. It is also a struggle to make India understandable amidst the complexities of tradition and modernity, poverty and prosperity, and peace and strife!

– Author's Note, 2016

India is undoubtedly one of the most fascinating countries in the world. For centuries, people around the world have cherished its historical and cultural richness. It is the land of *sadhus* (ascetics) and scientists; of color and contrasts. Its political and social landscape have been a complex mix of indigenous richness interspersed with a series of foreign interventions spanning several centuries, culminating in the British colonial period that lasted until the middle of the twentieth century. Since independence in 1947, over the last seven decades, India has attained the celebratory, albeit dubious, distinction of becoming the world's largest democracy. As a democratic polity, despite occasional wrinkles, India has been a beacon of the ballot and a champion of sustained institutional and procedural reliance on peaceful transfer of power. This record of democratic success is simultaneously marked with inequalities of wealth and disparities in development. In recent decades, India has recorded dazzling prospects and prowess in technological, military, and economic areas, but it has also been saddled with continuing challenges surrounding poverty, equity, public health, and governance. Together, these opportunities and challenges have generated widespread interest in understanding how this fascinating country is steering through them and whether it will be able to jostle out of its designation as an emerging power to one that has emerged.

This book is an attempt at introducing India and making it understandable. It seeks to underscore the importance of history and culture in understanding political, economic, and social trends in contemporary India. Beneath the visible changes that dot the landscape in contemporary India are deeper currents that shape its institutions, and, hence, the book contextualizes them in its rich history, complexity, and diversity. It might not be an understatement to suggest that it is impossible to make any generalizations about India. As stated above, it is a land of contrasts with varied richness and complexity. It is impossible to understand India without going into the depths and complexity that make it so unique and fascinating. For example, despite its economic boom in recent decades and the rise of a new middle class, millions of Indians continue to struggle with poverty and lack of resources. Despite an overall commitment and success in establishing a secular democracy, occasional bouts of religious riots by zealots – as witnessed in the riots that followed partition in 1947, the death of Indira Gandhi in 1984, and during the pogrom carried out in Gujarat in 2002 – remain a blemish on its record on secularism. There are numerous challenges that millions of people face as a result of lack of resources, education, infrastructure, and a social security and safety net. Yet, through it all, its 1.2 billion people remain optimistic about the human essence. Through it all, India has most commendably upheld the democratic tradition with its political culture, institutions, and processes.

Understandably, India's multifaceted and complex trajectory of changes and challenges has perplexed many. To anyone visiting India or learning about the country, the enigmatic nature of India's progress seems baffling. State-of-the-art, high-rise buildings coexist with slums. In 2010 and 2014, I accompanied a group of American college students to explore India. We visited Delhi, Agra, Jaipur, and Kolkata (Calcutta). We also spent time in *Shantiniketan*, the abode of peace, where India's Nobel laureate poet Rabindranath Tagore established *Vishwabharati*, or a world university, a place where music, art, and science instruction is often conducted in classrooms nestled in the midst of nature. We met and interacted with people from different walks of life. We visited historical and cultural landmarks, educational institutions, shopping malls, and children living in poverty in urban areas. Despite lessons and readings on India that students had done prior to the trips, visiting India unfolded a reality that easily surpassed what they had previously read about the country.

The contrasting landscape of India is fascinating. History coexists with contemporary reality in a working alignment. Cultural diversity lends color and beauty but has also been the source of occasional and sometimes lingering tension among groups. The gap between the rich and the poor was visible even during a casual stroll along the city sidewalks. Cows and cars jostle for space on the nation's urban thoroughfares, which are heavily bottlenecked with the chaotic influx of imported and locally manufactured vehicles, *auto-rickshaws*, and *rickshaws*. The students were fascinated by India's rich cultural heritage and history and also perplexed as to why so many people lived on the streets surrounding the rapidly rising high-rise residential complexes. They wanted to know how much the government of India spends on education, healthcare, social welfare, and defense. Other questions they had were how India compared with China, what the future of a U.S.-India partnership would be, would India resolve its differences with Pakistan, and what the status of women was. I found it intriguing that their questions addressed many of the historical continuities and discontinuities, as well as disparities about India. Such questions are also the ones that appear in op-eds, blogs, and narratives about the challenges of the new India – both within the country and outside. These questions serve as cues to a better understanding of the portrait of new India in the backdrop of the old, and they make the approach in this book unique.

Emerging from 200 years of colonial rule, since 1947 India has experimented with and maintained a democratic form of government that, despite its imperfections, has successfully sustained. Despite a largely non-violent overthrow of the British rule, the political history in the immediate aftermath of independence has been plagued with violence that continues to challenge the secular harmony in a multi-religious and multi-ethnic nation that somehow holds its tenuous balance. After colonial India sustained negative to zero growth, and low to modest growth in the early decades of independence, the economic progress of the past few decades has made India second only to China as the fastest-growing economy in the world. Yet as already indicated, the story of India's rise is mired with contradictions. On the one hand, there is significant economic progress, which has led to improvement in social indicators. "Life expectancy in India today (about 66 years) is more than twice what it was in 1951 (32 years); infant mortality is about one fourth of what it used to be (44 per thousand live births today as opposed to 180 or so in 1951); and female literacy rate has grown up from 9 per cent to 65 per cent" (Drèze and Sen 2013: 5). Opportunities and income in the service sector, particularly in information technology (IT), have grown significantly. Yet, India is saddled with inequitable distribution of this new income; real wages for the working class continue to be stagnant; and large sections of the population remain economically deprived: "Democratic pressures . . . have gone in other directions rather than rectifying the major injustices that characterize contemporary India" (Drèze and Sen 2013: 9).

Despite such flaws, India's democracy has been resilient as it seeks to work out power relations. In the contemporary world, such relations among classes and sections of people in more-established democracies are undergoing realignment. Apparent in Brexit and in the primary campaign season leading up to the 2016 presidential elections in the United States is significant voter angst with the respective establishment political parties. It appears that the party establishments in both of these countries are struggling to give voice to all sections of the population, especially those who feel they are forgotten. India's sojourn with multiple constituencies began decades ago. India has consolidated its democratic institutions through a process of power negotiation that involved social groups, political institutions, and leadership strategies: "First, a delicate balance has been struck, and struck again, between forces of centralization and decentralization. Second, the interests of the powerful in society have been served without fully excluding the weaker groups" (Kohli and Singh 2013: 2). Hence, although paradoxical, India's democracy and its economic rise represent a constant realignment among the powerful and those seeking power, trying to seek a voice and strike a balance.

To anyone visiting India or learning about the country, the enigmatic nature of India's progress is visible at the outset and seems baffling. As already stated and as we will see in the subsequent chapters in this book, since independence, India has followed a tale of two profiles: one that shows progress, the other that is stifled under age-old problems; one that calls for more emphasis on military and nuclear advancement as key to its position of power and progress, the other that calls for a larger emphasis on social and educational expenditures. This book will attempt to offer a picture of India's story and capture its historical and contemporary aspects of development and complexities, interspersed with firsthand narratives and analysis.

The scholarship on India is rich, complex, and varied. While many of these secondary resources have provided the backdrop for this analysis, there remain many important ones that the book has not been able to include. In its humble attempt to offer a simple portrayal of India, this book makes no pretension that it is an exhaustive analysis. Rather, it is an attempt to provide an introductory overview with a historical trajectory of the political, economic, and socio-cultural evolution of policies and trends that have shaped the country and continue to impact contemporary India. Each chapter attempts to provide an overview and contemporary trends that are set in a historical context, and each is primarily based on secondary reference and analysis. Hence, the chapters try to encapsulate what can best be described as a snapshot, creating the pathway to the major socio-political and economic aspects of India's development, with their challenges and opportunities. Books on India cover a wide variety of subject areas. Because of the complexity of the historical, social, cultural, political, and economic aspects of India's development, it is often a challenge to gain a basic overall understanding of the country. This book seeks to cover the major areas that anyone seeking to become familiar with India would be looking to acquire.

To reiterate, untangling the complex questions surrounding India's prospects as a leading economic power in Asia, and the world, is indeed a difficult task. Making a contribution that adds to the already burgeoning literature about contemporary India is formidable as well. This book will offer a glimpse into the reality and the dream that is the new India, struggling with nettlesome issues mired in history, culture, economic priorities, security challenges, governance, and the overall quality-of-life issues for the ordinary citizen. The framework will explore the questions one might have, just like my students had, upon confronting 'India,' attempting to make sense of the dynamic changes and the age-old processes and institutions that together make India so complex and fascinating.

Adopting this perspective, each chapter will begin with a reflection related to the topic of discussion as it is seen in contemporary India, trace its origins, and unfold the policies and changes pertaining to it. The approach will follow the format of the other books in the *Basics* series and introduce India to a general readership that is more informed now, having access to various forms of print and electronic sources of information.

Even though the book is on contemporary India, it will begin with a journey through the highlights of ancient India, which will enable readers to familiarize themselves with India's past as it is still witnessed and experienced, and with its bearings on the landscape of India's modern and contemporary life. Taking the lead from Jawaharlal Nehru's *The Discovery of India*, which he (India's first prime minister) wrote while in prison (1942–1946), Chapter 2 will present a brief survey of India's history since the days of the Indus Valley Civilization until the British colonial period. The key focus of the chapter will be on presenting India's historical continuity and its bearings on the landscape of the country's modern and contemporary life. Embedded in the portrayal are questions and debates surrounding issues such as how much of India's present is influenced by its experience with foreign rulers. Was democracy imported through any such rule? Can India look to its past to address any of its contemporary challenges? Some of these questions will weave their way throughout the book.

During our visits to Indian universities and meetings with political analysts, American students, who came with some understanding of India, had many questions that they sought answers to from experts. Such questions centered on: Did the British bring democracy to India? How does India's mystical past corroborate with its more contemporary reality of diversity and technological and scientific advancement? What makes India the largest democracy in the world, accommodating a diverse tapestry and the nexus of castes, religions, and languages? Taking a cue from Amartya Sen's *The Argumentative Indian* (2005), Chapter 3 will begin by examining the cultural aspects of India's democratic tradition, which lie at the root of promoting India's skeptical culture and allow for dialectical reasoning and policy formulation, essential for democracy.

As is expected, India's democratic traditions and challenges encompass a wide range of institutions and trends. The discussion in this chapter will focus on the roots of pluralism as embedded in its political culture and as represented in the constitutional structures and the party system. The discussion of pluralism is carried on to the next chapter, where the focus is on sectarian politics and the challenges to India's democratic governance that have emanated in the decades since independence.

Having looked at India's rich tradition of diversity, it is natural for any observer to ask why it is that, despite such democratic roots, India still faces problems of sectarian violence rooted in differences in religion, language, and caste, and why the mistreatment of the *Dalits* continues to plague the country. Even as India is successful at engineering impressive growth with widespread promise of prosperity, certain groups in India continue to be marginalized. Chapter 4 will begin the narrative with V. S. Naipaul's 1990 book, *A Million Mutinies Now*, which is an account of India by recounting progress, as well as the possibility of positive change in India (Naipaul 1990). It will take into consideration both Sen and Naipaul, and their hopes of regenerating

India, but also analyze some contemporary assaults on personal freedom and organized violence against religious groups, as in the 2002 Gujarat communal riots. In addition, it will address some of the challenges that India continues to face in the areas of sectarian and ethnic violence rooted in differences in language, religion, and ethnicity.

The ideological and pragmatic underpinnings of India's model of development and economic liberalization programs will be the focus of Chapter 5. The title of the chapter is derived from Gurcharan Das' *India Unbound* (2000). It will highlight the intersections of lingering challenges of spreading the benefits of economic growth more equitably among the population and focus on health, education, environment, and other aspects of human development.

The place of women in India's society is particularly perplexing. The large numbers of Hindus who worship female deities also engage in social and cultural practices that discriminate against girls and women. The constitution guarantees gender equality, and India's women are politically active. Yet, dowry deaths, trafficking and human slavery, and other practices continue to put India among countries where women's rights are not upheld. Deriving from a blessing for women in India to wish that they gave birth to a hundred sons, Elisabeth Bumiller's book *May You Be the Mother of a Hundred Sons* (1991) serves as the starting point of the narrative with such life experiences which seek to analyze and juxtapose the complexities of women's rights and gender equality. International norms, national policies and priorities, women's movements, and local NGOs are working to achieve more gender equality and respect for women's rights. Yet, it is puzzling to note how and why, despite marked progress on these scores, violence against women continues and arguably is even on the rise.

Indeed, alongside an economic boom in recent decades, India has also slowly but surely earned greater stature as a military power and catapulted its place and role as one with credible and impressive defense strength, with an arsenal that includes nuclear capability and weapons. Chapter 7 takes its cue from Stephen Cohen's *India: Emerging Power* (2001). India's stature in the world is very much determined by its relations with other nations, both in its backyard and throughout the world, including the United States and Russia. As India emerges as a major power, Pakistan and China continue to be a central focus, but there is marked change in India's decades-long foreign policy perspective that called for nonalignment with either Super Powers during the Cold War, and there is a renewed interest in more cordial relations with its smaller neighbors by and large: "A new realism in the Indian strategic community suggests that Indians will fantasize less about various plots to encircle and weaken it, without losing the expectation that India has a special role to play in the world" (Cohen 2001:309).

Indeed, that role in India is a critical one. It is, as N. R. Narayana Murthy suggests, to build *A Better India, A Better World* (2009). It is one in which the country has to balance its economic prowess with guaranteeing human security to its more than 1 billion citizens. It is one that makes a commitment to garner its military strength alongside cleaning of the air that one breathes, the rivers that remain the major lifelines of millions of coastal communities and more, and an infrastructure that has made remarkable strides but still has to improve to benefit both urban and rural populations. It is one that makes us cognizant of India's tremendous economic potential, of the fissures within the fabric of Indian society, and of the challenges of gender inequality. Thus, this chapter will assess India's soft power, innovation, and democratic potential. India is home of the largest film industry in the world, and the impact of Bollywood both on India's society and on defining India abroad will also be discussed. Through a balance of its hard and soft power, India can harness its role as a major power.

It may not be an exaggeration to suggest that contemporary India represents some struggles and challenges of decades past, but, in defining its gateway to the future, it is on a fascinating journey. Engaging in equitable and sustainable growth that is based on a strong infrastructure is critical. So is managing the rising aspirations of its citizens. Earlier generations of India's leadership were successful in charting the course of development for the country upholding it democratic institutions, albeit with a heavier state presence. Early on, Selig Harrison had identified regional interest, caste problems, and communism as some of the challenges to Indian democracy (Harrison: 1960). Even in the midst of challenging or 'dangerous decades,' India's democracy has time and again proved its resilience. In 1997, when India turned 50, the country and all those who believed in it were hopeful but ambivalent. India's progress has generated hope in the new economy, but those who have been excluded are beginning to demand a share in that progress: "There are now more arguments, more interests, more conception of what development is and what it means for India. It will not be easy" (Khilnani 1999: 106).

Indeed, it has not been an easy journey. Growth has sometimes faltered, and so has the stability of the party system. Over the past decade or so, however, India's economic growth model is showing signs of sustenance. India has not returned to a one-party dominant system, but the coalition model around major parties seems to be responding to the country's pluralistic aspirations commendably. It is this respect for pluralism and acknowledgement of the economic and social diversity that are pronounced in society and that will help India find its way through its challenges. India's achievements will be even more remarkable because it has aspired toward prosperity without sacrificing liberty. It has not opted for a state-controlled market before promising democracy. In doing so, it has had to wait longer than its East Asian neighbors, most notably China, to ascertain the path of economic growth. It has also meant decades of chaos when society was attempting to sort out its power relations. As already mentioned, that lesson from India, which may very well serve as a lesson for democracies elsewhere, is that because India has relied on "democracy as the oxygen of society" it will not rest easy with growth alone (Khilnani: 1999:106). For economic prosperity, especially where the results are not equitable, can never be the only goal for collective and individual freedom.

August 15, 2017, marked the seventieth anniversary of India's independence from British colonial rule and birth into nationhood. India's first prime minister Jawaharlal Nehru's vision of a new India was, as he framed it, a "tryst with destiny." The political freedom that came at midnight seven decades ago has come to a nation that is harnessed to history and propelled to the future at the same time. India's stature as a democracy and as a formidable military power, with the ability to exert indomitable soft power, makes it a fascinating country to study, to inhabit, to visit, and to be a part of somehow. Some are frustrated with India's continuing infrastructure problems, clogged roadways, and polluted air, especially in some of the major cities. Others are besotted with India's appeal, music, movies, foods, and festivals. Wherever one falls in this continuum, India remains a country that one cannot ignore, where classes and castes, religions, and ethnicities cohabitate, not always harmoniously but for the most part with respect for the dignity of all. This book is also an attempt to underscore the effect of India's rise on its own citizens, its neighbors, as well as those in far-off lands, all of whom remain much more interconnected in today's world.

To reiterate, Nehru's "tryst with destiny" speech that he gave welcoming India's freedom at midnight signaled a harbinger of the vision and dream for modern India: "Long years ago we made a tryst

MODERN INDIA   Made w/ Natural Earth Data

Note: This is a historical map and is included here for representative purposes. The international boundaries, coastlines, denominations, and other information shown do not necessarily imply any judgement concerning the legal status of any territory or the endorsement or acceptance of such information. For current boundaries, readers may refer to the Survey of India maps.

FIGURE 1.1   Modern India

with destiny, and now the time comes when we shall redeem our pledge. . . . At the stroke of the midnight hour, when the world sleeps, India will awake to life and freedom" (excerpt of Nehru's 'Speech delivered in the Constituent Assembly, New Delhi, August 14, 1947, on the eve of the attainment of Independence').

This introductory chapter thus opens the gateway to the promises and portends of contemporary India, and it concludes with a poignant reminder from a child of that midnight, bearing the birthmarks of a nation born into freedom at the cusp of day and night – still yearning to be free! "Yes, they will trample me underfoot, . . . because it is the privilege and the curse of midnight's children to be both masters and victims of their times, to forsake privacy and be sucked into the annihilating whirlpool of the multitudes, and to be unable to live or die in peace" (Rushdie 2006 [1981]: 533).

Discussion questions

1   Why India?
2   What are some of the points to remember before attempting to
    understand India?
3   What are the some of the fundamental aspects of India's political
    system, culture, and society?
4   Before being introduced to the book, what preconceived notions
    about India did you have?
5   What do you expect from a Basic Book on India?

Further reading

Baxi, U. and Parekh, B. (Eds.) (1995) *Crisis and Change in Contemporary India*, New Delhi: Sage Publications.

Brown, J. (1994) *Modern India: The Origins of an Asian Democracy*, New York: Oxford University Press.

Das, Arvind N. (1992) *India Invented: A Nation in the Making*, New Delhi: Manohar.

Forster, E.M. (1924) *A Passage to India*, New York: Harcourt Brace.

French, P. (2011) *India: A Portrait*, New York: Knopf.

Kapur, A. (2012) *India Becoming: A Portrait of Life in Modern India*, New York: Riverhead Books, published by Penguin.

Nilekani, N. (2009) *Reimagining India: The Idea of a Renewed Nation*, New York: Penguin.

Panagariya, A. (2008) *India: The Emerging Giant*, Oxford University Press, New Delhi.

Tharoor, S. (2000) *India: From Midnight to the Millennium*, New Delhi: Penguin Books.

Zakaria, F. (2003) *The Future of Freedom*, New York: W. W. Norton and Company.

References

Bumiller, E. (1991) *May You Be the Mother of a Hundred Sons*, New York: Ballantine Books.

Cohen, S. (2001) *India: Emerging Power*, Washington, DC: Brookings Institution Press.

Das, G. (2002) [2000] *India Unbound*, New Delhi: Penguin Books.

Drèze, J. and Sen, A. (2013) *An Uncertain Glory: India and Its Contradictions*, Princeton & Oxford: Princeton University Press.

Harrison, S. (1960) *India: The Most Dangerous Decades*, Princeton, NJ: Princeton University Press.

Khilnani, S. (1999) *The Idea of India*, New York: Farrar, Straus, & Giroux.

Kohli, A. and Singh, P. (Ed.) (2013) *Routledge Handbook of Indian Politics*, London: Routledge.

Naipaul, V.S. (1990) *India: A Million Mutinies Now*, New York: Viking.

Narayana Murthy, N.R. (2009) *A Better India: A Better World*, New Delhi: Allen Lane/Penguin Books.

Nehru, J. (1947) Speech delivered in the Constituent Assembly, New Delhi, August 14, 1947, on the eve of the attainment of Independence. Retrieved from:www.wwnorton.com/college/english/nael/20century/topic_1/jawnehru.htm.

Nehru, J. (2004) [1946] *The Discovery of India*, New Delhi: Viking/Penguin.

Rushdie, S. (2006) [1981] *Midnight's Children*, New York: Random House.

Sen, A. (2005) *The Argumentative Indian*, New York: Farrar, Straus & Giroux.

2

DISCOVERING INDIA

Prologue

"In my room there is a book, the Bhagvad Gita. What is this book, and what is its significance in India? Is it like the Bible?" This question from a student greeted me on the very first day of my group visit with American college students to India. As I struggled to find a satisfactory and uncomplicated response to the student's query, I realized that no question about India could be answered in simple terms. My task, to make India understandable to 19- to 22-year-olds, many of whom had not left New Jersey prior to boarding the plane to India, was daunting indeed.

The student had heard about the Vedas but not the Gita. Interestingly, the Vedas and the Gita are important and critical to understanding the socio-cultural landscape of ancient India. These were interesting works, but much too complex for a beginner, especially a student from the United States who had little exposure to the historical traditions of India, to digest.

The Vedas, Upanishads, and epics such as the *Mahabharata* and *Ramayana* and other works help us understand ancient India's cultural practices and social structures. They also reflect some timeless traditions that continue to affect and shape beliefs and practices in contemporary India. As this chapter will discuss, the Vedas explain the framework of a way of life, and the Upanishads provide a perspective of the real world and its transcendental meaning. Some consider that the latter bears close resemblance to Plato's vision and works: "Plato's idea of the good is very close to the supreme God of the Upanishads" (Singhal [1972] 1993: 32).

Chapter objectives and outline

India's present is rooted in its past and branches out into its future. A journey through the philosophy, culture, history, and statecraft that guided the past is critical to understanding contemporary India. Following Jawaharlal Nehru's *The Discovery of India*, which he wrote while in prison from 1942 to 1945, this chapter will present a brief survey of India's history since the days of the Indus Valley Civilization to the British colonial period. It will begin with a discussion of the influences of the country's history and how it still impacts life in contemporary India.

Ancient India: circa 3000 BCE–1000 CE

A reservoir of complex historical, political, economic, and cultural confluences, India is not just a country; it is a civilization, a culture, a paradox, and an enigma, which is cherished by those who have long acquaintance with it, as well as by newcomers. Whether it is a history of subjugation by foreign invaders or a cultural amalgamation of pluralistic tradition, "what was distinctive about India's past was its ability to transform invasion into accommodation, rupture into continuity, division into diversity" (Khilnani 1999: xiv). Through this long and textured history, the impact of its past continues to be relevant for contemporary politics and society. Through this diverse kaleidoscope of the country's history and the shared experience of its people, a syncretic culture gradually evolved.

The country's two given names, *India* and *Bharat*, carry some of the historical origins of the region and the nation-state. It is common to associate the name *India* with the Indus Valley Civilization. *Bharat* or *Bharat-Varsha*, or the land of King Bharat, is rooted in the writings of ancient texts, or the "Puranas" (Majumdar et al. 1978: 3–4). Even though it did not receive the same attention as the other

INDUS VALLEY CIVILIZATION

Based on "Mature Harappan Period" by
Avantiputra7; Made w/ Natural Earth Data

Note: This is a historical map and is included here for representative purposes. The international boundaries, coastlines, denominations, and other information shown do not necessarily imply any judgement concerning the legal status of any territory or the endorsement or acceptance of such information. For current boundaries, readers may refer to the Survey of India maps.

FIGURE 2.1 Indus Valley civilization

ancient civilizations, and there is not much available in terms of written records, archaeological excavations in the twentieth century have established agricultural, commercial, and other forms of activities, including trade relations of the Indus Valley Civilization, the earliest human settlement in India, that grew along the banks of the Indus and the Ravi (Majumdar et al. 1978: 15). Mohenjo-daro and Harappa were the two major urban nerve centers that helped develop a fairly sophisticated system of networks, navigation, and a functioning commercial system. In addition to such early evidence of commerce, there were cultural exchanges as well. The civilizations were also distinct in developing their indigenous forms of tools, instruments, ships, and other utility goods (Mansingh 2006: 258–260).

Unfortunately, around 2000 BCE, the Indus Valley civilization began eroding. The actual reason for the demise of these civilizations is not clear. It is also unclear whether Aryans emerged from central Asia or in India itself, but most scholars seem to concur that there is some sort of Indo-European descent associated with Aryans. Debunking centuries-old definitions of Aryans, historians now seem to agree that they are more of a linguistic group representing the origins of Indo-European languages, *Sanskrit* being one of the most well known (Bose and Jalal 1998: 14).

Ancient India and democratic values

The *Rigveda*, *Yajurveda*, *Atharvaveda*, and *Samaveda* became the foundations to guide culture, education, lifestyle, teachings, and other basic premises of social, cultural, and personal life. As for democratic roots during the Vedic Age, historians have found divergent strains. While the Rigveda idealizes a sort of hereditary monarchy, it also talks about the need for such kings to rule with the consent of the tribes they represent. The kings, or *rajans*, were revered as they tendered protection to their tribes. Their position was not geographically tied, as with the later dynasties, but marked the headship of the tribe. In one of the Vedas, the Atharvaveda, there is mention of electing the *rajans* as well. Such election might have been in the spirit of ruling with consensus through an assembly system, known as *samiti*, representing a republican system, rather than a full-fledged democratic election process (Majumdar et al. 1978: 28–29).

In addition, the Vedas also provided the foundational structure of society, the basic premises of which continue to this day in some form (Singhal [1972] 1993: Chapter 1). It was a male-dominated system, with the 'family' at the center of this social setup. Historical accounts demonstrate that despite the preference for the male child, people accepted baby girls and provided them with the same kind of access to education and intellectual growth. Women were also allowed some access to decision making at the local *samiti* (assembly) or *sabha* (committee) levels. The major contributions of what was known as Vedic society contain the origins of the functional division of social structure, which eventually led to the division of society into castes: "When they divided the primeval being (*Purusa*), the *Brahmana* was his mouth, the *Rajanya* became his arms, the *Vaisya* was his thighs, and from his feet sprang the *Sudras*" (Majumdar et al. 1978: 31). The four-part division of India's society as outlined in the *Rig Vedas* emanated from the *Purusa*, corresponding to the various needs of society, namely a Brahmin (priest/philosopher), a *Kshatriya* (warrior), *Vaisya* (merchants/businessmen), and the *Shudras* (the menial tasks in society). The Shudras were also called Untouchables, Gandhi's *Harijans*, or the children of God. They are the *Dalits*, or the oppressed.

In this scheme, there was no rigid barrier to social mobility or intermarriage among castes. This occupational division was further embedded in several sub-castes that emerged on the basis of birth or *jati*. But even though this dual setup of caste by *varna* and *jati* was widespread, its later association with 'karma,' with the advent of the Upanishads in the eighth and seventh centuries, brought with it the rigidity and lack of mobility that we see in later years (Bose and Jalal 1998: 15). The ramifications of what began as structural and functional division of labor, especially the discriminatory practices that ensued based on caste, stubbornly continue to plague contemporary India. The idea was that one was born into a particular caste based on one's deeds in a prior life. There was also a sense of structural immobility or finality, directing the lack of mobility from the caste group in which one is born.

Greeks, Mauryas, and the Guptas in ancient India

The conquests of Alexander the Great are historically significant to India. Between 327 and 326 BCE, Alexander marched through the Hindu Kush Mountains and crossed the Indus, overcoming rough terrain, turbulent waterways, and dense forests. In his grand conquest, Alexander finally met with resolve from the Indian king, Porus, or *Puru* (head of the *Pauravas*), who tried to prevent the onward conquest of Alexander, but later succumbed to him. Alexander had intended to foray into the area of the Ganges, but his army was already worn out, and the tribes around the riverbanks of the Ravi and Chenab presented valiant resistance. Thereafter, Alexander was wounded, and the demise of his empire began (Singhal [1972] 1993: 45–49). After Alexander's death in 323 BCE, the struggle for succession in his loosely acquired empire began, and Selecus, the leader in Syria, tried unsuccessfully to expand to India but met with resistance from Chandragupta Maurya in 306 BCE.

In the period following expansions and decline of the Aryan, Greek, and Persian influences, several Hindu dynasties emerged and even embraced the rise of Buddhism. Gautama Buddha, himself a Hindu prince, founded Buddhism in the fifth century BCE. Soon after came the rise of the Maurya Dynasty, with famous and powerful emperors such as Chandragupta Maurya, who conquered much of northern India. Emperor Ashoka spread the Maurya Empire further into central and eastern parts of India. According to some accounts, after a particularly bloody battle in the eastern province of Kalinga (Orissa), he renounced violence and became a Buddhist. After Ashoka's death, for about 500 years (200 BCE to 300 CE), there was a period of decentralized units, until about 320 CE, when the Gupta Dynasty, led by Chandragupta I, and then Samudragupta, brought about a revival of Vedic rituals and Brahmanical traditions. With its roots in the epic *Mahabarata*, it stressed Dharma, or duty, as the guiding force behind action. It provided a source of guidance and strength, not egalitarianism. It swayed from the Vedas and "was quite influential by the Gupta age" (Bose and Jalal 1998: 18–19). The Gupta period also marks the rise of the Brahmins and a period when art and culture flourished. Centuries later, some aspects of social change associated with this rise are seen through *Sanskritization*, or emulation of high caste Brahmins.

By the fourth century BCE, Buddhism began to spread and was embraced by Emperor Ashoka, but its success was more pronounced in other parts of Asia, outside its birthplace, India. Hinduism did flourish during the Maurya Dynasty and, particularly, the Gupta Dynasty, but it did not inform the political system. Religion was not the basis of unifying the country. Therefore, even though we examine the periods of ancient, medieval, and modern, they are by no means identical to Hindu, Muslim, and British periods (Bose and Jalal 1998: 13). In fact, the lack of any ideological or religious unity, and a fragmented identity, perhaps made it easier for subsequent invasions, leading to the Mughal and, subsequently, the colonial period. The complexity of each of these periods gives contemporary India a fractured as well as a pluralistic and culturally vibrant legacy that it is still attempting to grapple with.

Muslim dynasties and Mughal period: circa 1200–1857

What were some of the cultural and administrative legacies of the Muslims and, in particular, the Mughals? The impact of Muslim rule in India is manifold and complex. Between the eighth and sixteenth centuries, several dynasties – including the Lodhis, the Tughlaqs, and, finally, the Mughals – ushered in a series of invasions, which had deep socio-economic, political, and cultural changes and amalgamations throughout northern India.

This process was diverse and had differential impact: "Muhammadan rule in India consists of a series of invasions and partial conquests, during eight centuries, from Subuktigin's inroad in 977, to Ahmad Shah's tempest of invasion in 1761 A.D." (Hunter 1966: 323). Minor invasions, migrations, conquests, and spread of tribes and groups led by various conquerors and chiefs did not always result in despotic rule. Neither did they result in complete overthrow and destruction of local and native cultures, socio-political structures, or religious traditions and beliefs. The Muslims brought religious and cultural traditions that were in contrast with centuries-old Hindu customs and practices. But as Hunter goes on to say, "At no time was Islam triumphant throughout the whole of India" (Hunter 1966: 313). By the fourteenth century, the Turkish, Persian, and Afghan invasions

MUGHAL EMPIRE

Based on a map of the Mughal Empire from
GlobalSecurity.org; Made w/ Natural Earth Data

Note: This is a historical map and is included here for representative purposes.
The international boundaries, coastlines, denominations, and other information
shown do not necessarily imply any judgement concerning the legal status of any
territory or the endorsement or acceptance of such information. For current boundaries,
readers may refer to the Survey of India maps.

FIGURE 2.2   Mughal Empire

gradually assimilated into an Indo-Muslim culture, but the impact
was also geographically diverse. While a majority of Muslims in India
were Sunnis, there were pockets of Shia influence in the Sind and
Punjab areas. Many others, spreading over a huge territory spanning
from the Punjab to Bengal, were drawn to the teachings of the Sufi
mystics and to their music, which brought solace through spiritual-
ity. The Sufi teachings actually provided a "powerful impetus to the
bhakti movement in India" and coalesced on the unity of their belief

in reaching God through love and the teachings of spiritual leaders (Bose and Jalal 1998: 28–32).

In 1504, Babur (a descendant of the legendary Turkish leader Timur and Ghengiz Khan, the great Mongol from Central Asia) captured Kabul, the current capital of Afghanistan. The last emperor of the Delhi Sultanate, Ibrahim Lodi, fell to Babur, who in 1526 ushered in the Mughal period in India. In its early onset, the Mughal rule represented clearly distinct dynastic periods. Babur, who was a scholar, could only lay the groundwork for the great Mughal Empire. His son, Humayun, was weak and ineffective. Unable to confront the Afghan chief, Sher Shah Suri, Humayun fled and returned only after the death of the former. It was only after Babur's grandson, Akbar, came to the throne that the consolidation took place (Majumdar et al. 1978: 418).

Prior to the emergence and functioning of a nation-state in the European tradition, the Mughal rule (1556–1858) represented a fairly large administrative unit. In fact, the military conquests under Babur began earlier. After 1526, Babur defeated the Lodi Sultan, Rajputs, Afghans, and the Sultan of Bengal. However, he died in 1530, and the task of administrative consolidation fell on his successors, most notably on his grandson, Akbar. Akbar succeeded in strengthening the sources and forms of cultural intersection as well as brought more stability to administrative unification. His court featured and supported Persian, Indian, and European art and music. He married a Hindu princess, Jodhabai, and promoted an environment of tolerance and religious and cultural diversity. His army had Hindu generals and officers, some in high ranks and positions. He was well known for his concept of *Din-i-Ilahi*, or 'Divine Faith' through which he hoped to bring about a synthesis of Hinduism and Islam. His political successes were evident in the expansion of the empire from the Delhi region well into the South, as far as the Krishna River, although he was not as successful in consolidating the South (Hunter 1966: 347–52; Bose and Jalal 1998: chapter 4).

The legacy of Akbar continues to reflect a unique synthesis of Islam on the cultural marvel that is India. Indeed, many of the architectural masterpieces, which stand as historical testimony of this synthesis and a cultural kaleidoscope, have become the wonders and treasures of the world. Akbar had his capital in *Fatehpur Sikri*, housing a magnificent building complex, which, to this day, represents a symbol of cultural unity. Many of the buildings of this period, pillars, and gateways masterfully and artistically combine Islamic art with traditional Hindu North Indian architectural styles, paintings, and motifs. In 1605, Akbar's son Jahangir succeeded him. Jahangir's mark in history is not as stellar as that of his father or his son, Shah Jahan, who came to the throne in 1627. Shah Jahan also expanded the Mughal Empire, but he is most well known for the Taj Mahal, a wondrous marble mausoleum that he built in memory of his favorite wife, Mumtaz Mahal, in Agra. In addition, he is credited with building the Jama Masjid (which continues to attract large numbers of followers every day, and especially on holy days for the Muslims) and the Red Fort (which symbolizes the seat of invincible power and stature of the Mughals).

So, the impact of the Muslim rule in India, especially that of the Mughals up until the reign of Shah Jahan, remains as a historical reminder of conquest without absolute vanquishing, amalgamation of cultures and peoples without overcoming and forcing to give up their own traditions and religious beliefs, and considerable administrative infrastructure without consolidating or politically uniting the whole country. Indeed, as Shah Jahan began building more and more of his architectural masterpieces, it also meant that he needed more revenue and labor. Increased taxation brought about frustration among the people and paved the way for his son Aurangzeb to wrest power in 1658. While Aurangzeb is sometimes credited for administratively uniting the country, it came at a price. In stark contrast to Akbar, Shah Jahan, and the other Mughal rulers, Aurangzeb's style did not call for compromise or accommodation of people's identities and traditional beliefs and practices. This style bred local resistance against his treacherous practices, most notably from the Marathas from the West. Led by Maratha leaders such as Chattrapati Shivaji, they began to spread and give shape to feelings of Hindu identity and a nationalistic spirit, including allegiance to a religious banner. Coupled with family feuds over the throne, such resistance eventually led to the decline of the Mughal Dynasty, which reigned over much of India between the early sixteenth and late seventeenth centuries (Hunter 1966: 361–68).

We therefore see an impactful and mixed legacy of cultural contributions and administrative styles brought to India and adopted by the Mughals. Even though the Moghul rulers had different governing styles, they included local rulers in the administration and maintained continuity of social institutions (Schaffer and Schaffer 2016: 7). Hence, by and large, the Mughal Era remains, with varying degrees of success, a complex yet earnest attempt at amalgamating with existing socio-cultural and administrative systems.

British colonial period: 1757–1947

The complex rise of British colonial rule in India for over 200 years can be understood by focusing on three watershed years, spanning this time period, and emerging almost 100 years apart. The first happened in 1757, with the British defeat of the Bengal Nawab Shiraj-ud-daula; next came the 1857 Sepoy Mutiny and, finally, political independence of India in 1947. Each of these watershed years provides a useful framework to outline the socio-economic and political and cultural history of the rise and spread of British colonialism in India, which began with commercial interests and ended up with political and economic domination.

From commercial outpost to colonialism

Since the seventh century, India was gradually opened to the west via various sea and trade routes. Vasco da Gama reached India in 1498. Between 1596 and 1602, the Dutch arrived, eventually forming the Dutch East India Company. In 1600, Queen Elizabeth issued a charter to grant the East India Company proprietary authority and trading rights, and after a few years of forays in Southeast Asia, in 1608, overcoming opposition from indigenous merchants in Surat and by the Dutch settlers, the Company sought to set up factories in India. Eventually, it explored eastward and set up a factory by the Hooghly River in 1651. With the decline of the Mughal rule, and the rise of local princes and rulers, who often feuded with each other, the Company gradually found itself entangled in such conflicts. Much of it was to forge trade licenses and privileges to promote their commercial interests. After some failures and negotiations, eventually in 1690, Job Charnok successfully established a factory in Sutanuti. In 1698, the English were granted *zamindari* of the villages of Sutanuti, Kalikata, and Gobindopur, consolidated under the control of the newly created

Fort William. Thus, in Bengal, the Company enjoyed authority from a dual source. Over English subjects, it followed English laws, and it also acquired authority over Indian residents whom they ruled as a *zamindar* (Majumdar et al. 1978: 623–33). Consequently, especially in Bengal, the Company soon got entangled in local disputes.

Until 1757, Bengal's Nawab Siraj-ud-daula successfully resisted and was able to prevent the British initially from expanding into his

COLONIAL INDIA

Based on "Political Divisions of the Indian Empire" by the Edinburgh Geographical Institute; Made w/ Natural Earth Data

Note: This is a historical map and is included here for representative purposes. The international boundaries, coastlines, denominations, and other information shown do not necessarily imply any judgement concerning the legal status of any territory or the endorsement or acceptance of such information. For current boundaries, readers may refer to the Survey of India maps.

FIGURE 2.3 Colonial India

territory. Eventually, however, under the command of Colonel Robert Clive, he was handily defeated. Clive engineered a Machiavellian ploy in which Siraj's own commander Mir Jafar and other powerful bankers in Bengal betrayed him, and Clive struck a deal to receive a handsome grant in exchange for paving the path for Jafar to succeed Siraj-ud-daula. The Battle of Plassey (1757) was significant in that it laid the foundations of British political control on India, with all the commercial potential of the Ganges valley and ports in the coastal metropolises (Lamb 1975: 58–59).

In the aftermath of the Battle of Plassey, until 1786, Lord Cornwallis faced the difficulty of integrating Indian and Western concepts of governance. In the context of the corruption and greed of the Company officials, the Select Committee of 1781 was tasked with balancing the interests of Britain with those of the 'native inhabitants.' In addition to limiting abuse by Company officials, the committee ensured that the "rights of zamindars and landholders must not be superseded in order to increase the revenues. There must be even-handed justice for Europeans and Indians alike" (Dodwell 1963: 433). One way in which this became evident was how to apportion land revenues. Charles Cornwallis created a 'permanent settlement' system, whereby the 'revenue agents,' or *zamindars*, got more authority to actually exercise ownership rights rather than just collect taxes. After the *zamindars* paid their fixed amount of revenue to the British, they were free to impose further revenue burdens on their peasants, creating a landed aristocracy and a system that had the potential to breed extortion (Lamb 1975: 66).

By the turn of the century, through the 'subsidiary alliance' system, the English would offer protection to the Nawabs in exchange for honoraria, gifts, or subsidy. From Mysore in the South, to the Marathas in the West, the company exerted this kind of alliance building involving the rulers, financiers and bankers, and agrarian landholders, thus weakening the local potential for resistance and creating multi-pronged points of the nexus of loyalty. Even though some local rulers – such as those in Mysore, those in Punjab (Ranjit Singh), and the Marathas – provided courageous challenges to the company's forces, the British were able to weaken most of the local rulers, who, in order to pay off their tribute monies to the company, were often pitted against the landlords (*zamindars*) and bankers, creating distrust among them. By the nineteenth century, this alliance system faced challenges, mostly due to interventionist policies of governor-generals such as Clive, Wellesley, and Dalhousie (Bose and Jalal 1998: 60–62). Even as regional states resisted company control, the British were able to collude with 'merchant capitalists,' but very carefully and deftly they also made sure the latter did not become an albatross for them (Bose and Jalal 1998: 65). Thus, the British, who were keen on consolidating state power, also gradually eroded the potential for cultivating a viable economic infrastructure.

By the 1850s, with two-fifths of the territory directly governed, and the remaining areas controlled through subjugated Indian princes, India came under the administrative control of the British. The revolt that broke out in 1857 among the soldiers, also known as the Sepoy Mutiny, marked the first significant resistance against the British. The mutiny shook the British authorities as it started among its own soldiers, and, even though it was contained in certain parts of India, it showed the resolve and frustration of the people. It took them a year to quell the uprising, and, in 1858, India came under the total control of the Crown. With the 1876 Act of Parliament, Queen Victoria was declared Empress of India, and the entire territory of India, including the princely states, came under more direct British colonial rule (Lamb 1975: 68–70). For almost 100 years after that, the spirit of revolt that unfurled with the 1857 revolt laid the foundations for a series of challenges against unjust British laws and policies, culminating in India's independence movement and freedom as a nation-state in 1947.

Nationalism and political independence

India's nationalistic movement evolved out of a cultural revivalism and was interwoven with Indian and Western values. Looking at the evolution of nationalism, we find that there were three overlapping waves. The first was the period since 1885 and the establishment of the Indian National Congress. Following this, the two world wars complicated matters further for the British. The Indian nationalist movement was led largely by Western-educated liberals such as Nehru, right-wing leaders such as Vallabbhai Patel, the Muslim League, led by

Muhammad Ali Jinnah, and others who coalesced forces with Gandhi. This ushered in the largest non-violent freedom struggle, which helped secure India's political independence in 1947.

As the First World War went on, there were signs of mutiny and frustration among soldiers, but they did not lead to any large-scale protest movement in India. In 1915, there emerged a man, who, despite his humble presence, would become the voice and soul power of the Indian nationalist movement. Mohandas Karamchand Gandhi, a lawyer who was trained in Britain and then went to practice law in South Africa, was torn by the dual admiration and antipathy that he developed for the British. On the one hand, he admired the British allegiance to human liberty and equality.

Stirred by the racial discrimination he had witnessed and experienced in South Africa, Gandhi questioned the unequal treatment of Indians in India by the British. Over a decade, between 1909 and 1919, the British government made several overtures to grant some concessions to the rising Indian demand for greater representation in administration. The Indian National Congress (INC), whose leaders were Western educated but were discriminated against in their entry to the Indian Civil Service, made demands for access. In response, the British granted partial representation through elections in the provincial legislative councils and the central government. However, growing frustrations as well as new aspirations among Indian leaders and the end of World War I saw a change in the demands they made as well as in the leadership of INC. While both aimed for self-rule, there were strategic differences between the moderates, led by leaders such as Gopal Krishna Gokhale, who sought cooperation with the British, and the more extreme wing, led by Bal Gangadhar Tilak, who was an avid nationalist (Oberst et al 2014: 24).

Both groups criticized the British for their continual denial of self-determination. The moderates continued to hope for concessions and constitutional measures. The extremists grew increasingly frustrated by the foot dragging and discriminatory policies of the British when it came to giving access to civil service posts and self-government. This division within the INC represented a larger movement of cultural identity that accompanied the evolution and growth of the organization. The social reforms of the nineteenth century were spurred by this cultural revival and nationalist aspirations. The reform agenda included revisiting institutions and practices such as *Sati* (*Suttee*) or the practice of dying together (*sahamarana*), which effectively turned out to result in the burning of widows along with their deceased husbands. In addition, this also meant that other practices associated with Hinduism, such as the divisions and social discrimination brought about by the caste system, and others, would be examined. Most Western-educated reformers, and those inspired by liberal thinking, such as Raja Ram Mohun Roy, who was an ardent supporter of the abolition of *Sati*, were in favor of re-examining customs and social rituals based on Hinduism that were regressive in nature and would potentially lead to the decline of Hinduism in the face of more progressive and liberal ideas based on Western traditions. Through the 'Brahmo Samaj,' Roy and his followers promoted the idea to reform Hinduism through a liberal approach, moving away from idol worship and reliance on monotheism. The 'Arya Samaj,' on the other hand, was a movement that evolved around reviving the glory of Hinduism and, eventually, of Hindu nationalism (Oberst et al. 2014: chapter 2). Roy also promoted new opportunities for Western education and established the Hindu College (later Presidency College, and now Presidency University), which is still a prestigious university in India. Other iterations of Hindu revivalism are found in Ramakrishna and his disciple, Vivekananda, who brought his message to the United States and incorporated the idea of service to humanity through Hinduism (Lamb 1975: 120–124).

Despite this difference in perspective, this second wave of nationalist aspirations was distinctive in two ways. First, the moderates, led by Gokhale, became the more dominant players. Second, the phase elicited identity politics to the forefront. The Muslims, who had hitherto aspired for national self-determination simultaneously with the nationalists in the first phase, gradually became unsure of what an independent India led by Hindus would look like. The All India Muslim League was created in 1906. It allowed the Muslims to create a channel to make their demands for separate representation, and the British were also able to use this division to their advantage by inculcating a feeling of divisiveness in the already pluralistic Indian society.

By the third wave of nationalism, Gandhi had already entered the national scene. He galvanized large masses of people with his *satyagraha*, or 'soul force,' resorting to truth and civil disobedience against unjust laws. With the non-cooperation movement of 1921, the Salt March of 1930, and civil disobedience movements in 1933, the national movement was poised for demanding political independence from the British (Oberst et al. 2014: 25–27). Like an astute strategist, Gandhi combined *ahimsa*, or 'non-violence,' with *satyagraha*, or 'truth,' into a political weapon. His approach was grounded in pragmatism and prudence. He understood that India would not be able to stand against the might of the Empire. Practicing non-violence resistance requires courage, a steadfastness, and inner strength that the wielding of weapons does not. "The restraining value of non-violence, the leadership principle, and the Congress party organization which Gandhi was able to fashion his needs made it possible for him to launch powerful, yet controlled, mass movements" (Bose and Jalal 1998: 138–139). The frail and gaunt man that he was, Gandhi's fasts represented an effective strategy: a commitment that put pressure on the British as well as helped stop riots between feuding Hindus and Muslims.

Alongside Gandhi's meteoric rise in popular appeal, and its galvanizing effect on the masses, the INC also kept its pressure on the British in its pursuit of national autonomy. Starting in 1929, the INC began making demands for complete independence from the British government. Provincial autonomy came through the Government of India Act 1935, with a provision for partial representation at the federal level. Simultaneous forces and leaders that began to emerge at the time in India would become significant for identity politics on the cusp of independence and into the future. Of these, the Muslim League, led by Muhammad Li Jinnah, was the most vociferous in its demand for separate representation for the Muslims. Other groups such as the Kashmiri Muslims and the Sikhs in the Punjab also found leaders and political parties and groups, such as the National Conference and Akali Dal to represent their interests. Subsequent chapters of this book will examine the effects of such identity politics in independent India.

Meanwhile, by 1942, and Gandhi's call for 'Quit India,' it was evident to the war-torn British that India's independence was imminent. What was also apparent was that the nationalist aspirations of sectarian groups and parties put pressure on what an independent India would look like. The Muslim League clearly became the representatives of the Muslims, and their demand for separate statehood became a rational choice following communal violence between Hindus and Muslims, which seemed to be irreconcilable without it.

The much-commended peaceful transfer of power did not come smoothly or without corrosive outcomes. In 1946, a three-member Cabinet Mission of the British government visited India to facilitate political independence. In 1947, appointed Viceroy of India, Lord Louis Mountbatten, facilitated the British withdrawal. Lord Mountbatten also introduced several proposals to transfer power to the provinces, which Nehru resisted vehemently, fearing 'balkanization' of the nation. With utmost haste, Sir Cyril Radcliff, a lawyer by profession, drew up the lines of demarcation between provinces and districts (Tharoor 2016: 169–172).

Political freedom came to India at midnight on August 15 with the transfer of power from the British Crown to an independent India. It also marked the creation of the new state of Pakistan, for the Muslims. States with Muslim majority could opt to join Pakistan, as most did. Due to logistical and other political reasons, Kashmir, Junagadh, and Hyderabad were deemed part of India. The status of Kashmir remains a source of contention between India and Pakistan. The freedom bells brought an end to colonial servitude for the Indian people, but the joy was also marred by fierce violence between ethnic communities and families around border states undergoing the pain of separation of loved ones who had to choose which side of the dividing line they were going to live in, India or Pakistan. The birthmarks of ethnic conflict thus underscored, India's challenge was to create representative institutions within a parliamentary democracy that would also help the country make progress economically and socially.

Thus, political freedom came to India with partition, which in turn brought a huge toll in human suffering. On both, the West and the East, Hindus, Sikhs, and Muslims tried to resolve their new futures, millions had to be separated from their families and friends, and widespread riots broke out. Gandhi appealed for peace, and eventually the Congress leaders agreed to release Pakistan's share of assets from India. Many within the Congress Party considered Gandhi to be favoring Muslims, and right-wing Hindus were more militant against him. On January 30, 1948, a Hindu fanatic shot Gandhi while he was returning from a prayer service (Hardgrave and Kochanek 2000: chapter 2); thus occurred a new beginning of India with the ending of the life of *Bapu*, or the 'father' of the nation.

In addition to the force of the indigenous nationalist movement, there were some structural imperatives that showed the weaknesses of the British government. The impact of the two world wars was felt in the following areas, not always separable: administrative, political economy, and policy. The immediate need that became apparent was in the armed forces. The British army recruited heavily from India – in particular, from the Punjab – to meet the growing needs to fortify the army. About 60,000 Indian soldiers died serving for the British army in the war. To keep up the war efforts, goods needed to be sent, and defense expenditures increased. By the early twentieth century, the impact of the Second World War and the ensuing economic crisis of the 1920s also created malaise and frustration with the British government. Unable to control so many fronts in Europe as well as in the colonies, the colonial government showed signs of inevitable fracture (Bose and Jalal 1998: chapter 12).

Conclusion: reforms, reformers and impact of colonialism on contemporary India

In 2007, on the occasion of the sixtieth anniversary of India's political independence, Nobel Prize–winning economist Amartya Sen reflected on the impact of British colonialism on India. In his examination, Sen recounted the centuries-old tradition in India where settlers from a variety of countries impacted the country, its culture, and its economy, and he remains skeptical about the British contribution. He began his critique with a reference to Niall Ferguson, who in his book *Empire* had offered a "guarded but enthusiastic celebration of British imperialism" (Sen 2007: 4).

To the more commonly held claim that the British unified the country, Sen points out since the third century BCE, the Maurya, Gupta, Mughal, and other dynasties were successful in administratively uniting most of India. Sen agrees that 1757 marked a turning point, which the British authorities used well to bring most of the country under its suzerainty. It is erroneous to take the fragmented sense of India's unity in the mid-eighteenth century as reflective of the country's identity, because by then the country was suffering the aftermath of the remnants of a fractious and dwindling Mughal Empire. Furthermore, as our analysis has already shown, the British did engage in a Machiavellian plot and used betrayal by the Nawab's own general to bring about the victory. In fact, the British occupied a thriving and prosperous Bengal, and they misused their power to bring about its economic decline. Bribery and corruption benefited the East India Company, while causing widespread starvation and death in the Great Bengal Famine in 1769–1770. The British fostered political unity, but the country also had seeds of divisiveness around religion (Sen 2007: 8).

In terms of cultural revival, it is often cited that Western education influenced many of the leaders of the nationalist movement, which in turn also helped bring a series of positive social changes. In retrospect, one finds that the British government adopted a cautious approach to that. In general, the British government avowed that it would stay out of local customs and religious practices. Initially, the practice of *Sati*, for example, was not questioned and considered part of their policy of 'laissez faire' in terms of religion. In light of growing protests against the brutal practice, the British, in 1817, ruled that it was against Hindu law (Hardgrave 1998: 57–80). However, this did not stop the practice. Led by progressive voices such as Raja Rammohun Roy and the Governor General Lord William Bentinck, *Sati* was banned in 1829 (Majumdar et al. 1978: 816–819). Recent literature also highlights the reality that even though the practice was banned in the mid-nineteenth century, the British and the Indian perspectives seemed to suggest that the brutality of the practice violated the sacred scriptures and hence needed to be abolished (Mani 1986: 32–40). Evidently, then, the larger issues of the status of women and their fundamental human rights were not the driving force of such reforms.

In sum, despite some progressive policies, there was an absence of equity in treating Indian subjects that seemed to plague and tarnish the administrative unity and aspects of social progress that the British managed to successfully implement. Rabindranath Tagore, an internationalist, and the first non-European to win a Nobel Prize in literature, praised many of the liberal ideas the British stood for but was deeply disturbed with the denial of basic human rights and treatment of Indian subjects by their British colonial masters. He renounced his knighthood in the face of the mass murder of women and children in the Jalianwala Bagh shooting in Amritsar in 1919. In a letter to Lord Chelmsford, the Viceroy of India, Tagore wrote,

> I for my part wish to stand, shorn of all special distinctions, by the side of those of my countrymen, who, for their so-called insignificance, are liable to suffer degradation not fit for human beings.
>
> *(Tagore 1919)*

This summarizes the sentiments of millions in the first half of the twentieth century. It captures the impact of the British rule in India, a reverence for its values, but a bewilderment and frustration about its tactics and treatment of Indians as humans. India's soul was wounded, and its spirit needed to rise up, as it did with the nationalist movement. As the debate continues about the relevance of India's past on its present and future, Nehru's words seem timeless: "Each incursion of foreign elements was a challenge to this culture, but it was met successfully by a new synthesis and a process of absorption" (Nehru 2004 [1946]: 72). The democratic system that the country has been experimenting with since political independence in 1947, indeed the world's largest democracy, bears the seeds of conflict as well as a commitment to resolving often chaotic differences, albeit providing the foundations of a resilient democracy.

Discussion questions

1   What are some of the highlights and turning points in the history of ancient India?
2   What aspects of the history of India do you think have relevance to contemporary India?
3   What were the positive and negative influences of the Mughal rule in India?
4   What were the positive and negative influences of the British rule in India?
5   India would not have obtained a non-violent independence from the British without Gandhi – argue with opposing viewpoints.

Further reading

Akbar, M.J. (1988) *Nehru: The Making of India*, New York: The Viking Press.

Bayly, C.A. (1988) *The New Cambridge History of India, II.1: Indian Society and the Making of the British Empire*, Cambridge: Cambridge University Press.

Brecher, M. (1959) *Nehru: A Political Biography*, New York: Oxford University Press.

Brown, J.M. (1985) *Modern India: The Origins of an Asian Democracy*, New Delhi: Oxford University Press.

Brown, J.M. (1989) *Gandhi: Prisoner of Hope*, New Haven: Yale University Press.

Habib, I. (1982) *An Atlas of the Mughal Empire*, New Delhi: Oxford University Press.

Keay, J. (2011) *India: A History*, New York: Grove Press.

Metcalf, T.R. (1994) *Ideologies of the Raj*, Cambridge: Cambridge University Press.

Sarkar, S. (1989) *Modern India 1885–1947*, New York: Palgrave Macmillan.

References

Bose, S. and Jalal, A. (1998) *Modern South Asia*, New Delhi: Oxford University Press.

Dodwell, H.H. (1963) *The Cambridge History of India, Volume V*, New Delhi: S.S. Chand.

Hardgrave Jr., R.L. (1998) 'The Representation of Sati: Four Eighteenth Century Etchings by Baltazard Solvyns', *Bengal Past and Present* 117: 57–80. Retrieved from: www.laits.utexas.edu/solvyns-project/Satiart.rft.html.

Hardgrave Jr., R.L. and Kochanek, S.A. (2000) *India: Government and Politics in a Developing Nation*, Austin, TX: Harcourt College Publishers.

Hunter, W.W. (1966) *The Indian Empire: Its People, History, and Products*, New York: AMS Press.

Lamb, B.P. (1975) *India: A World in Transition*, New York: Praeger.

Majumdar, R.C., Raychaudhuri, H.C. and Datta, K. (1978) *An Advanced History of India*, New Delhi: Palgrave Macmillan.

Mani, L. (1986) 'Production of an Official Discourse on "Sati" in Early Nineteenth Century Bengal', *Economic and Political Weekly* 21(17): WS32–WS40. Retrieved from: www.jstor.org/stable/4375595.

Mansingh, S. (2006) *Historical Dictionary of India*, Lanham, MD: Scarecrow Press Inc., a subsidiary of Rowman Littlefield.

Nehru, J. (2004) [1946] *The Discovery of India*, New Delhi: Viking/Penguin.

Oberst, R.C., Malik, Y.K., Kennedy, C.H., Kapur, A., Lawoti, M., Rahman, S. and Ahmad, A. (2014) *Government and Politics in South Asia*, Boulder: Westview Press.

Schaffer, T.C. and Schaffer, H.B. (2016) *India at the Global High Table: The Quest for Regional Primacy and Strategic Autonomy*, Washington, DC: Brookings Institution Press.

Sen, A. 'Imperial Illusions', *The New Republic*, December 31, 2007. Retrieved from: https://newrepublic.com/article/61784/imperial-illusions.

Singhal, D.P. [1972] (1993) *India and the World Civilization*, Calcutta: Rupa.

Tagore, R. (1919) Public letter to Lord Chelmsford, Viceroy of India, published by *The Statesman* (June 3, 1919), and in the *Modern Review* (July 1919). Retrieved from: www.indiaofthepast.org/contribute-memories/read-con tributions/major-events-pre-1950/320-tagore-and-the-jallianwala-bagh-massacre-1919.

Tharoor, S. (2016) *An Era of Darkness: The British Empire in India*, New Delhi: Aleph.

3

INDIA'S 'ARGUMENTATIVE' CULTURE

Democratic institutions and the party system

Prologue

The students I was traveling with recalled from their readings that the British had left India in 1947. For a long time, Calcutta served as the British capital. But the original villages that comprised the city were Kolkata, Sutanuti, and Gobindopur. Decades after the British departure, reverting the name of the city to Kolkata, a derivation of one of the original villages, marked a move to reassert the indigenous identity of the city and its populace. Naturally, they tried to match what they had learned with what they started witnessing upon landing in the 'City of Joy.'

The bus meandered through the eastern section of the city, which at one time would be considered the outskirts but has, over the past decade, witnessed rapid expansion and the emergence of skyscrapers alongside sprawling slums. The hotel was located on Camac Street, the heart of the business district, and so the bus had to divert through the northern section of the city to get to the hotel from the airport. It was still early in the morning, but the traffic already started clogging up the narrow streets. The residential buildings had an old-world charm but also one of lack of upkeep, perhaps due to the skyrocketing cost of maintenance.

The streets were also lined with colorful flags representing different political parties. Often we would come across certain neighborhoods heavily inundated with flags of a particular political party, and sometimes they would occupy opposite sides of the same street. There were political slogans calling for equality and reducing the gap between the rich and poor, marking the signature of the Communist Party of India and its affiliates. There were claims of what the national Congress party accomplished, the Bharatiya Janata Party (BJP), as well as the Trinamool Congress, led by Mamata Banerjee in the state of West Bengal, of which Calcutta (Kolkata) was the capital. As evident from even this casual encounter of the streets, democracy and diversity seemed very alive!

– Author's Note 2014

Chapter objectives and outline

During our visits to universities around India and meetings with political analysts, American students, who came with some understanding of India, had many questions about political parties and how they work in the Indian democratic system. Such questions centered on whether it was the westerners who brought democracy to India. How does India's mystical past corroborate with its more contemporary reality of diversity and technological and scientific advancement? Or what makes India the largest democracy in the world, accommodating a diverse tapestry and the nexus of castes, religions, and languages?

Taking cue from Amartya Sen's book *The Argumentative Indian* (2005), this chapter will begin by exploring the ethos of India's democratic tradition that lies at the root of promoting India's skeptical culture and that allows for dialectical reasoning and policy formulation, essential for democracy. It will present the governmental structure and institutional processes that India adopted to establish its democratic political system. The focus will be on India's democratic political culture and institutions, primarily the growth and development of the party system and how it adapts to India's diversity and plurality. Over the last seven decades, political parties in India have worked within a federal system with national and state priorities, and they have been challenged by and adapted to the structure and functioning of ideological and identity-based politics, the dominance and erosion of the Congress Party, and coalition politics. Through it all, they have been able to muddle through and sustain a parliamentary system of government, however challenged and flawed. The discussion will continue on to the next chapter, which will focus on the cultural roots and fissures in the Indian political system that have given rise to much discontent and the state's attempts to address them.

Roots of India's democratic political culture

In an attempt at contextualizing democratic trends and systems, Amartya Sen has examined the universality of the concept of democracy. Like Robert Dahl, Sen argued that ancient Greek city-states, where democracy arguably took roots for the first time, gave expression to democratic participation in its most direct form. It then traveled in various iterations across continents. The cultural component includes opportunities for public discussion of issues and priorities. It is a combination of these opportunities that has prompted Sen to also examine and conclude that opportunities for public discourse lay at the heart of a successful democracy. In *The Argumentative Indian* (2005), Sen thus considers the *argumentative nature* of the Indian ethos that goes deep into its roots to contribute to its democratic culture and ethos (Sen 2005: chapter 1).

This chapter provides a narrative of how the parties hold together India's 'working democracy.' It is commonplace to identify democracy with *majority rule*. By inference, there is a structural and political element to this concept. The electorate has the political freedom to choose those who are to govern and hold the seat of power during a stipulated, limited tenure. Majoritarian politics, however, has its downside. Minorities tend to get sidestepped; their needs and wants ignored. Amidst its diversity, the democratic experiment in India gives expression to this reality. India is coming to terms with its own past and moorings to sort out the democratic challenges.

Essentially, the point that Sen emphasizes the most is perhaps the need to explore the premise that "the practice of democracy gives citizens an opportunity to learn from one another, and helps society to form its *values and priorities*" (Sen 1999:10 [emphasis added]). In order to accomplish this aspect of democracy, a society has to encompass a qualitative and holistic view of democracy as a symbiosis of *process and institutions*, and *society and culture*. It is difficult to capture all the facets of the institutions and processes and their genesis here. As already mentioned, this chapter will focus primarily on the functioning of national political parties and how they have adapted to sustain a parliamentary democracy. Chapter 4 will focus on state-society relations and the mobilization of groups based on language, religion, caste, and ethnicity.

India's democratic government: legacy and adaptation

Albeit not perfect by any standard, India's democratic system has been commended for its resilience and stability amidst challenges. A parliamentary political framework and a state-guided economic model were at the heart of creating the post-independence framework of governance. Since the initial decades of independent India, the twin goals of political and economic development have been the chief arteries providing challenges as well as stability of the polity.

Recounting the legacies of the Raj, Ramesh Thakur (1995: chapter 2) begins with the caution that unlike the impact of the British in other colonies, the case of India was rather unique. Impact of the British entanglements on the economy and social relations, culture, and the creation of a middle class notwithstanding, the political legacies can arguably be identified. Those legacies "include a rise of political consciousness; tools, machinery, and experience of government; party politics; and civil disobedience as a legitimate technique of political protest" (Thakur 1995: 41).

As Thakur continues to explain, three important landmark legislations helped to formalize the political institutions and structure of the national or central government and its governing principles. First were the Morley-Minto Reforms of 1909. These reforms addressed issues such as how to expand suffrage, on what bases to elect members of legislatures, and how to distribute power between central and regional political units or provinces. The Montagu-Chelmsford reforms of 1919 outlined the basics of the parliamentary governmental structure, distribution of powers, and two chambers of the legislature, and they marked the beginnings of shared governance between central and provincial governments. Finally, the Government of India Act of 1935 consolidated many of these features and expanded the franchise, although it did not include all adults, and it restricted on the basis of qualifications based on property ownership. Many Indians learned about conventions and norms that guide parliamentary democracy (Thakur 1995: 42). Leading up to the Government of India Act of 1935, even though the British rulers granted these and other concessions, they did not respect or give expression to the 'political aspirations' of the nationalist leaders and the people at large, and this resulted in alienating them. One can perhaps argue that denial of civil liberties that followed might have ignited more of a yearning for political independence and the importance of creating a governance system that granted civil and political freedoms. It is no surprise that the Congress Party served as the mouthpiece for such motivation to institute parliamentary democracy in India. Along with Gandhi's transformational leadership, which inspired and unified the country, the Congress Party provided the political insights by winning a majority of the legislative seats in the elections in 1937–1939.

These early experiences gave the party administrative acumen and opportunity to envision the models of political and economic development. The Congress Party leadership rested on Western-educated liberals who were schooled and socialized in the merits of the British system of parliamentary government and citizen participation (Oberst et al. 2014: 29). This perspective was shared by the framers of the Constitution who wanted a politically representative model of democracy but also aspired to a form of 'democratic socialism' to accommodate all socio-economic groups and ensure civil rights and religious freedom. The Preamble of the Constitution pledges a sovereign, socialist, secular, democratic republic. Part III of the constitution ensures the Fundamental Rights of all peoples, and Part IV lists the Directive Principles of State Policy. The latter are not enforceable but outline a set of responsibilities that the state ought to fulfill toward its citizens.

The Indian governmental structure is derived in part from the British parliamentary system and is based on a fusion of powers where the legislative and executive powers are hardly separable. The president is the *de jure* executive head but is more of a ceremonial chief. The prime minister works as the executive and legislative head of government. An electoral college comprising all elected members of state legislative assemblies elects the president for five-year terms. Under the direction of parliament and the prime minister and her/ his cabinet, the president is entrusted to declare emergency in the face of crisis, military threats, or natural and economic disasters. The president addresses joint sessions of parliament and makes judicial and public appointments. The vice president of the country is elected by the two houses of parliament, is the *ex officio* chair of the Rajya Sabha, and complements the functions of the president. The *de facto* or actual head of the government is the prime minister and the cabinet and the council of ministers. Even though the president selects the prime minister, the leader of the majority party in the lower house usually assumes the position.

The party system, particularly at the national level, thus goes on to determine and guide the pathways of India's democratic governance structure and process. Parties also serve as a barometer of the representative model in that their success depends on the extent to which they are able to represent the interests of various groups competing for resources. As the analysis below will show, national political parties have had to depend on state parties for their success, and the functioning of the party system is a key to understanding India's democratic culture.

The party system: from one-party dominant system to coalition politics

In the seven decades since the inauguration of the constitutional democratic system in independent India, one of the most striking trends in terms of transformation has been in the party system. The structure, ideology, and rise of political parties reflect the political and social change to which India has had to adapt since the 1950s, giving expression to growing aspirations of the people through a complex set of sectarian and identity politics. At the national level, political parties in India are often examined on the basis of their ideology and the phases of influence through which they have evolved.

I. 1950–1975: one-party dominance, decline of Congress, and rise of authoritarian politics

Tracing its origins to the 1885 creation of the Indian National Congress, in the initial decades, until 1967, the Congress Party emerged as a centrist and 'catch-all' party, giving rise to a one-party dominant system in India. The Congress Party was able to play this dominant role by accommodating diverse standpoints and flexibility of approach, especially in the early decades. With its organizational efficacy, it was able to accommodate the opposition and factional demands within the party. Even though the Congress Party dominated, it did not generate a "one-party" state, as there was opposition from the left and right throughout the 1950s and 1960s (Harriss 2010: 57).

After Nehru's death in 1964, a fractured identity within the party began to threaten its solidarity. A 'polycentric' decision-making system evolved, in which the various organizations within the party and the state-level entities struggled to establish their identities and success as they vied for effectiveness in the face of rising opposition parties. The first setback for the Congress Party in its dominance came with the 1967 elections in which it suffered losses in several states, resulting in the removal of several state-level party bosses. The Syndicate, which worked as a power broker, bargained for Indira Gandhi's prime ministership, while Morarji Desai became deputy prime minister. However, Indira Gandhi broke ties with the Syndicate, and the chaos within the party crystalized further (Hardgrave and Kochanek 2000: 251–253).

Prior to this, there was broad consensus that the path of political development was parallel to the ones that scholars of comparative politics identified from a Western perspective (Chatterji 2009: 2). Essential to this perspective is the notion of political parties as representing diverse interests. Within this, the 'Congress system' provided the necessary framework for national cohesion and representation: "The Congress system of power consisted not simply in the 'consensual' accommodation of various groups and in the factional interactions between them; it also provided a single framework of power, a degree of policy commitment, and a certain measure of internal consistency and discipline which at the same time provided a 'system' of politics for the whole country" (Kothari 1967: 1490). Likewise, W.H. Morris-Jones' view of the one-party dominant system of the Congress Party also contended that the opposition forces could work out their dissent in cooperation in the Congress era and even bring about necessary changes in the leadership (Morris-Jones 1966: 451–466). It is interesting to note, however, that after the Congress Party's losses in several states in the 1967 election, Kothari was mindful of the need for a realignment but also cautioned against feudal or communal loyalties and discouraged 'parochial behavior.' It is not surprising, therefore, that his writings also welcomed "Indira Gandhi's strategy of personalizing the state and *etatizing* (statalizing) the society through subordination of civil society" to prevent the political fragmentation during that time. Subsequently, after the spate of authoritarian policies of the Congress Party in the 1970s, Kothari reiterated the importance of liberal democratic institutions and self-governing groups constituting a healthy civil society as a buffer between the individual and the state (Chatterji 2009: 2).

Evidently, by the late 1960s, the party had split, and Indira Gandhi rose to power with her populist style and ignored both the party's cohesive culture and the institutional norms surrounding the efficacy of a representative parliamentary government. In 1971–1972, following on the heels of her victorious role in the conflict with Pakistan that led to the creation of an independent Bangladesh, she and her party scored decisive victories in the general and state assembly elections. Riding on this wave of popularity, though, Indira Gandhi adopted authoritarian policies and decimated any opposition from within the party at the national and state levels. In 1975, in the face of widespread unrest and dissatisfaction with her policies and tactics, she declared a state of Emergency, suspending all civil liberties and democratic processes in the country (Oberst et al. 2014: 90–91). India faced its first hurdle in democratic governance.

In retrospect, the 1967 split was critical in that it weakened the core of the Congress Party at state levels, a loss that crippled the party

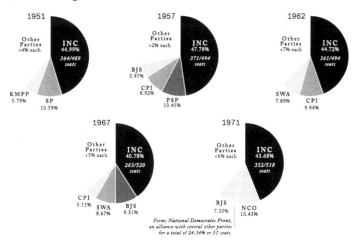

FIGURE 3.1   Election results, 1950–1975

for decades. In some ways, it proved more damaging than the Emergency. In its quest for suspension of civil rights, the latter had mobilized the civil society and renewed faith in constitutionalism and civil rights. "But the Congress split, by wrecking the oldest political institution, created a huge vacuum in the political space that was not easy to fill" (Chatterji 2009: 10).

II. 1977–1989: return to democracy, populism, and rise of pluralism

In the 1977 general elections, voters clearly sent a message protesting against the authoritarian policies and abrogation of democratic institutions and civil rights by Indira Gandhi's administration during the Emergency. The results of the 1977 elections shocked Congress. Indira Gandhi lost her own parliamentary seat. She and her son, Sanjay, lost in this referendum against the brief interlude to their authoritarian policies, which included forcible sterilization, draconian demolitions to clear slums, and disenfranchisement of the lower classes and castes, who had previously been a major part of Indira Gandhi's support base (Hardgrave and Kochanek 2000: 263–265). This election was more of a mandate to restore democracy. Rural and urban voters shared this perspective (Weiner 1977: 621). The Janata Party coalition won decisively, grabbing 330 out of 542 seats in the Lok Sabha. Congress won only 34.5 percent of the votes and 156 seats, and a coalition of Janata Party came to power.

Evidently, the political system was still adapting to coalition politics. The coalition was formed in light of the widespread curtailment of civil rights and disenfranchisement during the Emergency. The splinter party of Congress, the Congress for Democracy (CFD), formed an alliance with the Janata Party and appealed to a wide spectrum of ideological sentiments ranging from the Communist Party of India–Marxists (CPI-M), the Akali Dal in Punjab, and the Dravida Munnetra Kazagham (DMK) in Tamil Nadu in the South. This alliance thus attempted both geographical alignment and shared views on issues surrounding the restoration of democratic principles and processes. Having lost its solo dominance, Congress aligned with the Communist Party of India (CPI) and the All India DMK (AIADMK) in Tamil Nadu. The Janata coalition gave expression to voter disillusionment, but the coalition government lacked a clear platform and stability.

In many ways, the periods preceding and following the 1977 elections mark important turning points in the maturing of India's democratic trends. They reflected what analysts have called the 'awakening' and 'decay' in the Indian electorate and political system. The rise of discontent was evident especially among lower socio-economic classes and rural masses. They were not willing to vote according to the wishes of their landlords; they learned to assert their demands. The effect of all this was that the Congress Party machinery could not control dissent as it had previously done successfully (Manor 1988: 72–74). The Janata government, unable to handle the complexities surrounding dissatisfaction and dissent, fell in 1979. Despite being short-lived, the phenomenon of coalition politics became an important vehicle to assert growing divergence of voters' aspirations and choices and the limits of state power. Social forces started gaining momentum, and they began to emphasize that the state could not continue in its coercive role and had to give vent to people's aspirations; sometimes the parties or the state were not able to fulfill that role. This meant there was a schism between social groups and political institutions, with the former relying less on the latter (Manor 1988: 73). The state as an agency of social change was losing its legitimacy and momentum, giving rise to various ideological and geographical priorities and aspirations, which it was clearly not able to deliver.

Meanwhile, in the face of dissipation of the effectiveness of the Janata coalition, Indira Gandhi returned to her personality-based leadership and created Congress (Indira), which successfully came back to power in 1980 with resounding victory in both Lok Sabha (351 out of 539 seats) and state assembly elections (15 out of 22 states). The period between 1975 and 1980 saw dramatic swings in the party system as well as the strengths and weaknesses of the Congress Party and Indian democracy. The factional struggle within the opposition parties demonstrated that India was not yet ready for coalition politics.

The Congress Party too was fractured with defection of long-time veterans such as Jagjivan Ram, and gradually it eroded the Nehruvian culture of consensus building and built a system based on suspicion that led to cronyism, with only those who were close to Indira Gandhi holding the reins of party power. She also focused on grooming her succession through her son, Sanjay Gandhi. Saddled with unrest in Assam and the northeast, the separatist movement in the Punjab (which will be discussed in the next chapter), the Soviet invasion of Afghanistan (which complicated India's close relationship with the Soviet Union), inflation, and drought, Indira Gandhi faced several challenges. Sanjay's unexpected death in an airplane crash in June shook her further, and she brought in her elder son, Rajiv Gandhi, for support. Internal dissidence within the party continued, and it seemed that with its routing in parliamentary elections in the South, particularly its defeat in Andhra and Karnataka to local and opposition parties respectively, Indira Gandhi's Congress was in serious trouble. Following Indira Gandhi's assassination in October 1984, the Congress Parliamentary Party rallied around Rajiv Gandhi, who became the prime minister. They held elections in December, in which he won 48.1% of the vote and 396 parliamentary seats: an unprecedented and massive mandate (Oberst et al. 2014: 92).

> Jawaharlal Nehru had bequeathed to his daughter, Indira Gandhi, a unified nation; a highly institutionalized political order

and a basic national consensus of the government's socioeco-
nomic and foreign policies; and a reasonable climate of public
morality. Indira Gandhi bequeathed to her son a divided nation;
a highly centralized and personalized system of power; and a
criminalized, weak, and corrupt party of sycophants.

(Hardgrave and Kochanek 2000: 272)

Curiously, during this pendulum swing of the rise, decline, and
return of the Congress Party, it also became evident that the Indian
voters were maturing as they rejected authoritarianism of the Emergency period, reinstated the party with its promise of organizational
and national cohesion, and denounced the chaos and inefficiency of
the coalition parties.

Perhaps it was a swell of sympathy vote following Indira Gandhi's
assassination; perhaps it was a compelling desire for the electorate to see
a unified India. Whatever the impetus, never before did the Congress
Party do as well in the general elections as it did with Rajiv Gandhi at
the top of the ticket. Was Rajiv able to utilize this mandate? Unfortunately, as already mentioned, Rajiv inherited a country that was suffering from a fractured sense of unity with separatist movements, as in
Punjab and other dissatisfied states. He also inherited a party that was
rotting at the core with the personality cult and deep distrust among
members that had been developing since the late 1960s into the 1970s.
Despite early signs of reforms that brought in new players and sought
to prevent floor crossing and dissent within the party, Rajiv too fell
prey to a sense of crony politics and populism that he inherited.

The following year, the assembly elections bore evidence of the
continuing distrust of southern states of Andhra and Karnataka and
Sikkim in the northeast, which voted against the Congress I. In fair-
ness, Rajiv's successes did include the development of a more concil-
iatory tone toward regional and ethnic demands and the signing of
accords with Assam and Punjab. However, between 1984 and 1989, he
and his administration became saddled with several scandals, including
the Swedish Bofors arms scandal, alleging corruption in a defense deal.
Rajiv's liberalization policies did not seem to benefit the large masses,
and he failed to overcome the internal weaknesses of the party, despite,
or perhaps because of, frequent attempts at cabinet reshuffles. Above

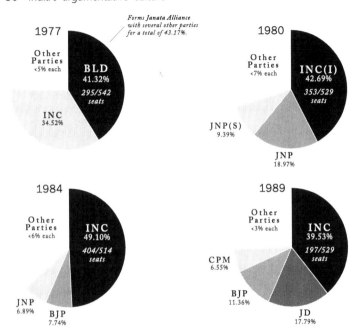

FIGURE 3.2 Election results, 1977–1989

all, he continued his mother's legacy of surrounding himself with crony followers described as "back-room boys" (Sharma 2003: 79).

III. 1990–2004: caste politics, coalition governments, and democratic pluralism

During the 1990s, state parties began to institutionalize politics emanating as other backward classes (or OBC) and caste identities. Following the recommendations of the Mandal Commission Report, political mobilization based on social justice issues gained momentum. The other backward classes included what is also known as the *Bahujans*. At one level, there was an attempt to give political voice to the OBCs overall. Another trend was to politically align the OBCs and members of Scheduled Castes or *Dalits*. In states such as Uttar Pradesh and Bihar, there were brief, albeit unsuccessful, attempts at combining the OBC and *Dalit* interests through coalition governments. Caste-based organizations and parties such as the Bahujan Samajwadi Party (BSP) and others are mired in local realities and a sense of identity that are rooted in state politics and remain a challenge in terms of their national impact (Palshikar 2016: 97–102).

Just before the 1991 elections, while on the campaign trail, Rajiv Gandhi was assassinated by a suicide bomber from a disgruntled Tamil separatist group in Sri Lanka, the Liberation Tigers of Tamil Elam (LTTE). As already mentioned, Rajiv had successfully mediated a peace settlement with the Sri Lankan government, the terms of which included sending Indian forces to uphold the peace treaty and became a source of discontent with the LTTE. Unlike previous tragedies, though, there was no groundswell of support for Congress this time. However, it did help Congress (I) come back to power. The Congress (I), led by P.V. Narasimha Rao, did manage to form the government after garnering the support of smaller parties and pulling a coalition together. It was also able to last the whole term. Despite this, voter ambivalence with Congress (I) was clearly evident. Even though the party was able to gain a few more seats by 1991 and 1992, including most from Punjab, it was routed in state legislative elections, losing to the *Janata Dal* and the rightist Hindu *Bharatiya Janata Party* (BJP). Congress (I) lost in powerful states in northern and central India: Uttar Pradesh, Rajasthan, Gujarat, Orissa, Bihar, Madhya Pradesh, and others (Oberst et al. 2014: 92).

It was clear that India was witnessing a surge of renewed pluralism, and Congress (I) was not able to represent the different voting groups it easily swept in earlier decades. It was able to improve its performance compared to 1989, but the political landscape was clearly changing. The voters in the Hindi-speaking belt of northern India rejected Congress (I). In addition, the BJP continued to build its platform around upper-class backlash against reservationist politics and Hindu fundamentalism, or *Hindutva*. Even though it lost in 1991, it garnered more seats than in previous election cycles, and it won 20% of the votes, a rise from the 11% in 1989. It also spread its influence in key states such as Uttar Pradesh, Madhya Pradesh, Gujarat, Himachal Pradesh, Bihar, and Rajasthan. This period thus witnessed the declining dominance of the Congress (I) and the rise of issue and identity politics surrounding the Janata Dal and the BJP. These trends would collude to the next phase of electoral politics, and party loyalty split into coalition governments again.

Saddled with losses in 1996 and in 1999, the Congress (I) in its part went through several changes in internal leadership, catapulting Sonia Gandhi, Rajiv's widow, to the party presidency, with mixed and limited success. Meanwhile, the BJP clearly was engaged in assessing its electoral futures and reinventing itself. By the 1998 general elections, it had spread its support beyond the northern states by entering into alliances with several regional and state-based parties, such as the Shiv Sena in Maharashtra and the Samata Party in Bihar, among others. It adopted a more pragmatic and less extreme and rhetorical posture toward *Hindutva* and realized it had to extend its reach to lower caste voters. The leadership of a moderate Atal Behari Vajpayee strengthened this appeal further. Even though it managed to secure 182 seats (25% of the vote), its dependence on alliances proved to be critical. The coalition government it formed lasted only one year, but, at the 1999 elections, the BJP came back with a more sound strategy toward coalition formation. After doing well at the state level parties, "the BJP was well placed to

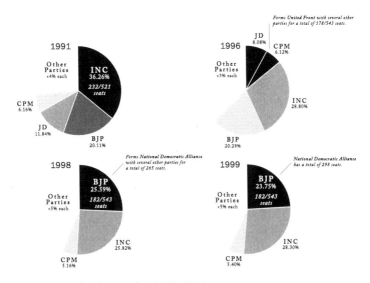

FIGURE 3.3   Election results, 1990–2004

strike up at least junior partnerships with them in the elections of 1998 and 1999 and concurrent and subsequent state elections" (Sridharan 2003: 145). Trinamool Congress in West Bengal and Biju Janata Dal (BJD) in Orissa were two examples of how the BJP was able to cut across the ideological platforms of these parties, which would have made them alliance partners in other coalitions. It formed the National Democratic Alliance (NDA), with a similar majority as in 1998, but having spread its breadth across the country more effectively, and with a pragmatic posture, was able to provide a more stable coalition.

IV. 2004–2014: solidifying coalitions, the Hindu party, and the way forward

Prompted perhaps by its own success at this new wave of coalition building and the fractured opposition, and/or by a strong growth-producing economy (of approximately 7% to 8% annual growth rate) since the liberalization policies took effect ambivalently under Rajiv Gandhi, and more intentionally under the Rao government, an early election seemed in favor of the Vajpayee government. Polls suggested a hands-down mandate for the NDA, characterized in the media as a "Landslide for Atal" (Tummala: 2004: 34). As already discussed, coalition building became the norm since the 1990s. However, it was the Congress-led alliance, the United Progressive Alliance (UPA), that outwitted the NDA in the 2004 elections. It won 36% of the vote and 222 seats, which was 36 more than the NDA won but not enough to form government. It was only with the support of the leftist parties, under the CPI (M), that UPA obtained the needed majority to form government. Other factors leading to the NDA's loss were associated with its anti-minority stance, especially against Muslims, as well as Christians. The BJP's failure to adequately condemn and address the pogrom in Gujarat in 2000 and violence against Christians is considered to have had an effect on the unpopularity of the BJP. Economic growth also seemed to have left a vast majority of the Indian populace behind. About 740 million rural people did not benefit from economic liberalization programs. Focus on trade and less emphasis on agriculture led to the unfortunate situation of poverty despite food sufficiency; peasant suicides in the face of failure to pay off loans also led to dissatisfaction with the NDA government (Tummala 2004: 39).

Several factors are said to have led to the return of the Congress-led UPA government, which performed better than in 2004 and gained 61 more seats in the 2009 elections. With a total of 206 seats out of 543, Congress was able to solidify its strength. Ganguly and Mukherji (2011) contend that by getting more votes in populous states such as West Bengal, Kerala, Rajasthan, Madhya Pradesh, Uttar Pradesh, and Uttarakhand, Congress actually got more seats as they get allotted based on the actual number of votes cast at the state level – more votes means more seats, and the chances of getting this in states that are highly populated are greater. In addition, Congress was able to dilute the impact of caste-based voting by appealing to larger masses of poor and lower socio-economic brackets, people who had been left out of the BJP's 'India Shining' campaign but benefited from the former's welfare policies. BJP continued to hold on to its popularity among higher caste groups, but the success of regional parties such as the Trinamool National Congress (TNC) in West Bengal and the DMK in the South strengthened the UPA coalition and Congress further (Ganguly and Mukherji 2011: 134–137).

By 2014, a combination of factors – including lackluster leadership and economic performance, high inflation, and government inefficiency – were instrumental in the unpopularity of the Congress Party. On the other hand, careful engineering of vote conversion into seats, realigning outside the upper-caste base, and promise of economic progress catapulted the BJP to a convincing victory in the 2014 elections. Lacking an identifiable and stable social base, the Congress Party has had to shift strategies to cultivate support, and this left them even more disorganized. Meanwhile, its main contenders, the BJP and BSP, have been able to get the support of upper-caste Hindus and OBCs and Scheduled Caste voters. From its image of a national level 'catch-all' party, it was reduced to a 'catch-none' party (Chacko and Mayer 2014: 525). By focusing on issues that appeal to the poor in general, such as social protection schemes like the Mahatma Gandhi National Rural Employment Guarantee Act (MGNREGA), which guarantees 100 days of employment, success has been achieved but is limited by some local- and state-level party officials. Whereas in some states, such as Chhattisgarh, the BJP government helped implement it successfully, making the role of the Congress Party in effective governance of such schemes questionable (Chacko and Mayer 2014: 525–526).

Conversely, the BJP seemed to have addressed its earlier shortcomings in garnering more support and converting votes to seats, and it has been able to widen its spatial reach to states beyond the northern and central states. Its coalition also managed to align with upper-caste groups as well as OBCs and received more Scheduled Castes and Scheduled Tribe votes than Congress. One analysis maintains that BJP was able to capture some rising trends and realignments in Indian politics. It received support from a rising middle class, which grew five times in a decade and had rising expectations of less state intervention in the economy. This break from India's traditional reliance on state regulations and subsidies came at a time when the Congress Party was saddled with corruption scandals ranging from coal, housing, Commonwealth Games, and a host of other sectors that also included extended members of the Gandhi family. Clientele politics such as extending reservation or affirmative action benefits to Jats, who represent rural castes in northern India, raised questions among the public as well as the Supreme Court and the National Commission for Backward classes. In desperate moves, the UPA government also resorted to populist measures such as providing gas cylinders and other low-cost provisions such as food grains. While these populist and pro-poor measures, such as MGNREGA, were supported in principle, the corruption and lackluster government was seen to be inept at their implementation (Chibber and Verma 2014: 1–3). Finally, there was also the *Modi lahar* or wave of support based on the charisma of Narendra Modi as prime minister, and his ability to attract 'vote mobilisers' who used their visibility and media access to attract votes (Chacko and Mayer 2014: 526; Chibber and Verma 2014: 4). The fuller and longer-lasting impact of these campaign strategies will be evident through the BJP's ability to translate the expectations and promises to policies and effective governance, which help to consolidate the realignments.

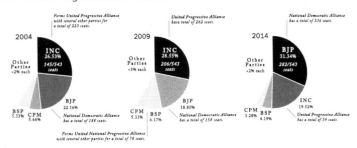

FIGURE 3.4 Elections results, 2004–2014

Conclusion: the party system, pluralism, and democracy

This overview of the party system has traced its path from a one-party dominant system to fragmentation and rise of alternative national- and state-level parties. What does this story reflect about the deeper currents of democratic governance and pluralistic representation? Does the party system capture India's rising socio-political and economic aspirations of its vast and diverse constituencies?

The party system and whether and how it has evolved to address the rising aspirations of the people is one aspect of this understanding. As a corollary, the other related aspect lies in the role of the state and its success and limitations in giving expression to all its citizens. The latter, also seen from the perspective of center-state relations, or essential to the federal structure of the state, have appeared as challenges that threaten democratic governance in India.

After the demise of the one-party dominant system, in addition to the institutional decay of the Congress, and perhaps because of it, there also arose numerous other political parties and coalitions centered around the National Front (1989), the Janata Dal and United Front (1996), and, more recently, the UPA and NDA. As the above analysis has shown, some of these coalitions have been more stable than others; some have accommodated state parties and interests more deftly than others. A party like the BJP realized that it had to move past rightist Hindu sentiments and *Hindutva* to have wider appeal and to spread its influence geographically beyond the northern states, and it also had to reach beyond the upper-caste Hindu base. The system that has evolved since the decline of the one-party dominant system is what has been called India's unique version of a multi-party system, based on "spatial compatibility" in India's "vast heterogeneous federation." This is a system "in which coalescing parties do not compete in each other's political strongholds, a development that is made possible by the fact of a federal polity and state-based parties. State parties are able to trade assembly and parliamentary seats with the coalition's dominant national partner" (Sridharan 2003: 141). It remains to be seen how the BJP fares in terms of governance and policy formulation to do justice to its wider base and campaign promises of a more robust economy. This is not surprising. Despite the common perception of the dominance of the Congress Party, it was never a monolithic system. It always had links to the states and multi-party systems (Brass 1968: 1175). Thus the seeds of dissent and state parties' aspirations were always there; they just asserted themselves at different times and through various arrangements of coalition politics as the above analysis has demonstrated.

Indeed, seven decades later, India is a work in progress, and its democratic ethos, however imperfect, seems persistent. When trying to understand the political culture of India, it is commonplace to attribute all of India's challenges and failures to democracy. Pratap Bhanu Mehta has posed the issue in a comprehensive but pithy perspective, noting,

> Discussions of Indian politics suffer from a kind of over-attribution to democracy. Middle-class despair of democracy tends to blame almost every symptom of our discontent to excess democracy. In response, populists, intellectuals and others blame every ill on the lack of democracy. Both responses are unilluminating.
>
> *(Mehta 2003: 24–25)*

Mehta goes on to propose that it does not help to surmise that democracy has impeded growth and wellbeing. Neither does it help to hold on to the idea that democracy will resolve all of India's ailments. But it appears that the changes apparent in the evolution of the party system in India are clearly a demonstration of India's deep democratic ethos. India has not settled for a top-down model of politics; it represents a vibrant, albeit chaotic, system of aspirations and expectations of groups and interests. Following Sen, it is not so much a matter of whether India is 'fit' *for* democracy but is getting 'fit' *through* it (Sen 1999: 4). Democracy is a much more complex system with a myriad of variants, some of which are polemical and even produce and promote conflict. India is one such experiment, a continual one, with a 'Million Mutinies,' which will be the focus of the next chapter. The debates surrounding India's evolving democracy, in its many iterations, are therefore not a limitation but an asset that helps the healthy regeneration of aspirations and critiques of the ruling elites and institutions – emanating from the quintessence *Argumentative Indian*.

Discussion questions

1   Does India owe the success in its experiment with democracy to the British and Western influences?
2   What is the one-party system, and how did the Congress Party become the flag-bearer of this system?
3   What led to the decline of the one-party system?
4   Do India's coalition governments reflect a failure or success of democratic governance?
5   Does the rise of the BJP indicate that India has abandoned secularism?

Further reading

Gould, H. and Ganguly, S. (Eds.) *India Votes: Alliance Politics and Minority Governments in the Ninth and Tenth General Elections*, Boulder, CO: Westview.

Hasan, Z. (Ed.) (2002) *Parties and Party Politics in India*, New Delhi, Oxford University Press.

Kothari, R. (1988) *State Against Democracy: In Search of Humane Governance*, New Delhi: Ajanta Publications.

Mitra, S.K. and Chiriyankandath, J. (Eds.) (1992) *Electoral Politics in India: A Changing Landscape*, New Delhi: Segment Books.

Manor, J. (Ed.) (1994) *Nehru to the Nineties: The Changing Office of Prime Minister in India*, Vancouver: UBC Press.

Oldenburg, P. (Ed.) (1990) *India Briefing 1990*, Boulder, CO: Westview.

Pylee, M.V. (2012) *Constitutional Amendments in India*, New Delhi: Vikas.

Rudolph, L. and Rudolph, S.H. (2008) *Explaining Indian Democracy: A Fifty Year Perspective – 1956–2006*, New Delhi: Oxford University Press.

Weiner, M. (1978) *India at the Polls: The Parliamentary Elections of 1977*, Washington, DC: American Enterprise Institute.

References

Brass, P. (1968) 'Coalition Politics in North India', *American Political Science Review*, 62 (4), 1174–1191.

Chacko, P. and Mayer, P. (2014) 'The Modi *Lahar* (Wave) in the 2014 Indian National Election: A Critical Realignment?' *Australian Journal of Political Science* 49(3) 518–528. Accessed from *Political Science Complete*, EBSCO-host (accessed May 5, 2016).

Chatterji, R. (2009) 'Political Development in India', in R. Chatterji (Ed.) *Politics India: State-Society Interface*, New Delhi: South Asian Publishers.

Chibber, P. and Verma, R. (2014) 'The BJP's "Modi Wave": An Ideological Consolidation of the Right', *Economic and Political Weekly* 49(39): 50–56. [Web document appears as pages 1–7].

Ganguly, S. and Mukherji, R. (2011) *India Since 1980*, Cambridge: Cambridge University Press.

Hardgrave Jr., R.L. and Kochanek, S.A. (2000) *India: Government and Politics in a Developing Nation*, Austin, TX: Harcourt College Publishers.

Harriss, J. (2010) 'Political Change, Political Structure, and the Indian State Since Independence', in P.R. Brass (Ed.) *Routledge Handbook of South Asian Politics*, London: Routledge.

Kothari, R. (1964) 'The Congress System in India', *Asian Survey* 4(12): 1161–1173. Retrieved from: http://as.ucpress.edu/content/4/12/1161.

Kothari, R. (1967) 'India's Political Transition', *Economic and Political Weekly* 2(33/35): 1489–1497. Retrieved from: www.jstor.org/stable/24477855.

Manor, J. (1988) 'Parties and Party System', in A. Kohli (Ed.) *India's Democracy: An Analysis of Changing State-Society Relations*, Princeton, NJ: Princeton University Press.

Mehta, P.B. (2003) *The Burden of Democracy*, New Delhi: Penguin Books.

Morris-Jones, W.H. (1966) 'Dominance and Dissent', *Government and Opposition: A Quarterly of Comparative Politics*, March, 451–466.

Oberst, R.C., Malik, Y.K., Kennedy, C.H., Kapur, A., Lawoti, M., Rahman, S. and Ahmad, A. (2014) *Government and Politics in South Asia*, Boulder: Westview Press.

Palshikar, S. (2016) 'Regional and State Parties', in A. Kohli and P. Singh (Ed.) *Routledge Handbook of Indian Politics*, London: Routledge.

Sen, A. (1999) 'Democracy as a Universal Value', *Journal of Democracy* 10(3): 3–17.

Sen, A. (2005) *The Argumentative Indian*, New York: Farrar, Straus & Giroux.

Sharma, S. (2003) 'Indian Politics', in S. Ganguly and N. DeVota (Ed.) *Understanding Contemporary India*, Boulder, CO: Lynne Rienner.

Sridharan, E. (2003) 'Coalitions and Party Strategies in India's Parliamentary Federation', *The Journal of Federalism* 33(4): 135–142.

Thakur, R. (1995) *The Government and Politics of India*, New York: St. Martin's Press.

Tummala, K.K. (2004), 'The 2004 General Election in India and Its After-math', *Asian Journal of Political Science* 12(2): 31–58. Available at *Political Science Complete*, EBSCO*host*.

Weiner, M. (1977) 'The 1977 Parliamentary Elections in India', *Asian Survey*, 17(7), 619–626.

4

"A MILLION MUTINIES"

State-society relations in India

Prologue

In *India after Gandhi* (2007), Ramchandra Guha begins his chapter "Minding the Minorities" with a diary entry of an American doctoral student, Granville Austin (which was published in *The Hindu* in 1994). Austin wrote about a scene in front of the prime minister's residence on the day India's first prime minister, Jawaharlal Nehru, died, in 1964. Among the mourners were Dr. Syed Mahmud, long-time associate and partner of Nehru, who Austin observed being comforted by Jagjivan Ram, who was a senior Congress Party leader and hailed from a low caste. Guha quotes from Austin's reflection that this constituted "a scene symbolic of Nehru's India; a Muslim aided by an Untouchable coming to the home of a caste Hindu." Guha then continues the account observing, "Between them, Muslims and Untouchables constituted one-fourths of the population in free India. Before 1947, two leaders had most seriously challenged Congress' claim to represent all of India. One was a Muslim, M. A. Jinnah, who argued that the party of Gandhi and Nehru represented only the Hindus. The other was a former untouchable, B.R. Ambedkar, who added the devastating rider that the Congress did not even represent all Hindus, but only the upper castes" (Guha 2007: 365).

Fast forward to 2016. In January, a student of New Delhi's Jawaharlal University, Kanhaiya Kumar, was arrested following the complaint by another student group affiliated with the Hindu nationalist Bharatiya Janata Party (BJP) about Kumar's role in a demonstration that observed the anniversary of the execution of a convicted terrorist who was involved in an attack on the Indian parliament that had taken lives of innocent people. The terrorist was said to have ties with a radical Islamic group in Pakistan. The demonstration was considered to be 'anti-national' This spurred a nationwide controversy about free speech and nationalism in the BJP-ruled India since 2014 (*Burke* 2016). Questions that have challenged the resilience of Indian democracy since independence – namely, state-society relations, identity politics, and the meaning of nationalism – came to the forefront again.

Chapter objectives and outline

Having looked at the roots of India's democratic governance structure and the party system, the focus of this chapter will be on India's democratic governance as a nation-state in the face of political mobilization by language, caste, and religion: that is, on identity-based politics. Over the last seven decades, various groups have mobilized to assert their identities and aspirations. The chapter will analyze some contemporary assaults on personal freedom, organized violence against religious and ethnic groups, and national unity amidst sectarian identities and civil rights in India.

State-society relations

By and large, as we saw in Chapter 3, India's model of a democratic system has been upheld by the constitutional government and electoral politics guided by a party system that evolved over the last seven decades. During this time, national unity in the face of sectarian and separatist tendencies has certainly challenged the government at the center in New Delhi. Rajni Kothari suggests that given India's colonial and fractious past, the leadership had to confront the challenge of achieving national integration and economic development together (Kothari 1976: 194–195). Atul Kohli (1988) highlights scholars such as Samuel Huntington and others who argue that when the state fails to accommodate demands of groups empowered by economic development, it faces turmoil and even decay (Kohli 1988: 12–13).

Chapter 3 examined the challenges that India faced in the realm of state-society relations emanating from the political deinstitutionalization of the party system. It began with Indira Gandhi's authoritarian tactics and policies, rendering the central government and party structurally and functionally weak and incapable of responding to local and regional aspirations. This decay became evident in the issues based on linguistic identity with language politics and ethnicity in the separatist demands by the Sikhs. Identity politics rooted in religion, and challenging India's commitment to secularism, has also become important in contemporary India.

Class and caste-based politics centered on the mobilization of such groups and the rise of parties seeking to voice their opinions are also rooted in the continuum of decline of the one-party system and the rising aspirations of mobilized groups. During its period of dominance in the 1950s and 1960s, the Congress Party had relied, to their success, on populist leadership styles to reach the poor. In the ensuing decades after the 1960s, social groups including the 'middle peasants' from the success of the Green Revolution, the Scheduled Castes (as in the *Dalits*) and Scheduled Classes, and Other Backward Castes (OBCs) asserted their identities and challenged the nexus of the dominant classes and political institutions (Kohli 1988: 12–16). In the northern state of UP, for example, the 1977 defeat of Indira Gandhi was a demonstration of mobilization of the backward castes behind the Janata Party and the defection of Muslims and Scheduled castes in northern India (Brass 1997: 35). As some of the issues and cases discussed in this chapter will show, inter-caste, communal and particularly, Hindu-Muslim relations form the vortex of rising violence in contemporary India. However, studies have demonstrated that communal riots are interrelated and become a challenge to national unity. Moreover, the narratives of their sources and impact on politics are politicized and complex constructs: "They are used by state and national Muslim politicians to mobilize the Muslim minority, on the one hand, and by militant Hindu nationalists to consolidate Hindu communal sentiments, on the other hand" (Brass 1997: 11).

Sectarian issues in contemporary India – language, religion, caste, and national identity

Language and politics

"Language has been the subject of continued conflict in the state of the Indian Union. India has 1,652 'mother tongues,' and of these, the government has recognized 18 regional languages as 'official' in the eighth schedule of the Constitution" (Hardgrave and Kochanek 2000: 152). Early on, recognizing the importance of linguistic identity, the Congress Party committed to linguistic states or provinces in independent India. While supportive of the idea, Gandhi recognized its "fissiparous tendencies" and its impact on promoting parochial as opposed to a united national ethos (Chandra et al. 2000: 98). Following Gandhi's assassination in 1948, and the country's challenges, including displaced refugees following the partition on the eastern and western flanks (East and West Pakistan), war in Kashmir, and the urgency to set up the political and economic infrastructure, Nehru and other leaders became more cautious about proceeding with the guarantee of linguistic states right away. This caused some dissent in the Constituent Assembly where party members speaking languages such as Marathi, Gujarati, Oriya, Telegu, Kannada, and so on demanded their separate language-based states. A committee – headed by Nehru, Patel, and Pattabhi Sitaramayya – called the JVP reinforced national security and economic progress and advocated that "every separatist and disruptive tendency should be rigorously discouraged" (Guha 2007: 192) for good governance.

However, late in 1952, following protests, Nehru acquiesced to the formation of the state of Andhra Pradesh. But in so doing, he feared that he had stirred the 'hornet's nest.' The States Reorganization Committee (SRC) was appointed, which conducted opinion surveys, which demonstrated that the masses were heavily in favor of linguistic identity. "The movements for linguistic states revealed an extraordinary depth of popular feeling. For Kannadigas and Andhras, for Oriyas and Maharastrians, language proved a more powerful marker of identity than caste or religion" (Guha 2007: 206–207). However, discounting fears of 'balkanization,' the process actually helped India recognize plurality through a pragmatic unity, allowing diversity to thrive through provincial identity based on language. In the eastern state of Assam, where the natives spoke Assamese, there were also a large number of Bengali-speaking people, from neighboring West Bengal, domiciled in the state. When the state legislature adopted Assamese as the only official language, widespread protests broke out, largely from the Bengali-speaking people in the state, demanding the decision be reverted and include Bengali as an alternative. Ultimately, the government had to make appropriate accommodations to calm the protests and civil disobedience.

Even though such movements and recognitions are harbingers of democratic aspirations and trends, the State Reorganization Commission (SC) assessed its threat to national unity and in its 1955 report discouraged the "one language one state" approach. Prime Minister Nehru did not disagree with this perspective. Based on this report, there were to be 14 states and six union territories in India. Each state would be based on a dominant language, along with the presence of other languages and linguistic groups (Hardgrave and Kochanek 2000: 144–145). The colliding perspectives of states as administrative units versus them as entities for linguistic and ethnic identity came to loggerheads at several other instances over the decades.

Some of the demands were temporarily halted but resurfaced decades later. One such complexity arose in the Punjab, where language, religion, and communal rivalry coalesced into exacerbating the issue of linguistic lines dividing state borders. By 1956, Punjab hosted three main linguistic groups who spoke Punjabi, Hindi, and Pahari. In the Punjabi-speaking part of the state, the Sikhs, led by the Akali Dal, demanded a separate Punjabi-speaking state, arguing that the language used *Gurmukhi* script and hence was a Sikh language. The Hindu communalists, supported by the Jana Sangh, naturally opposed this. The opposition was based on a fear that this would, under the banner of linguistic identity, create a Sikh majority state. Nehru and the leaders of Congress, along with SRC, were opposed to dividing states on religion and communal grounds. But the demands for a Punjabi state continued for a decade. In 1966, Indira Gandhi facilitated the split of the state into Punjabi- and Hindi-speaking units of Punjab and Haryana, respectively. They shared the capital city of Chandigarh, which was declared a Union Territory. The Pahari-speaking area was merged with the state of Himachal Pradesh (Chandra et al. 2000: 101–102).

Several other states had similar grievances and demanded separate state boundaries. By the 1970s, much reorganization took place in the northeastern part of India, giving birth to states such as Manipur, Tripura, and Meghalaya, and Union Territories such as Mizoram, which later became a state as well. In the late 1980s, the territory of Goa became a state. It is important to note, however, that not all of these demands were based on linguistic groups demanding separate statehood. Often times, regions and groups within a state felt that they were economically neglected and needed separate identity and resources (Hardgrave and Kochanek 2000: 146–151). Such territories or states continued their unsuccessful bids and demands for statehood for decades. Recently, some of them, including Uttarakhand (from Uttar Pradesh in the north), Jharkhand (from Bihar in the east), Chattisgarh (from Madhya Pradesh in central India), and, finally, in 2014, Telengana (separated from Andhra) attained statehood, bringing the total number of states and territories in India to 29 and seven, respectively.

On balance, by recognizing the need for linguistic reorganization of states, Indian federalism has in fact survived, proving fears that it will lead to a disintegration of national unity to be moot. Noted scholars such as W.H. Morris Jones and Rajni Kothari have upheld the ways in which recognizing linguistic identity has facilitated more willingness of the units to work in tandem with the central government. By overcoming early reservations and responding to the rising demands of linguistic identity by the people in the states, New Delhi's compromise has made the union more cohesive. Needless to say, some of these demands may have language issues entangled in

TABLE 4.1 Official Scheduled Languages as of 2001

Language	Speakers (millions)	Percentage (%) of Total**
Hindi	422.0	41.0
Bengali	83.4	8.1
Telugu	74.0	7.2
Marathi	72.0	7.0
Tamil	60.8	5.9
Urdu	51.5	5.0
Gujrati	46.1	4.5
Kannada	37.9	3.7
Malayalam	33.1	3.2
Oriya	33.0	3.2
Punjabi	29.1	2.8
Assamese	13.2	1.3
Maithili	12.2	1.3
Santhali	6.5	1.2
Kashmiri	5.5	0.5
Other[1]	13.0	0.1
Total	993.3	100.0

Source: Census of India 2001. Retrieved from www.censusindia.gov.in/Census_Data_2001/Census_Data_Online/Language/Statement4.aspx.

* Excludes figures of Paomata, Mao-Maram, and Purul sub-divisions of Senapati district of Manipur for 2001 Census.

** The percentage of speakers of each language for 2001 has been worked out on the total population of India excluding the population of Mao-Maram, Paomata, and Purul subdivisions of Senapati district of Manipur due to cancellation of census results.

1 Includes Nepali, Sindhi, Konkani, Dogri, Manipuri*, Bodo, and Sanskrit.

more complex political and economic demands as well. The Constitution, through Article 30, recognizes the right of minority communities to set up schools using instruction based on the mother tongue and to not be subject to any discrimination. However, many minority groups and languages continue to struggle for identity. Urdu is the largest minority mother tongue of India. Urdu speakers are scattered in many different parts and states of India. While many in India align the language with communal discord with Muslims, the richness and beauty of the language and its impact on enriching the cultural contributions in poetry, music, and performing arts remain strong and popular (Chandra et al. 2000: 102–105).

Religion and politics

In a complex and diverse country like India, religion, language, caste, and ethnicity often get entangled in the nexus of identity politics. Although the constitution declares India as a secular state, the presence of religion and how it inevitably weaves into the political discourse is difficult to avoid. India's commitment to secularism did not emerge in the similar ethos of religious fundamentalism as in the West or the American concept of separation of the church and state. It was primarily geared to quell religious and cultural fanaticism between Hindus and Muslims (Bhargava 1998: 1). At the outset, Nehru and the Congress Party tried their utmost to maintain secularism. In fact, after Gandhi's assassination in 1948, Nehru, Maulana Azad, Sardar Patel, and other leaders in independent India advocated secularism, and communal politics was kept at bay. Even though India was not declared to be a secular state until 1976, Nehru's commitment to a socialistic pattern of development following secular principles and priorities guided India in the initial years after independence. In reality and in terms of defining individual identities that often overflow into political ones, there is a complex relationship between religion and other forms of social structures and institutions.

In terms of the breakdown of religious groups, the presence of majority and minority religions is obvious. Despite a slight recent dip in numbers, Hindus have been and continue to be the dominant religious group. According to 2011 census reports, there are six major religions, and numerous others practiced in India. For the first time in India's history, Hindus fell from the 80% mark to 79.8% of the population, and the Muslim population was at 14.23%. Among the other major religious communities, there were 2.3% Christians and 1.72% Sikhs. Buddhists and Jains constituted 0.7% and 0.4%, respectively (Singh, *The Hindu*, August 25, 2015). These changes in the 2011 census are reflected in Table 4.2. They can be contrasted with corresponding figures in the 2001 census, as reflected in Table 4.3.

Hinduism, however, is more than a religion. It is a way of life. A Hindu majority does not necessarily translate into advocacy of Hindu beliefs and practices. In fact, the diversity of these practices

TABLE 4.2 Indian population by religious community 2011

Religious group	Number (millions)	Percentage (%) of total
Hindus	966.3	79.8
Muslims	172.2	14.2
Christians	27.8	2.3
Sikhs	20.8	1.7
Buddhists	8.4	0.7
Jains	4.5	0.4
Other[1]	10.8	0.9
Total	1,210.8	100.0

Source: Census of India 2011. Retrieved from www.censusindia.gov.in/2011census/ C-01.html.

[1] Includes persons not identified by religion.

TABLE 4.3 Indian population by religious community 2001

Religious group	Population (millions)	Percentage (%) of total
Hindus	827.6	80.5
Muslims	138.2	13.4
Christians	24.1	2.3
Sikhs	19.2	1.9
Buddhists	8.0	0.8
Jains	4.2	0.4
Other[1]	7.3	0.7
Total	1,028.6	100.0

Source: Census of India 2001. Retrieved from www.censusindia.gov.in/Census_Data_ 2001/India_at_glance/religion.aspx.

[1] Includes persons not identified by religion.

and beliefs has a built-in tolerance in the religion itself. But the social context of religions can hardly be overlooked (Thapar 2013: 6): "As a secular state, the government could not in any way favor Hinduism, but as a nation-state it had the right and duty to promote Indian culture. This culture, however – its art, literature, music – is saturated and colored by Hinduism, as the European Middle Ages were by Christianity. What was to be the place of other religions with different and, at times, conflicting cultures?" (Embree 2003: 221).

Thus, a culture dominated by religious ideals finds it hard to become secular. Since the 1980s there have been strong arguments about the success of secularism in India. Tracing the somewhat different ethos of India's culture and structure of democratic institutions, Madan, Nandy, and Chatterjee contend that India is not suited for secularism and the latter is not only able to prevent religious fundamentalism but could actually fuel it (Bhargava 1998). The politicization of communal aspirations as well as the activities of political parties to assuage religious minorities in post-independence India point to the validity of such arguments questioning India's readiness for secularism. Interestingly, within the Nehru-Gandhi dynasty, secularism has undergone paradigm shifts. Nehru's version of *secular tolerance* was replaced by Indira Gandhi's *secular arrogance* and Rajiv Gandhi's *secular innocence*. In India, where secularism never meant the separation of the church and the state, the latter has muddled through variants and interpretations of secularism. Nehru had managed to keep the state 'equidistant' from all religions. Indira Gandhi's alliance with the religious leader Sant Bhrindanwale to curb the more moderate Akali Dal (discussed later in this chapter) demonstrated that she was using religion to attain her political goals. In the 1980s, Rajiv Gandhi and his Congress Party got entangled into religion in the Shah Bano case (Varshney 2003: 78–82).

A related note to keep in mind is that in the case of India, communal identities and the politics surrounding it often seep into those based on caste. As will be seen in our discussion of caste and politics, the boundaries between caste and communal identities often become obfuscated. Intersectionality or cross-cutting cleavages often guide political mobilization. The Hindu-Muslim outbursts in northern India are based on communal demands, whereas, in the South, they often align with the fallout of caste politics. For example, in parts of South India, where the anti-Brahmin movement was weak, Muslims found an opportunity to advance their communal identity-based demands (Béteille 1969: 50).

Empirically speaking, from early on, communalism did not disappear, as the nationalist leaders had hoped. Whether it is for votes, or to give representation to minority rights, secularism faces challenges as it gets entangled as the state acts as mediator between communal and ethnic groups and their demands. This becomes even more challenging with state involvement in communal riots (Wilkinson 2004). Occasional outbreak of religious fanaticism and riots have plagued India and, alongside, raised questions about the role of the state in assuaging and fueling them. Organizations such as the RSS, the Jana Sangh, Jamaat-e-Islami, Muslim League, Akalai Dal, and Christian groups operated in different parts of the country. Geographically, they spread from Punjab to Kerala, Tamil Nadu, Andhra Pradesh, West Bengal, and Orissa (Chandra et al. 2000: 434–435). The very birth of India and Pakistan saw communal riots and violence following the Partition. Subsequently, several situations and cases demonstrated the complex relationship of the politicization of religion. These include issues surrounding Shariyat or Muslim Personal Law, the Babri Masjid controversy in the late 1980s and early 1990s, the Sikh demands for separate homeland, and the unresolved status and ensuing instability in the state of Kashmir, which is a complex issue involving many aspects of democratic governance, including religious identity.

 Even though a champion of secular ideas in independent India, Congress began relying on the Muslim vote early on. Several trends and events, and the gradual waning of the party's dominance in the 1960s, made it necessary for the rise of several platforms through which the Muslim community, sometimes through interest groups politics, sometimes through advocacy, tried to remove overt Hindu influence on educational curricula, recognize the Urdu language and the Muslim Personal Law (or Shariyat), and establish other ways to maintain the identity of the community, especially where there was a sizable Muslim minority. The Congress Party and its policies during the Emergency had a negative impact on displacing poor Muslims in the pretext of slum clearance as part of the Poverty Removal or Garibi Hatao campaign. The Muslim community felt that the Congress Party, which had protected their interests in the past, was less sympathetic to their needs. They felt alienated and also began to mobilize around issues that affected their community.

Subsequently, the Congress Party tried to assuage Muslim sentiments for political gains. In the 1980s, a court decision favored Shah Bano, a 62-year-old Muslim woman from Indore, who appealed that her former husband, Ahmad Khan, be responsible for her maintenance support after divorce. Section 125 of the Indian Penal Code required alimony support be paid to Bano, like any other woman, regardless of religious identity. This went against Muslim Personal Law, or the Sharia Law, which allows for such maintenance only for three months after the divorce. Following the court's decision, Muslim leaders mobilized nationally, arguing that Muslim Personal Law was in in serious trouble of being jeopardized. The Congress Party under Rajiv Gandhi responded to this by initiating and passing the Muslim Women (Protection of Rights of Divorce) Act, 1986, which upheld the Sharia Law of Iddat (or that alimony was restricted to three months following divorce, as per Muslim Personal Law). The title of the act implied that it was to 'protect' Muslim women, but its underlying intent was to appease the Muslim orthodox voices and guarantee the community's votes. The power of Muslim clerics in establishing the pre-eminence of Sharia Law was further strengthened in the 1990s (Basu: 2009: 314–315). While the actions of the Congress Party government appealed positively to the Muslims, in parts of northern India that some call the Hindu Belt, or conservative bastions of the BJP and its allies, as well as among many Hindus in general, this was a clear case of religious and minority appeasement. Not long after the Shah Bano case, the Ayodhya case started flaring up.

Even though the controversy surrounding the Babri Masjid in Ayodhya in Uttar Pradesh (UP) escalated in the 1980s, its roots go back centuries. In 1528, the founder of the Mughal Dynasty, Babur, had built several mosques where Hindu temples once stood. One such mosque was the Babri Masjid, allegedly built on the holy ground believed to be the birthplace of Lord Rama (*Ramjanambhoomi*), a Hindu legendary god. Since the sixteenth century, this had troubled some Hindus, and they tried several times, especially after the country became independent, to reinstate the temple of Lord Rama on that site. Fearing religious strife between Hindus and Muslims over the issue, the local government sealed the mosque off so as to not allow entry to anyone. In 1986, a district judge allowed Hindus to worship in the temple/mosque, unleashing angry communal riots in many parts of the country. In 1989, the Viswa Hindu Parishad (VHP), representing the sentiments of Hindu extremists, mobilized its followers to construct a Rama temple at the site of the mosque. In 1990, L. K. Advani, the leader of the BJP, organized a national rally or *rath yatra* to further consolidate its efforts to construct the temple. In early December 1992, a large procession of Hindu zealots, approximately a million strong, rallied near the temple, and a small group from among them razed Babri Masjid, unleashing nationwide unrest, protest, and violence (Chandra et al. 2000: 442).

The days and weeks following the demolition of the Babri Masjid revealed several layers of complexities and challenges underlying India's commitment to secularism and the role and strength of religious identities and sentiments and how they affected political and social stability. At the institutional level, the central government was clearly unable to control the wave of religious fervor from the rightist Hindu organizations and their political supporters in the BJP. In terms of the climate of religious fervor in the country, the incident and its aftermath clearly signaled deep fissures in communal harmony stemming from religious discord – hence a blow to India's constitutional commitment to secularism. Riots broke out in Calcutta, Bombay, Bhopal, and other areas of the country. The violence resulted in the deaths of more than 3,000 people, including Hindu and Muslim casualties (Chandra et al. 2000: 442). Whether having the secular Congress Party at the helm helped scale down the violence or whether they could have been more intentional and effective in curbing it is subject to debate. Whether a BJP government at the center would have endorsed the right-wing rally and mosque demolition remains unknown. However, this latter question was addressed somewhat by the lingering issues surrounding the Babri Masjid-Ram Janambhoomi or Ayodhya controversy and events erupting in the years following its immediate aftermath. Some analysts find this to be less a religious issue, and more a communal one, in which religious identity is used to foster a communal interest (Chandra et al. 2000: 442–443).

To be sure, secularism in India has a new meaning in the context of the rise of the Hindu Party, the BJP. Following a pragmatic path, the BJP straddled between cultivating and nurturing its support base, which came largely from conservative Hindu followers, mostly from rural India, and its political ambition of becoming a national party. It assuaged the former by focusing on culturally restoring the golden years of Hinduism by revising textbooks and historical accounts and glorifying Hindu legends, myths, kings, and victories. As for gaining national status politically, it gradually drew strength, largely under the leadership of Atal Behari Vajpayee and relatively moderate and skill-ful management of the party prominence through coalition building through the National Democratic Alliance (NDA). With this strategy, the BJP-led NDA managed to acquire political power at the national level between 1999 and 2004. The party's success at the national level was not matched at the state levels, but it remains unclear whether it helped foment further militancy surrounding the Ayodhya controversy.

Whether as a mark of confidence garnered by the BJP's national presence, or as a reminder that the Ayodhya controversy was far from resolved, communal violence erupted again surrounding the issue. In 2002, a group of Hindus were on board a train on their return from a visit to Ram Janambhoomi. In the Godhara district of Gujarat, the train was set ablaze by local Muslim slum dwellers, killing 58 pas-sengers. To counter this brutal insanity, angry radical militants carried out systematic torture, murder, and property destruction of Muslim community members throughout the state. Amidst accusations that Chief Minister Narendra Modi and his BJP government in the state did not intervene to curb the violence against Muslims in his state, the central government instituted President's Rule, and by-elections were held after the situation calmed down. That the country was far from having resolved communal issues surrounding the controversy was evident. For one, the BJP coalition at the center took no further action against alleged state inaction in this context. Second, in the by-elections that were held later in the same year (2002), the BJP attained a resounding victory (Ganguly and Mukherji 2011: 141–147).

Amidst the Ayodhya controversy and the rising levels and extent of communal violence, it is natural to despair over India's secular democratic system. One might surmise that in the aftermath of the 2002 Godhara incident, the rightist Hindu religious fervor in the state might have felt they had tacit support of the BJP government. Even as there was widespread criticism of government inaction at the state and national levels, when the by-elections took place in December of the same year, Gujarat Chief Minister Narendra Modi succeeded in gaining the state mandate through his charismatic image and strategic vision of economic resurgence through technocratic changes. More than a decade later, in 2014, he was elected the prime minister of the country, and, among other factors, the glamour of the Gujarat revitalization was a centerpiece of that victory. It remains to be seen if leftover resentment and religious strife among the Hindus and Muslims flare up again under his and the BJP's national leadership.

On balance, however, "[t]he crimes of commission or omission in Gujarat notwithstanding, the constitutional dispensation of Indian secularism remains intact, and its practice is not dead – yet. But its health is poor, and it may be facing a slow demise. . . . If secularism breaks down decisively in India, this will spell the rise of 'illiberal democracy'" (Ganguly and Mukherji 2011: 147–148). There is also the call for an ethical grounding of the idea based on 'common good' through participatory democracy, with the backing of a rights-based secularism (Bhargava 1998: 536). India's sojourn, especially with the BJP at the helm, would be to institutionalize such prospects of secularism. Failure of the political apparatus at the center and of the states to handle such questions have been evident in the complexities of the Sikh demands for resources and cessation from the union.

Political entanglements and the Sikh community

Decades after the Congress Party's dominance dissipated, a process that started in the 1960s, as well as under Indira Gandhi's leadership, communal disharmony (especially religious strife) began to take center stage in Indian politics. Nowhere was this complexity revealed more clearly than in the chasm that developed between what is apparently cited as one between the Sikhs and Hindus, emerging from the status of the Akali Dal. The state of Punjab was created in the mid-1960s, but the religious identity got entangled with the political aspirations of the Akali Dal and its aspirations to hold on to power in the state. After its fall from power, roughly from 1980, the party began its demands for resources and identity. In a bid to quell such demands, and even while the Akali Dal was in power, the Indira Gandhi–led Congress Party tried to create a wedge by surreptitiously supporting the radical wing leader, Sant Jarnail Singh Bhindranwale. The Dal, which was never a united front to begin with, reacted to the government's reluctance to negotiate peacefully or responsively, by strengthening its opposition. Against the backdrop of a government, which seemingly lacked resolve and a clear and rationale perspective, the extremist wing began to garner more support. Gradually, Sant Bhindranwale became a lethal force, using the holy site of the Sikhs, the Golden Temple, to launch many of his offensives against Hindus (Hardgrave and Kochanek 2000: 158–159).

Thus, what began as aspirational politics of statehood and resources for the Sikhs became a religious schism by the early 1980s. It also ushered sustained periods of terror in the state and region. By the middle of June 1984, Bhindranwale-led terrorism was responsible for hundreds of deaths. Desperate and unable to prevent the rise and escalation of violence, the government launched Operation Bluestar, which was an offensive that was gravely injurious from many angles. For one, it meant that the army had violated religious space by entering into the Golden Temple, the holiest shrine of the Sikhs, and the strategic staging ground of the Sikh extremists. Major General R.S. Brar, himself a member of the Sikh community, who was in charge of the operation, lamented the assault on the sanctity of the Sikh religion and praised the tenacity of the militants. Many who had despised Bhindranwale's tactics prior to the incident sympathized with him and praised him for his courage to protect the holy shrine (Guha 2007: 563–564). Reacting to this offensive and to heavy casualties, extremism spread to other states as well, and widespread resentment against the government by Sikhs in general developed. The worst of the violence followed the assassination of Indira Gandhi by her Sikh security guards on October 31, 1984. New Delhi became the fulcrum of atrocities against Sikhs by angry mobs, and the violence spread to other parts of the country as well. In Delhi alone, more than 1,000 Sikhs died as a result of the violence that followed Indira Gandhi's assassination (Guha 2007: 565). It was reportedly carried out by angry mobs comprised of slum dwellers, many of them Untouchables, Muslims, and from Congress (I). Although many Hindus provided protection for their Sikh friends and neighbors, such acts of kindness could not allay the fears and communal mistrust among the latter that the aftermath of Indira Gandhi's assassination fueled (Hardgrave and Kochanek 2000: 163).

Rajiv Gandhi, who took over the prime ministership after his mother's demise, took several steps to open dialog with leaders of the Akali Dal and reached some accord, but, due to ongoing factionalism and violence among the different political actors in the state and party, peace was yet to come to Punjab. In 1989, Prime Minister V.P. Singh, representing a coalition government of the National Front with the Janata Dal, tried to mend the divide but was beholden to the BJP for support, and hence he could not make much progress. Punjab was under central government rule for about a decade, as elections were marred by violence and distrust of the central government. In 1996–1997, the Akali Dal, under the leadership of Prakash Singh Badal, came to power in the state, and in the 1998 general elections he supported the BJP government in New Delhi (Hardgrave and Kochanek 2000: 166). In essence, then, the issues surrounding Sikh militancy began and ended with political aspirations and settlements. Despite such events and outbursts of violence based on religious and other forms of identity politics, however, by and large, optimists share the promise of the prevalence of secularism in India.

Caste and politics

As with complexities surrounding other forms of religious and ethnic identities, caste lies at the cusp of social, economic, and political inequality and conflict. Caste represents a unique aspect of India's history and culture with its alignment to the notion of hierarchical status and pollution, tracing back to ancient beliefs and practices (Dumont 1980). The Constitution of the Republic of India, promulgated in 1950, has sought to uphold equality through several of its basic principles and provisions. Mirroring the Bill of Rights of the U.S. Constitution, the Indian Constitution enshrines the Fundamental Rights as well as the Directive Principles of State Policy, which serve to determine platitudes of social and political targets of development, embodying goals and objectives. It also seeks to redress long-standing discriminatory practices based on language, race, ethnic background, caste, sex, or place of birth.

During the formative days of India's democracy, Dr. B. R. Ambedkar, a chief architect of the Constitution and a social reformer and lawyer, ensured through Article 15 the prohibition of discrimination on grounds of religion, race, caste, sex, or place of birth. However, Ambedkar also noted how tenacious and complex the issue of caste is, and how difficult it would be to remove its scourge. Caste intersects with social and economic inequality. He cautioned the complex contradictions that are embedded within inequality (Sen 2005: 36). M.N. Srinivas contends that the intersections between class and caste were evident in that despite new prospects being open to all irrespective of caste or class, it was clear that higher castes, which traditionally had access to better education, were able to take advantage of economic and other opportunities. In the face of such developments, some lower caste members were able to exploit and take advantage of economic opportunities. Such a low caste member then began emulating the ways of members of higher castes, a process Srinivas called Sanskritization. In addition, others in their community realized that they too could rise up and improve their economic condition: "It was as though they suddenly woke up to the fact that they were no longer inhabiting a prison" (Srinivas 1966: 90–91).

Aside from this notion of movement is the concept of caste as a hierarchy based on the purity-pollution axis exemplified by the uppermost Brahmans and the lowest caste, the Untouchables. According to this perspective, the caste system is based on ideas and values, backed by religious beliefs (Dumont 1980:91). Scholars have contested this by pointing to the politicization of horizontal caste categories, as in the rise of the bullock capitalists or the middle peasants. While this is most evident in independent India, the colonial impact on strengthening caste identification is also apparent in that the British gave the Brahmans added importance, which they began to use to exert local influence. As early as in 1909, through the Morley Minto reforms, separate electorates were introduced, giving non-Brahmans a distinct identity. Other reforms gave more access to the so-called polluting or Untouchables castes. Political independence gave legal equality to all citizens, and gradually elite castes began to be challenged by newly empowered 'peasant castes'(Gupta 2005: 409–427).

The story of the amalgamation of caste and class and the politicization of caste is an interesting one. Caste-based identity became interwoven in party politics in a multiparty system that thrives on diversity. Such diversity was often a result of a complex set of factors that rested on identity politics surrounding caste, class, education, rural-urban cleavages, language, etc. A trend that is unique in India is the 'politics of accommodation,' which seems to give the democratic system its resilience, but it has not come without its share of challenges and disruption. Whether it was the Kammas supporting the Communists in Andhra and the Reddy backing the Congress, or rival castes vying to control Congress as in Mysore, or caste divisions based on hierarchy as in Madras (between Brahmins and non-Brahmins), or surrounding land ownership as in Bihar, the issue of caste was present since the outset, and a constitutional pledge of non-discrimination based on caste did not prevent political mobilization based on it. By the late 1970s, the Other Backward Classes (OBCs), intermediate castes between the higher ones and the Scheduled Castes in many states, which gained economic power through agricultural reforms, became "dominant castes." Some of their successes were evident in Madras with the DMK, and in the Janata coalitions, for example with Lok Dal and the Socialists (Guha [2007: 597–599] cites Srinivas who used the phrase "dominant caste" and "vote bank" – the latter implying the political effectiveness of the OBCs).

Such electoral and economic successes of the OBCs often obfuscate the reality of the Scheduled Castes and Scheduled Tribes (SC and ST), or *Dalits*. Land reforms or political mobilization did not alleviate them from dire poverty and illiteracy. In fact, many of the rising castes included in the OBCs in the rural areas exploit agricultural laborers who happen to be members of SCs (Chandra et al. 2000: 450). In 1990, the Mandal Commission reported that almost 50% of India's population was considered "backward." Throughout the 1980s, the *Dalits* attempted to mobilize through the Bahujan Samajwadi Party (BSP) in states such as Uttar Pradesh, Punjab, and Madhya Pradesh, and challenged that the higher castes were exploiting them electorally and economically. The electoral performance of the BSP has improved between 1996 and 2007, especially at the legislative assembly elections, but it has also had to align with other parties such as Congress (I) in coalition as well as accommodate candidates from upper castes. In 2012, the BSP was not successful in capturing the state assembly elections in Uttar Pradesh, caving into the Samajwadi Party (Oberst et al. 2014: 105–106). While it is true that the BSP has had to align with other parties and candidates, the Dalit Movement is broader than electoral victories. Their goal is social transformation. "They have exploded a large number of myths created by Brahminical ideology and the Western liberal framework. The Dalit Movement has also successfully built up a great deal of pressure on the ruling classes and compelled them to give concessions to Dalits" (Shah 2001: 230). The relationship between caste and politics thus remains a complex and dynamic aspect of the Indian democracy, exceeding the limits of hierarchies based on religious sentiments and values alone.

Testing liberal democracy and nationalism: Kashmir

One of the lingering issues that challenges democratic governance is the Indian government's handling of affairs in Kashmir. It is also the quintessential case representing a confluence of religious and ethnic nationalism, territorial dispute, and governance. At the cusp of independence in 1947, the rulers of princely states had the option to join India or Pakistan. Depending on their geographic location and the sentiments of the majority, most made the choice easily. Three states – Kashmir, Hyderabad, and Junagadh – faced the difficult choice of accession and religious identity. Hyderabad, largely a Muslim state, with the Nizam at the head, was deep in Indian Territory and geographically impossible to accede to Pakistan. Junagadh was largely Hindu, with a Muslim ruler, who acceded to Pakistan. Both of these territories were eventually merged with India. The third state, Kashmir, had issues that were much more complex and remain in a stalemate today.

Kashmir had a Muslim majority and was close to the Pakistan border. Its Hindu ruler, Hari Singh, preferred independence and a Standstill Agreement with both countries. During this uncertain period, a tribal army from the Muslim-dominated Poonch area launched demands and a guerilla attack to wrest Kashmir forcibly. However, in response, Pathan tribesmen from Pakistan launched a guerilla attack to wrest Kashmir forcibly. This gave Hari Singh a basis to approach India for assistance and security. He also signed the instrument of accession, which made Kashmir a formal part of India. The government of India agreed to hold a plebiscite, whereby the people of Kashmir would have a say in the union of their choice – i.e., whether they would join Pakistan or remain within India. Article 370 of the Indian Constitution was introduced to give the state special autonomy to manage the governance of the area (Das 2001: 23–24). Even with the brief incursion, the intruders managed to control a third of the state. Addressing questions regarding the accession of Kashmir, several scholarly sources have established Pakistan's role in inciting the incursions and have underscored the legality of the state's inclusion within the Indian union (Ganguly 1998: 11–13).

Beyond the India-Pakistan wars over Kashmir in 1947, 1965, and 1999, the complexities surrounding governing the region, the impact of the stalemate on the lives of the people of Kashmir, and Hindu-Muslim relations need closer examination. The National Front, which dominated the region, failed to represent the spirit of the people. Politically speaking, the Indian government under Indira Gandhi leveraged its 1965 and 1971 victories with Pakistan and ignored the Kashmiri's people's ethno-national and cultural aspirations or *Kashmiryat*. Several attempts were made to forcibly integrate the state with the Indian federation. Repeated unrepresentative governments in Kashmirundermined the political influence of Sheikh Abdullah and his son, Farooq Abdullah. The latter succeeded in rousing the anti- New Delhi rhetoric. In this environment, the militants took the opportunity to organize, train, and cause instability in the area. Following the 1984 elections, New Delhi engineered a dismissal of the legitimately elected National Conference government in Kashmir, which had won a sizable victory in all major constituencies of the Kashmir Valley. This cemented the failure of trust between *Kashmiriyat* and the central government, fomenting extremism in the state (Das 2001: 39).

Since 1987, following dissatisfaction about state elections, the Jammu and Kashmir Liberation Front (JKLF), founded in 1965, and several other separatist groups began using violence to accentuate their demand for independence. Since this insurgency, clashes between the Indian army and various groups in the area have continued to cause consternation amongst the people. Meanwhile, the Hiz-ul-Mujahideen (HUM), supported by the Jamaat-e-Islami party of Pakistan, have continued their attempts at secession of Kashmir to join Pakistan. Throughout the 1990s, violence between the Kashmiri militants trained in Pakistan and armed forces from the Indian side escalated, causing instability and often harming civilians in the process (Hardgrave and Kochanek 2000: 167–170). A terrorist attack on the

Indian-administered Parliament in Srinagar and continued violence in the Kashmir Valley in 2001 strained relations between India and Pakistan and destabilized the region further. Since the early 2000s, the security situation in the Kashmir valley has remained volatile. The government continues to rely on the Armed Forces Special Powers Act (AFSPA). Protestors and separatists respond to the army's killings by violent overtures, and allegations of human rights violations by the government forces mount. The central administration and the government led by the National Conference have gradually experienced an erosion of the peoples' support because of election corruption, human rights violations, and use of military force.

In retrospect, the Kashmir imbroglio demonstrates a multi-pronged case of ethno-religious mobilization. There was religious division in the area between the Muslim-dominated Kashmir Valley and the Hindu-dominated Jammu. The National Conference used its collusion with the Jamaat-e-Islami party as a threat and a bargaining chip with New Delhi. Because of its geographic location, Muslims in the rest of India were not able to integrate with those in Kashmir; on the other hand, the location also facilitated infiltrations and training of insurgents who became a viable force in destabilizing the area (Ganguly 1998: 39–42). Land reforms, economic development, and educational opportunities also seemed to be skewed to disfavor the Muslims. Bureaucratic jobs went mostly to the Hindus, and, even if Muslims were employed, they faced discrimination (Das 2001: 39). "Furthermore, as secular and institutional pathways of expressing political dissent were curbed, political mobilization and activism increasingly proceeded along ethno religious dimension"(Ganguly 1998: 42).

Conclusion

Thus, in some ways, unfulfilled and rising aspirations and socio-economic developments have mobilized caste groups, the Sikhs in Punjab, and Muslims in Kashmir, to name a few. Paul Brass has argued that the "relentless centralization and ruthless, unprincipled intervention by the center in state politics" during Indira Gandhi's tenure has had incendiary effect as in Punjab. As the above analysis has shown, this strategy is also at the root of the Kashmir imbroglio. Rajiv Gandhi attempted to assuage some of it, but, when he came to power in 1985, he was faced with a "wave of Hindu militant nationalist sentiment that supports centralization, national unity, and intolerance towards aggressive minority demands" (Brass 1988: 212). Moreover, Rajiv Gandhi was ineffective as a leader and failed to effectively address institutional decay. According to Atul Kohli, "Leadership incompetence was only a part of the problem. The larger and more important reasons lay in the nature of state-society relations in India's democracy, especially the weakness of systematic authority links between the state and society" (Kohli 1988: 332). Kohli continued that India needed parties and programs to address and solve such problems.

One such wrinkle in state-society relations or the failure of it was evident in the violence that has erupted since the 1960s with the Naxalite movement in West Bengal and that has subsequently spread to neighboring states. The leaders of the Marxist-Leninist wing of the Communist Party, Charu Mazumdar and Kanu Sanyal, took on the campaign to end the extortionist feudal structure of landownership. They represented the poor in rural areas whose demands were not met even through the land reforms instituted by the leftist government in the state. Inspired by Maoist tactics, Mazumdar's brand of militancy yielded some positive results for rural peasants. Indira Gandhi suspended the democratic process and used presidential rule to have central police round up and kill Naxalites (Kohli 1990: 123–133). The Congress Party's crackdown on the movement, which had spread to other states and educational institutions, thwarted the unrest but was not able to eradicate it. In the 1980s and 1990s, the movement, although subverted, spread to rural areas in several states including Andhra Pradesh and Maharashtra. In 2004 the splinter groups of the Naxalites formed the Communist Party of India (Maoist). The network of Maoists, with their belief in armed struggle against rich landlords, spread from states bordering Nepal, including Bihar and extended to Jharkhand, Orissa, Andhra Pradesh, Madhya Pradesh, and Maharashtra. The state's handling of this insurgency represents a duality. As a matter of policy, there is realization on the part of the state that the Naxalites and Maoists give voice to disgruntled and deprived peasants. However, the tactics that the state has used, including torture and violation of civil rights, have put a blemish on its ability to handle dissent, albeit armed struggles, democratically. The state's violent response to the nascent movement in the 1960s only resulted in its spread and irresolute future (Banerjee 2010: 382–398).

To be sure, a vital part of that system is the ability of the central government in New Delhi to work with local governments and regional parties and disgruntled groups. In a pluralistic and heterogeneous society like India's, cultural identity and socio-economic inequality can ignite passionate mobilization in states and communities to assert civil rights. Social unrest and movements in tribal areas in Bihar, Orissa, Madhya Pradesh, Maharashtra, West Bengal, and Uttar Pradesh continue in varying degrees. In 1998, the BJP's national agenda included the creation of several new states: Uttaranchal, Jharkhand, and Chattisgarh, truncated from Uttar Pradesh, Bihar, and Madhya Pradesh respectively (Hardgrave and Kochanek 2000: 170). In 2014, Telengana was granted statehood after decades-long protests that it was neglected in terms of socio-economic development, becoming India's twenty-ninth state. In the 1950s, Nehru had resisted balkanization on the basis of linguistic identity in the region, and lamented, but realized when it came time, that for representative government to work effectively, the party and government at the center needed to respond to such protests and demands.

Thus, deinstitutionalization of the Congress Party under Indira Gandhi and the culture and structure of the Congress Party she nurtured have been a source of much of the erosion of state-society relations. As discussed in Chapter 3, the party system in India has undergone a change in the last two decades. After a spate of unstable and short-lasting coalition governments in the 1990s, the coalitions around the NDA and UPA seemed to address some of these demands. In 2004, the popular verdict sent a message to the government that economic disparities needed to be addressed. In 2014, the voters again sent a message to the anemic Congress-led government and brought the BJP back to power. It remains to be seen what the BJP delivers in terms of maintaining a secular agenda and sustainable economic prosperity. Contemporary India's sojourn with democracy continues to rest on the structural and institutional ability of the party system to serve as representative government as much as to deliver on its economic promise.

Discussion questions

1 How did the national government in India respond to the linguistic demands in the early decades?
2 Discuss state policies with regard to reservations and whether they help with caste discrimination or generate more fissures among the people.
3 With the rise of the BJP, what is the state of secularism in India?
4 How could the demands of the Sikhs be met without generating a wave of secessionist demands in the rest of the country?
5 What are some hopeful ways to address the unrest in Kashmir?
6 Given the sectarian 'mutinies,' and the government's response, can India still be called a democratic state?

Further reading

Akbar, M.J. (2003[1985]) *India: The Siege Within: Challenges to a Nation's Unity*, New Delhi: Roli Books Pvt. Ltd.

Béteille, A. (1991) *Society and Politics in India: Essays in a Comparative Perspective*, London: Athlone Press.

Brass, P.R. (2005) *The Production of Hindu Muslim Violence in Contemporary India*, Jackson School of International Relations, Seattle, WA: University of Washington Press.

Chaddha, M. (1997), *Ethnicity, Security, and Separatism in India*, New York: Columbia University Press.

Corbridge, S. and Harriss, J. (2000) *Reinventing India: Liberalization, Hindu Nationalism and Popular Democracy*, Cambridge: Polity Press.

Dasgupta, J. (1970) *Language Conflict and National Development*, Berkeley: University of California Press.

Harrison, S.S. (1960) *India: The Most Dangerous Decades* Princeton, NJ: Princeton University Press.

Sen Gupta, B. (1996) *India: Problems of Governance*, New Delhi: Konark Publishers.

Singh, Y. (1993) *Social Change in India: Crisis and Resilience*, New Delhi: South Asia Books.

References

Banerjee, S. (2010) 'Radical and Violent Political Movement', in P. R. Brass (Ed.) *Routledge Handbook of South Asian Politics*, London: Routledge.

Béteille, A. (1969) *Castes: Old and New*, Bombay: Asia Publishing House.

Basu, P. (2009) 'Religious Cleavage, Politics, and Communalism', in R. Chatterji (Ed.) *Politics India: State-Society Interface*, New Delhi: South Asian Publishers.

Bhargava, R. Ed. (1998) *Secularism and its Critics: Themes in Politics*, New Delhi: Oxford University Press.

Brass, P. R. (1988) 'The Punjab Crisis and the Unity of India', in A. Kohli (Ed.) *India's Democracy: An Analysis of Changing State-Society Relations*, Princeton, NJ: Princeton University Press.

Brass, P. R. (1997) *Theft of an Idol: Text and Context in the Representation of Collective Violence,* Princeton, NJ: Princeton University Press.

Chandra, B., Mukherjee, M. and Mukherjee, A. (2000) *India After Independence: 1947–2000*, New Delhi: Penguin Books.

Das, S. (2001) *Kashmir and Sindh: Nation-Building, Ethnicity and Religious Politics in South Asia*, Kolkata: K P Bagchi & Company.

Dumont, L. (1980) *Homo Hierarchus: The Caste System in India and Its Implications*, Chicago: University of Chicago Press.

Embree, A.T. (2003) 'Religion', in S. Ganguly and N. DeVota (Ed.) *Understanding Contemporary India*, Boulder: Lynne Rienner.

Ganguly, S. (1998) *The Crisis in Kashmir: Portents of War, Hopes for Peace*, Cambridge, UK: Cambridge University Press and Washington, DC: Woodrow Wilson Center Press.

Ganguly, S. and Mukherji, R. (2011) *India Since 1980*, Cambridge: Cambridge University Press.

Guha, R. (2007) *India After Gandhi*, New York: Harper Collins.

Gupta, D. (2005) 'Caste and Politics: Identity Over System', *Annual Review of Anthropology* 34: 409–427.

Hardgrave Jr., R.L. and Kochanek, S.A. (2000) *India: Government and Politics in a Developing Nation*, Austin, TX: Harcourt College Publishers.

Kohli, A. (Ed.) (1988) *India's Democracy: An Analysis of Changing State-Society Relations*, Princeton, NJ: Princeton University Press.

Kohli, A. (1990) *Democracy and Dissent: India's Growing Crisis of Governability*, Cambridge: Cambridge University Press.

Kothari, R. (1976) 'Integration and Performance: Two Pivots of India's Model of Nation-Building', in R. Kothari (Ed.) *State and Nation Building*, New Delhi: Allied Publishers.

Oberst, R.C., Malik, Y.K., Kennedy, C.H., Kapur, A., Lawoti, M., Rahman, S. and Ahmad, A. (2014) *Government and Politics in South Asia*, Boulder: Westview Press.

Sen, A. (2005) *The Argumentative Indian*, New York: Farrar, Straus & Giroux.

Shah, G. (2001) 'Dalit Politics: Has It Reached an Impasse?', in N.G. Jayal and S. Pai (Ed.) *Democratic Governance in India: Challenges of Poverty, Development, and Identity*, New Delhi: Sage.

Singh, R.S.V. (2015), 'Muslim Population Growth Slows', *The Hindu* [Census 2011, Religion Data], August 25. Retrieved from: www.thehindu.com/news/national/census-2011-data-on-population-by-religious-communities/article7579161.ece.

Srinivas, M.N. (1966) *Social Change in Modern India*, Berkeley and Los Angeles: University of California Press.

Thapar, R. (2013) 'The Secular Mode for India', *Social Scientist* 41(11–12), 3–10. Retrieved from: www.jstor.org/stable/23610452.

Varshney, A. (2003) *Ethnic Conflict and Civic Life: Hindus and Muslim in India*, New Haven: Yale University Press.

Wilkinson, S.I. (2004) *Votes and Violence: Ethnic Riots in India*, New York: Cambridge University Press.

PHOTO 1   Gateway of India, Mumbai. Photo: A. Mazumdar

PHOTO 2   Roadside cricket is popular in contemporary India. Photo:
G.T. Woolston

PHOTO 3   Taj Mahal, Agra. Photo: A. Mazumdar

PHOTO 4   South Park Street Cemetery, Kolkata. Photo: R. Datta

PHOTO 5   Raj Ghat, Delhi. Photo: R. Datta

PHOTO 6   India welcomes visitors. Photo: R. Datta

PHOTO 7   A city street before the elections. Photo: A. Mazumdar

PHOTO 8   Rajiv Gandhi Memorial Rally. Photo: A. Mazumdar

PHOTO 9   Beth el Synagogue, Kolkata. Photo: R. Datta

PHOTO 10   Roadside temple. Photo: R. Veit

5

INDIA'S ECONOMY 'UNBOUND'

From state control to liberalization

Prologue

As I was walking down a narrow alley in North Calcutta (Kolkata) on a bright sunny winter morning, I was struck by the uncommonness of a common sight. It was that of a man taking a bath at a roadside public faucet. Growing up in the city, I was familiar with the long lines in front of public roadside taps like that where women, men, and children would collect drinking water. It was not an uncommon phenomenon. Public space for private use such as this one meant a lot of things. The city faucets were for community use. It meant that there was a collective acquiescence that not everyone had running water at home, or even proper showering facilities. Scorned by a Western audience as an affront to one's dignity to take a bath on city streets in public, it was not something most Indians would cringe at.

Usually, someone taking a bath on the pavement would ignore the passersby, and the latter would also maintain a respectful distance and silent acknowledgement without any judgment, without any intrusion. There is this underlying notion of respecting the economically deprived and the poor that is unique to Indian culture. There is no shame in being poor. There is also a sense of community ownership of public space, be that the pavement, or the facilities by the sidewalk. It almost exudes a deep sense of the culture of democratic equality through a shared perspective and tacit understanding of community needs. Yes there is deprivation and disparity, but there is by and large no indignity or sense of shame or laziness associated with poverty. On this day, though, I noticed that as soon as the man saw me with a group of foreign students, he cowered and tried to get some privacy by moving behind a sparkling red Toyota vehicle that was parked not too far from the faucet gushing out bubbling water that seemed to wipe away all disparities and differences in the city. The sparkling red car in a middle-class neighborhood was also a sign of India shining. Yet people are continuing to have to take baths on city sidewalks. How does one make sense of India's newfound economic prosperity amidst continuing disparity?

– Author's Note from 2014

Chapter objectives and outline

Somewhere in between the "million mutinies" and the "million reformers," contemporary India is shining. Its urban centers are bustling with malls and food chains that one would not associate with India even two decades ago. Upscale foreign-made vehicles cohabit its streets with Maruti and Tata brands, as well as stray cows and dogs. The enigmatic nature of India's model of development is clearly evident in its economic history, policies, and outcomes. Inspired by a planned model of development, often associated with socialist and communist systems, India also followed several short-term as well as longer and more sustained economic liberalization efforts since the 1980s. The policies that were associated with such efforts have introduced periods of growth in recent decades that are unprecedented by Indian standards and commended worldwide.

Questions about whether the economic prospects will sustain and whether the upward mobility will reach all regions and classes across the country continue to rile economists and policy makers alike. This chapter will highlight some of these trends and also look at the impact of and prospects for sustained economic development in contemporary India. It will begin with a conceptual overview of economic development and political democracy. It will then examine India's state-guided, post-independence economic models since the early 1950s. This will be followed by a discussion of the liberalization efforts and its discontents from 1980 onward. In conclusion, the chapter will reflect on the sustainability of India's growth model and its impact on human development.

Economic development and political democracy: a conceptual overview

Historically speaking, most analyses of democracy, rooted primarily in the western hemisphere, have established a link between industrial development and democracy. Institutional arrangements that provide for structural arrangements for people to express their freedom of electoral choice are important attributes of a democracy (Schumpeter 1950: 250, cited in Lipset 1994: 1). According to Atul Kohli, liberals, conservatives, and Marxists emphasize the importance of democracy and markets. These explanations range from the likelihood of democratic systems growing under capitalism, their success and sustainability, and also the presence of checks and balances that help countries thrive as democracies (Kohli 1988: 6). Agreeing with the Marxist position, Barrington Moore has stressed the role of both agrarian and urban sectors in the establishment of democracy: "[A] vigorous and independent class of town dwellers has been an indispensable element in the growth of parliamentary democracy. No bourgeois, no democracy" (Moore 1966: 418). Samuel Huntington has warned of 'political decay' in societies with rapid industrial development in the absence of corresponding mature political institutions. He demonstrated that when social change mobilizes new groups in the political system, and the corresponding political institutions to accommodate them have not arisen at the same pace, there is likely to be political instability:

> Social and economic change – urbanization, increases in literacy and education, industrialization, mass media expansion – extend

political consciousness, multiply political demands, broaden
political participation. These changes undermine traditional
sources of political authority and traditional political institutions combining legitimacy and effectiveness.

(Huntington 1968: 5).

While most industrial societies have been successful at install-
ing and maintaining functioning democracies, two important questions surround their efficacy. One is the issue of equality. Here, Kohli
separates economic from political/legal equality. Capitalism, more
precisely, its support of private property, presupposes economic inequality. Democratic state power has the ability to separate political
equality from economic inequality and establish legitimate governments in 'inegalitarian' societies (Kohli 1988: 7). Seymour Martin
Lipset goes further, calling for new democracies to establish legitimacy through a more "equalitarian economy" in addition to reducing strife among elite and other groups and creating democratic
electoral and administrative structure (Lipset 1994: 7): "What new
democracies need, above all, to attain legitimacy is efficacy – particularly in the economic arena, but also in the polity. If they can take the
road to economic development, it is likely that they can keep their
political house in order" (Lipset 1994: 17). Economic development is
therefore key for democratic stability, but there can be strains from it,
causing instability, as Lipset goes on to show.

India's sojourn with economic growth or the lack of it at the cusp
of independence and later resurgence contains some of these elements,
but India's is also a unique story. Moore captured the paradoxical nature
of India in no uncertain terms: "That India belongs to two worlds is
a familiar platitude that happens to be true. Economically it remains
in the preindustrial age. . . . But as a political species, it does belong to
the modern world. . . . There is a paradox here, but only a superficial
one" (Moore 1966: 314). Five decades since Moore expressed the paradoxical nature of India's development, India has evolved into a market economy, albeit cautiously, and with setbacks and successes. And
its commitment to a 'socialistic pattern of society' and how it blends
it with capitalist influences is the challenge that the country faces to
fulfilling its commitment to state-guided development and democracy.

India's economic development: from a state-centric model to liberalization

To be sure, the state is at the epicenter of India's development models; hence, state-society relations that are fundamental to establishing the political foundations of democracy are integrally linked and relevant for India's economic progress and models adopted to achieve growth. There has been no bourgeois revolution, no conservative revolution from above, and no peasant revolution. The planned model of development that India adopted since Independence partially followed the Soviet model, with state-generated emphasis on agricultural and industrial development and the coexistence of private enterprise. The model drew support from the Soviet Union because of its commitment to the public sector-led development enterprises. India's political stance of nonalignment in the Cold War politics, although a cause for consternation for both super powers, served its model of development well. During the 1950s and 1960s, India received assistance from both the United States and the Soviet Union for its major industrial projects. On balance, it appears that more than its model of development per se, it is the 'mismatch' between it and the state's capacity to direct and provide guidance to social and economic change that constitutes the "Achilles heel of Indian political economy" (Kohli 2004: 258).

Nationalism, development, and the state: 1950–1965

The reliance on the state to generate growth and spearhead the economy was recognized even before independence. The Karachi Resolution (1931) of the Congress gave the state control of major infrastructure areas such as railways, waterways, shipping, transportation, other utilities, and key industries including defense and services. As president of the Indian National Congress, Netaji Subhas Chandra Bose introduced the idea of a National Planning Committee and appointed Jawaharlal Nehru as its first chairman. In 1952, after a brief change during the Interim Government of 1946, it took a more established form and structure as the Planning Commission.

The goal was to address the country's infrastructure development and alleviate poverty through a unified vision while maintaining participation of local bodies (Dandavate, Foreword 1997: 5). Between 1956 and 1966, Nehru and noted economist Prasantha Mahalanobis helped launch the Second and Third Five-Year Plans, introducing in India the Soviet model of planned development. Widely known as the Mahalanobis Plan after one of the chief architects, these early plans emphasized investments and industrial growth to the detriment of the service sector and household goods sector. Mining, manufacturing, and infrastructure development for transportation were some of the areas that the government invested in, including the setting up of three steel plants in the public sector (Chandra et al. 2000: 342–343). The policies clearly favored industrialization over agriculture, with the former's promise of boosting employment. Import substitution was implemented through state protection. Nehru believed in a mixed system, which relied on state intervention as well as liberal political and economic institutions – 'a socialistic pattern of society.' "The building of industrial capitalism was combined with the radical rhetoric of a political democracy as a means of reconciling economics and politics" (Nayyar 1998: 3124).

Indeed, Nehru had a vision, and it blended well with nationalistic aspirations toward industrial development on the heels of independence and the need to strengthen the country's economic infrastructure. Early on, land reforms, public investment in infrastructure development, science, and technology were all undertaken in that spirit. Despite its 'socialistic' elements, it was a veritable alternative to communism. It provided a 'non-capitalist' path to development, and a welfare state based on social democratic values (Nayyar 1998: 3124). This model also gave rise to the licensing system, which meant private businesses were subject to greater state control.

Between 1951 and 1965, or the first three plan periods, industrial production was impressive (7% industrial production growth rate per year), particularly in the newer industrial initiatives in basic metals, engineering, rubber, chemicals, and pharmaceuticals, to the detriment of jute and textiles, which were stagnant. Foreign assistance also increased during this period (Patnaik 1979: 708). By the Third Five-Year Plan, India's growth spurt and the efficacy of the planned model of development began to show signs of decline. Agriculture, which had already succumbed to a lower priority than industrialization in the first three plans, was further stymied by droughts in 1965 and 1966. Inflation rose from 3% in 1963 to 12% between 1965 and 1968, accompanied by a 20% per annum rise in food prices. Facing severe food shortages and balance of payments deficits, external lending agencies such as the World Bank and the International Monetary Fund (IMF) as well as the United States imposed three conditions on India. They included trade liberalization and relaxation of industrial controls, rupee devaluation, and a new agricultural strategy (Chandra et al. 2000: 352). After Nehru's death in 1964, India seemed to have learned the lessons of capital-intensive rapid industrialization and neglect of agriculture, and heavy reliance on the PL-480 program, which the United States refused to renew in the context of the 1965 war with Pakistan. The Shastri government limited the power of the Planning Commission. Emphasis on agriculture, rupee devaluation, liberalization of imports, and more private and foreign investment were the other priorities of the new government (Ganguly and Mukherji 2011: 66).

On balance, whereas the first three plan periods (between 1950 and 1965) brought some growth, they were also marked by challenges. The Nehruvian consensus was, however, more easily attained through his vision. Albeit not always perfect, there was a sense of nationalism and the challenge to establish the new and independent state. Facing capital shortage, the state injected substantial public investment in the economy; import substitution was implemented to protect domestic industries. Land reforms were introduced, and the *panchayati raj* system gave more institutional access to villagers (Nayyar 1998: 3124). How far India was able to reconcile the outcomes of some of the investments in public spending and what their impact was on various sections of the people, as well as how the institutional framework of the party system was able to mesh with such policies, would determine the reality of the development model in decades to follow.

The impact of external shocks on the Indian economy was evident in the decline in growth rates following the border war with China, and the conflicts with Pakistan in 1962, 1965, and 1971 respectively. It further intensified with the influx of refugees after the 1971 war and successive droughts in 1971-72 and 1972-73, and the oil shock of 1973 (Panagariya 2008: 47).

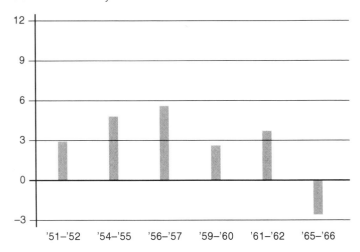

FIGURE 5.1 GDP growth rate at constant prices, 1950–1965

Note: The tables showing GDP growth rates at the different periods outlined in this chapter are reconstructed from data from the Planning Commission of India, retrieved from: http://planningcommission.nic.in/data/datatable/data_2312/DatabookDec2014%2010.pdf.

State intervention, growth, and populism from 1967 to 1991

As already discussed in previous chapters, the political backdrop to these changes was complex and critical to understanding the economic policies outlined above. The 1967 elections demonstrated that the country was undergoing a fundamental realignment. The Congress Party had begun to lose its grip over the Nehruvian consensus. In fact, the consensus of the early decades was yielding place to shifting political alignments and rising expectations, especially by newly mobilized groups such as the newly wealthy peasants: "It was this rich peasantry which captured the benefits of the land reform legislation, the community development programme, the *panchayati* raj system and the network of cooperatives" (Nayyar 1998: 3125). After its significant loss, especially in the northern belt, the Congress Party coalesced with leftist parties and adopted populist platforms such as *garibi hatao* (remove poverty), and it promised 'radical socialist policies' (Chandra et al. 2000: 353).

To reiterate, the narrative of India's development policies was rooted in the political process as much as in the economic policies during this period. It reflected a complex relationship between the state, economic growth, and the readjustments in the institutional set up of political parties – in particular, the deinstitutionalization of the Congress Party and the rise of opposition parties and coalition politics. Other policies and outcomes that strengthened the state included the success of the Green Revolution, the abolition of the privy purses, growth in savings and investment, and Indira Gandhi's leadership in the 1971 Bangladesh War. This phase thereby saw the consolidation of Indira Gandhi's populist and authoritarian rule (Nayyar 1998: 3125). However, the "solutions became a part of the problem." The government became stronger, but consolidation of power in New Delhi weakened the institutional base, neglecting the structures and processes that could negotiate and channel demands at regional and local levels. The party-system, in particular the Congress Party, weakened, and over time, without the structural base to mobilize voters at the local levels, it made room for money in politics, particularly during elections (Nayyar 1998: 3127).

By the mid-1960s, economic performance suffered as a result of crop failures, which led to price rise and balance-of-payments difficulties. Facing sluggish economic growth and balance-of-payments arrears, Indira Gandhi gave in to foreign pressure and devalued the rupee, which was much criticized (Ganguly and Mukherji 2011: 67). In separate moves, tariffs aimed at protecting Indian companies from foreign competition ended up making the former less competitive. Government controls meant increased bureaucratic hoops leading to slow and inefficient performance in public sector enterprises (Chandra et al. 2000: 352–353).

Between 1966 and 1980, as a result of these and related challenges, industrial growth slowed. Import substitution strategies in sectors such as machinery and manufacturing had reached an optimal stage, and there was demand for more equitable distribution of results of such protection. These challenges overflowed into political discontent. Dissent expressed through uprisings such as the Naxalbari movement and others, that demanded more equitable distribution prompted the above-mentioned *Garibi Hatao* or 'poverty alleviation' programs.

The government realized that despite the economic success of the first few plan periods, inequality and poverty had to be addressed. They laid the groundwork for anti-poverty programs (Nagaraj 2016: 193). Deep down, these trends became the harbingers of future policies that could not ignore equity in development and its concomitant dissent. More extreme measures addressing poverty with a goal to redistribution became a centerpiece of the government's 20-Point Economic Program during the Emergency period in the mid-1970s (Frankel 2006: 548). These were aimed at land redistribution, wages, and other measures to alleviate poverty and rejuvenate the rural agrarian economy. However, the outcomes were embroiled in a confusion of political rhetoric and implementation roadblocks. Even though some rural employment opportunities were created, there was no sustained plan for capital investment, which slowed further employment (Frankel 2006: 548–579). The fallout of many of these misconceived policies was mired in political economy and revealed the growing weakness of the Congress Party, as previously discussed.

To reiterate, the fallout became visible between the 1970s and the 1980s, and India was clearly ready for a shift and a revisit of state interventionist economic policies and other structural issues that increased debt and hamstrung economic growth overall. In the mid-1970s, reflecting on an average of 3.5% to 4% economic growth rate, noted economist and member of the Planning Commission Raj Krishna called it the "Hindu rate of growth" (Ahluwalia 1995: 1, Ganguly & Mukherji 2011: 60). By the 1980s, the country was facing serious economic and financial crises, and the stage was set for relaxing regulations on the private sector and on foreign investment.

In essence, the need for reforms in the macro and microeconomic scales were beginning to be reckoned by Indira Gandhi in the beginning of the 1980s. In a 2006 study, Atul Kohli listed some of the 'pro-business policy reforms' that Indira Gandhi and her government initiated since the early 1980s. These included removing restrictions through the MRTP that restricted big businesses and allowed them to expand and compete in areas hitherto restricted only to public sector enterprises, including power generation and others (Kohli 2006: 1256). After her assassination, her son Rajiv Gandhi took office and continued the reform program, although in lukewarm fashion.

Measures such as reduction of income tax were coupled with reforms mandated by the World Bank and the IMF. The call for reforms had effectively begun before the conditionalities imposed by these financial institutions. The Industrial Policy of 1980 began the path of decentralization and the lifting of restrictions for private sector investments. The decades of remaining at the mercy of bureaucrats to secure licenses, or the License Raj, was coming to an end. During Rajiv Gandhi's tenure as prime minister, the government took several steps toward deregulation. It became more lenient with legislation such as the Monopolies and Restrictive Trade Practices (MRTP) Acts and raised the allowable assets for companies (Ganguly and Mukherji 2011: 70–75). Thus, from 1985 onward, in terms of the drivers of growth in India's liberalization efforts, the private sector gradually earned its place among the public enterprises.

Evidently, some obstacles that needed additional macroeconomic policy changes to bring about positive changes toward liberalization continued. Foremost among them was the culture of corruption. Even before Gurucharan Das wrote about the new economy and the associated cultural antecedents leading to *India Unbound*, economist Jagdish Bhagwati identified the process of India's transition from

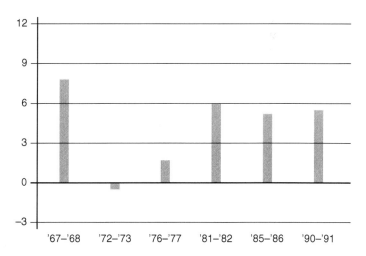

FIGURE 5.2   GDP growth rate at constant prices, 1967–1991

the so-called 'permit raj' with its ancillary institutions of bureaucratic delays and red tape, bribes to maneuver the system, and corrupt practices that meant one would be successful in business if one knew the right people, a sort of nepotistic culture. People had learned to accept it reluctantly. "The time was ripening when an assault on the system would be greeted with a sense of relief" (Bhagwati 1993: 82). How this situation turned around for India in economic terms to become *India Unbound* is an interesting tale.

Liberalization and its discontent: 1991 to 2000

In terms of overall strategy of enhancing economic growth, there were several associated areas that needed to be strengthened. It was in fact a combination of government efforts and private businesses that ushered in much of the growth, although they helped big business more than small and medium sized private enterprises. Kohli attributes much of the transition from India's "Hindu rate of growth" to a gradual upswing during the 1980s to Indira and Rajiv Gandhi's policies that favored the operation of private business. However, this growth-based model resting on private big businesses primarily had two interrelated obstacles. The first, according to Kohli, had to do with politics, and the second with political economy. With the narrowing of the "ruling alliance," the Congress Party began mobilizing the poor using a variety of 'ethnic sensibilities.' The BJP's potential and future strength also increased in this context. Second, "on the political economy front, given the nature of power in the Indian state, the embrace of a state-capital-alliance-for-rapid-growth model of development could never fully replicate East Asia; India's authority structure was and remains too fragmented, and given democracy, the underlying class basis of state power could never be too exclusively pro-business" (Kohli 2006: 1258). Kohli thus argues that the political aspect was demonstrated in the Congress leadership attempting to reinstate its outreach to ethnicity-based party loyalty to mitigate some of the effects of its narrowing support base by aligning with big business. The political economy aspect was also evident from this, that Congress, or for that matter any government, could not be too narrowly wedded to business. The very fissures that make for a viable democracy in India needed space and time to vent, and not dance to the tune of pro-business government all the time. The pressures on the government to exercise caution in collecting revenues, and also to widen public expenditures, led to increased borrowing, as Kohli points out, and even the steering of funds toward internal fiscal balances, paving the way for the fiscal crisis of 1991.

The rumblings of the crisis had started in the mid-1980s. Despite growth, expenditures offset the budget balance. In the 1980s, India's foreign exchange reserves fell as a result of external debt and debt servicing, and the country's credit rating was downgraded (Bhagwati 1993: 68). Coupled with this were domestic and international political turmoil between 1989 and 1991, including the first Gulf War and its impact on oil (Sharma 2011: 157).

The reasons for the financial crisis notwithstanding, the watershed moment for India was that the country was going through a culture shift in terms of the role of the state in regulating the economy and growth, underscoring the impact of ideology on political economy. By mid-1991, led by Prime Minister Narasimha Rao and the minority Congress government, India introduced economic liberalization with a greater role of the market and reduced role of the state in the economy. Furthermore, the demise of socialist-based regimes, symbolized by the fall of the Berlin Wall and the retraction of the Soviet collectivist systems, ushered in a renewed faith in liberalism. By the 1990s, there was thus a divide between those who desperately wanted to cling on to the old regime ideology, and the rise of the new middle class, making it evidently clear that the latter was feeling vindicated in the early 1990s. There was optimism surrounding multinational corporations, the technology sector, telecommunications, and investment in the stock market. Telephone connections rose from 23 million to approximately 672 million, with more than 600 million of them being mobile phones. Apart from reflecting the success of the private sector, the rise in mobile phones also meant that they were better able to connect the rural areas (Ganguly and Mukherji 2011: 93). In addition, the Indian political landscape and the political parties that were viable embraced market reforms, regardless of their ideological disposition. The state parties mirrored the commitment of the parties at the central or federal level to market reforms (Sharma 2011: 160–163).

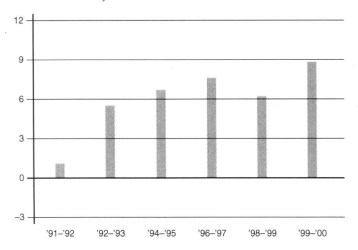

FIGURE 5.3 GDP growth rate at constant prices, 1991–2000

Given India's previous attempts, skepticism surrounding the longer-term sustainability of reforms looms large. Alongside such macro political economy approaches, institutions needed to be changed to respond to some of the new policy changes and challenges associated with them. To be successful and sustainable, such structural reforms needed cultural and institutional shifts as well, which needed to complement the move away from the heavy reliance and control of the state. Over the last three decades, India has witnessed several new policy initiatives leading to foreign collaborations in automobile and other industries, telecommunication and information technology, and other sectors. One example is the enterprise of Sam Pitroda and creation of the Centre for Telematics in 1984, which has ushered in a telecommunications revolution of sorts as well as the government's willingness to make room for autonomous bodies affiliated with it (Ganguly and Mukherji 2011: 70–95). Along with the policy initiatives and infrastructure investments, it appears that there was a gradual emergence of a 'national consensus' on the importance of reforms toward liberalization of the economy. Even though there were differences among parties and interest groups, and not all changes favored trade unions and farmers, by and large, there was no organized dissent powerful enough to derail the reforms or the commitment to them.

2000–2014: sustainability, disparity, and the way forward

The interplay of politics and economics and the pragmatism of the ruling BJP in the NDA coalition government in 1999 went hand in hand. While the nuclear tests of 1998 were a show of the BJP's commitment to hawkish nationalistic defense policy, trade and monetary policy were much more accommodating. Overall, it lowered interest rates and taxes and tariffs and opened up "the economy further by inviting foreign investment in the automobile and power sectors. It fully honoured India's commitments under the World Trade Organization and eliminated all quantitative restrictions on traded goods by 2001" (Chaddha 2014: 109). It also lowered interest rates, but only after some initial hiccups. As expected, sanctions followed the 1998 tests, and had their impact on fiscal policy. As a precautionary measure, the Reserve Bank raised interest rates despite low inflation (3% to 4%), causing a dent in investments, which, fortunately, was short-lived; and, by 2000, India recovered, interest rates were lowered, and foreign exchange reserves rose.

The NDA implemented significant reforms that led to the breaking of the monopoly in power generation through the Electricity Act in 2001, inviting private organizations to generate and distribute power, and also gave state governments authority to work with private companies for use of the state power grid (Chaddha 2014: 110). Despite such forward-looking strategies and economic accomplishments, or perhaps because of them, the BJP-led government succumbed to the Congress-led UPA coalition at the general elections of 2004. Part of the reason attributed by the media to this outcome was that this spate of 'India Shining' policies promoted by the NDA left the poor, or the common, ordinary person (Aam Admi) behind. Others argued that it manifested a 'revolution of rising expectations,' and essentially the NDA lost because they could not keep up with the rising expectations generated by the economic promise and improvements with the new policies.

Dr. Manmohan Singh, who became prime minister under the UPA umbrella, was a primary architect of export promotion strategy and, as finance minister under the Rao government in 1991 had, along with like-minded policy advocates, supported many private sector oriented reforms. Indian companies, however small, even smaller ones such as Airtel, could enter into joint ventures with foreign companies, while bigger ones such as Tata and Infosys became global players (Ganguly and Mukherji 2011: 78–95).

This, however, does not mean that the reforms have been without complexities or criticism. Despite significant reforms and overall manifestations of 'India Shining,' the question of how far the reforms reach all economic classes has remained a formidable question. Part of the issue lies in the inherent challenges of 'market interests' and 'democratic principles.' Unlike welfare states, market reforms aimed at aggregate growth can displace and alienate groups and classes. The latter tend to express their discontent through electoral processes – i.e., by using the vote. In view of the UPA's success in 2004, scholars note the uniqueness of India's experience with this alliance between reforms and democratic impulse, to the point of turning "standard democratic theory on its head: the lower the caste, income, and education of an Indian, the greater the odds that he will vote" (Varshney 2007: 2). The preceding paragraphs have recounted some of the impressive gains and positive outcomes of the reforms in trade, tariff, devaluation, and deregulation, making India more welcoming for foreign investors and many sectors of the country's industries. But how equitable has that growth been? Have the benefits reached all sections of the population?

Noting some unique features of the phenomenon of growth in India, Atul Kohli demonstrated it was "pro-business" rather than "pro-market." As such, rather than the market creating more competition and opportunities, "India's growth acceleration is instead being accompanied by growing inequalities, growing capital intensity of the economy, growing concentration of ownership of private industry, and nearly stagnant growth in employment in manufacturing industries" (Kohli 2006: 1368). Furthermore, there is a growing concern in contemporary India about nonperforming assets (NPAs) of public sector banks (PBS) and restructured assets and loans to businesses (Iyer

2016: *Indian Express*). If these NPAs and loans are not carefully regulated, it might lead to further fiscal uncertainty and instability.

To be sure, when one compares some of the basic indicators of development, it appears that India has been showing steady progress over the decades. India's GDP at constant prices increased from 5.2% in 1980 to 7.6% in 2010–2011. In previous decades, for example, between 1950 and 1980, it hovered around 3.5% on average. Between 1951 and 2011, life expectancy at birth has increased from 32 to 66 years. During this same period, female literacy has risen from 9% to 65%, and male literacy has increased from 27% to 82% (Drèze and Sen 2013: 5–7). Amidst the visible signs of affluence in urban India and the bustling of economic activity, some stark reminders of uneven growth and continuing disparity linger. Just as highways and buildings have mushroomed, so have temporary dwellings and sprawling slums, especially in outskirts of major metropolises and city underpasses. "Poverty has clearly decreased since the reforms began, when roughly a third of the country was below the poverty line, but close to a fourth of the population still lives on less than $1 a day" (Varshney 2007: 6). The disparity between the privileged and underprivileged is growing, yet the channeling of the demands and needs of the latter seem to be co-opted. In contemporary India, the 'relatively privileged' groups, constituting about a quarter of the population, often put forward their demands as those of the 'common people'. For example, they might demand higher salaries and better fuel prices. Political parties and the media treat and channel such demands as 'populist'. In this mix, those who are poor, displaced, and discriminated on the basis of their caste often get ignored, whereas the privileged affluent are often the ones who benefit from public policy that responds to 'populist demands' (Drèze and Sen 2013: 267–69). Another disparity is visible in agricultural growth. Compared to the steady growth of the economy at a rate exceeding 6%, agriculture has grown at a rate of below 3% on average. Farmer suicides in several states are said to result "largely due to a movement from subsistence to commercial agriculture." Farmers tend to have to take more risks in the lure of higher returns, and, when the ventures fail, they do not have any safety nets to turn to (Ganguly and Mukherji 2011: 97–98).

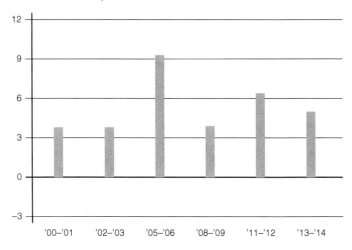

FIGURE 5.4 GDP growth rate at constant prices, 2000–2014

Other areas that India's growth model needs to address are in areas known as human security. Broadly defined, they cover areas such as education, healthcare, nutrition, and so on. Public expenditure on health in India constitutes 1.2% of its GDP, compared to 2.7% by China, and a global average of 6.5%. India relies largely on private healthcare. Lack of resources (only one-third of health expenditure is on public health) means there is an acute shortage of public health facilities. In a state such as Bihar, primary health centers lack electricity and even toilets. Whereas the poor are the most affected by the lack of access to public healthcare facilities, the affluent who can afford private facilities often become victims of fraud, unnecessary surgeries, and other expenses (Drèze and Sen 2013: 148–151).

Conclusion

Clearly, there is still much to be done. The Tenth Five-Year Plan (2002–2007) underlined what has been called a 'human face' to economic reforms, and it made a commitment to address the human security challenges outlined above by reducing poverty and hunger and promoting literacy and longevity. In November 2016, in a bid to crack down on corruption and illicit funding of terrorism, Prime Minister Modi introduced the demonetization of the popular Rs. 500 and Rs. 1,000 notes. After initial commotion and difficulty that millions of people, especially small business operators who depend on cash to conduct their business faced, the situation seems to be under control. However, it remains to be seen whether the move truly has cracked down on the shadow economy or whether it is a true harbinger of more transparency, without hurting India's growth and its poorer sections of the population. Overall, by all accounts, it looks like the reform process, of which the recent demonetization is only a part, has a new consensus that it is irreversible. In the area of market reforms, as recent years have shown, so entrenched is the faith in them that even the recession and financial crisis of 2008 did not usher in any call to revert back to a command economy.

Quintessentially, to India's credit, the reforms in general and the commitment to democracy, with challenges nonetheless, have raised the country's profile and potential as a globally significant power. While it remains true that the new liberalization efforts have yet to realize full eradication of extreme poverty and securing of human development comparable to neighboring countries and China, the path has so far been less than disastrous or dangerous. In 1966, assessing the possible price of India's path to peaceful change, Barrington Moore had concluded, "Barring some technical miracle that will enable every Indian peasant to grow abundant food in a glass of water or a bowl of sand, labor will have to be applied much more effectively, technical advances introduced, and means found to get food to the dwellers in the cities. Either masked coercion on a massive scale, as in the capitalist model including even Japan, or more direct coercion approaching the socialist model will remain necessary" (Moore 1966: 410).

In the last few decades, India has managed somewhat of a miracle in rapid growth and food production, and it continues toward the path of reforms and liberalization and, in the process, has remained steadfast to political democracy, averting both, and deftly averted sustained coercion and socialism. Even so, Moore had warned that the poor would bear the greatest burden regardless of whether the journey is a capitalist or a socialist one. While India's poor may be patient and endure their hardship even as India unleashes its economic might unbound, as Moore suggested, denying its existence is the "the acme of both intellectual and political irresponsibility" (Moore: 1966: 410). That, in essence, is the challenge that the policy makers, intelligentsia, and affluent need to heed to with diligence.

To end with a note of cautious optimism, the political economy perspective seems bright with two hopeful possibilities. The first is the conviction of a coalition consensus in growth. What this means simply is that since 1991, from Congress, to the reign of rival BJP (NDA) and Congress (UPA) led coalitions, from Prime Ministers Narasimha Rao, Atal Behari Vajpayee, Man Mohan Singh, and now Modi, the commitment to change for progress seems to be a shared vision. In retrospect, even Nehru's vision of state-focused change was geared toward progress: "Nehru was a pragmatic first and a socialist second. The policy frame-work that emerged under him resulted principally from the objective of self-sufficiency" (Bhagwati and Panagariya 2013: 211). While there is good news on the growth and revenue fronts, "300 million or more citizens remain below the official poverty line. Moreover, since the official poverty line is itself below set at the subsistence level, many among the officially non-poor are far from having a comfortable existence" (Bhagwati and Panagariya 2013: 96).

This is sobering and an important clarion-call for the leadership and the lay person to focus on a growth-oriented national policy, focusing on private and public sectors and all regions of the country. A more equitable growth, along with India's democratic ethos and institutions, will help the country steer toward a more just and equitable society, with widely distributed prosperity.

Discussion questions

1 Discuss fully the meaning of 'Hindu rate of growth.'
2 Are political parties in India aligned to particular development models?
3 Should India have introduced economic development before attempting to establish a political democracy?
4 Discuss the costs and benefits that the economic liberalization process has brought to India.
5 Will India's growth model sustain? What are its challenges?

Further reading

Ahluwalia, I. and Little, I.M.D., 2nd Ed. (2012) *India's Economic Reforms and Development: Essays for Manmohan Singh*, New Delhi: Oxford University Press.

Bardhan, P. (1984) *The Political Economy of Development in India*, Oxford: Basil Blackwell.

Bhagwati, J. and Panagaria, A. (Ed.) (2013) *Reforms and Economic Transformation in India*, New York: Oxford University Press.

Chakravarty, S. (1987) *Development Planning: The Indian Experience*, Oxford: Clarendon Press.

Chand, V. (Ed.) (2010) *Public Service Delivery in India*, New Delhi: Oxford University Press.

Drèze, J. and Sen A. (1995) *India: Economic Development and Social Opportunity*, Oxford: Oxford University Press.

Drèze, J. and Sen A. (Ed.) (1996) *Indian Development: Selected Regional Perspectives*, New Delhi: Oxford University Press.

Frankel, F.R. (1978) *India's Political Economy, 1947–1977: The Gradual Revolution*, Princeton, NJ: Princeton University Press.

Kochanek, A.A. (1974) *Business and Politics in India: The Politics of Reform*, Cambridge: Cambridge University Press.

Lewis, J.P. (1995) *India's Political Economy: Governance and Reform*, New Delhi: Oxford University Press.

Nayar, B.R. (1990), *The Political Economy of India's Public Sector*, Bombay: Popular Prakashan.

Sachs, J.D., Varshney, A., and Bajpai, N. (Eds.) (2000) *India in the Era of Economic Reforms*, New Delhi: Oxford University Press.

References

Ahluwalia, M.S. (1995) *First Raj Krishna Memorial Lecture: Economic Reforms for the Nineties*. Retrieved from: http://planningcommission.gov.in/aboutus/speech/spemsa/msa033.pdf.

Bhagwati, J. (1993) *India in Transition*, Oxford: Clarendon Press.

Bhagwati, J. and Panagariya, A. (2013) *Why Growth Matters*, New York: Public Affairs, a Council on Foreign Relations Book.

Chaddha, M. (2014) *Why India Matters*, Boulder, CO: Lynne Rienner Publishers Inc.

Chandra, B., Mukherjee, M. and Mukherjee, A. (2000) *India After Independence: 1947–2000*, New Delhi: Penguin Books.

Dandavate, M. (1997) Foreword in S. Bhattacharya compiled, *Subhas Chandra Bose: Pioneer of Planning*, New Delhi: Planning Commission. Retrieved from: http://planningcommission.nic.in/reports/publications/pub_scbosh.pdf.

Das, G. (2002) [2000] *India Unbound*, New Delhi: Penguin Books.

Drèze, J. and Sen, A. (2013) *An Uncertain Glory: India and Its Contradictions*, Princeton & Oxford: Princeton University Press.

Frankel, F.R. (2006) *India's Political Economy 1947–2004*, New Delhi: Oxford University Press.

Ganguly, S. and Mukherji, R. (2011) *India Since 1980*, New York: Cambridge University Press.

Huntington, S. (1968) *Political Order in Changing Societies*, New Haven: Yale University Press.

Iyer, P.V. (2016) 'Bank Insecurities', *Indian Express*, February 9. Retrieved from: http://indianexpress.com/article/opinion/columns/rbi-bad-debts-psb-npabank-insecurities/.

Kohli, A. (Ed.) (1988) *India's Democracy: An Analysis of Changing State-Society Relations*, Princeton, NJ: Princeton University Press.

Kohli, A. (2004) *State-Directed Development: Political Power and Industrialization in the Global Periphery*, Cambridge, UK: Cambridge University Press.

Kohli, A. (2006) 'Politics of Economic Growth in India, 1980–2005: Part I: The 1980's', *Economic and Political Weekly* 41(13): 1251–1259. Retrieved from: www.jstor.org/stable/4418028.

Lipset, S.M. (1994) 'The Social Requisites of Democracy Revisited: 1993 Presidential Address', *American Sociological Review* 59(1): 1–22.

Moore, B. (1966) *Social Origins of Dictatorship and Democracy*, Boston: Beacon Press.

Nagaraj, R (2016) 'India's Economic Development', in A. Kohli and P. Singh (Ed.) *Routledge Handbook of Indian Politics*, London and New York: Routledge.

Nayyar, D. (1998) 'Economic Development and Political Democracy: Interaction of Economics and Politics in Independent India', *Economic and Political Weekly* 33(49) (December 5–11). Retrieved from: www.jstor.org/stable/4407443.

Panagariya, A. (2008) *India: The Emerging Giant*, New York: Oxford University Press.

Patnaik, P. (1979) 'Industrial Development in India Since Independence', *Social Scientist* 7(11): 3–19.

Schumpeter, J. (1950) *Capitalism, Socialism, and Democracy*, New York: Harper and Row, cited in S.M. Lipset (1994) 'The Social Requisites of Democracy Revisited: 1993 Presidential Address', *American Sociological Review* 59(1): 1–22.

Sharma, C.K. (2011) 'A Discursive Dominance Theory of Economic Reform Sustainability: The Case of India', *India Review* 10(2): 126–184.

Varshney, A. (2007) 'India's Democratic Challenge', *Foreign Affairs*, March/April. Retrieved from: www.foreignaffairs.com/articles/india/2007-03-01/indias-democratic-challenge.

6

"MOTHER OF A HUNDRED SONS" NO MORE

The changing status of women

Prologue

"Miss, please don't leave. Promise that you will come back soon," a little girl, barely 6 or 7 years of age, whom I will call Meena (to protect her identity), said as she clung to me. Her frail hands cradling my neck, she refused to let go of me. It was the last day of my stay in India, and I had come to say good-bye to the girls of the Rainbow program at Loreto Day School, Sealdah, my alma mater. Established in the same year as the Sepoy Mutiny, since 1857, this Irish missionary school and the Loreto order has pioneered an education for girls that served as an epitome of India's secular appeal, bridging cultures. This was the school where our close friends were of many faiths – Christian, Muslim, Sikh, Jewish, Parsi, and Hindu. This was the school where we celebrated each other's festivals, foods, and heritage.

Since the 1980s, under the leadership of Sister Cyril Mooney, an Irish nun who made India her home and educating under-privileged girls her mantra, the school opened its doors to street children who were abandoned, trafficked, worked as domestic servants, and otherwise would not have had a chance to get an education. Integrating underprivileged children from the slums and streets with other fee-paying students in an inclusive environment where students mentor each other and share resources offers lifelong lessons in human rights and inclusivity. It was a daunting undertaking: "[T]he school had conducted a survey of Kolkata with the help of other non-governmental organizations (NGOs) and our school students in which they searched for and found 44,000 children not in school. Through advocacy with the local government, 100 schools were created to take in 5,000 of those children, while we got another 10,000 children into existing vacancies and trained 1,200 more young people from the slums to cater to another 26,000 children in 400 small centers of 50–80 children each" (Sr. M. Cyril, 'Human Rights Education in School: Loreto Sealdah,' available at: (www.hurights.or.jp/archives/human_rights_education_in_asian_schools/section2/2005/03/human-rights-education-in-school-loreto-sealdah.html).

Even as this serves as a model for inclusive education, and has created positive outcomes whereby many of the girls in the Rainbow program have pursued higher education and obtained vocational careers, it remains a daunting task. The following year when I went back to the school and looked for Meena, I was told that she went home for vacation and never came back. Sometimes the families of the girls don't see value in their education. When they go home during vacations, they are placed in employment, married off, or even sold; they don't return to school.

– Author's Note 2011

Chapter objectives and outline

The place of women in India's society has always been paradoxical and complicated. In contemporary India, it is particularly perplexing. Some of the cultural conundrum associated with the status of women in society stems from religious and cultural practices and beliefs. They are deeply rooted in patriarchal norms and practices and have led to structural violence against women. The constitution outlines gender equality, and India's women are by and large economically and politically active. Yet, dowry deaths, trafficking, child marriage, sexual and domestic violence, and other practices continue to put India among countries where women's rights are at best disregarded and at worst violated. UN Women reported that a 2012 study conducted in New Delhi revealed that 92% of women there report some sort of sexual violence in public places in their life time (UN Women, Undated). The National Crimes Records Bureau reported that almost 90% of the trafficking victims were girls and half of them were children (*Indian Express*, September 1, 2016). Even if we consider that reporting in recent years has increased due to heightened awareness and more vigilance, the overall rise in crimes against women remain disturbing.

In contemporary India, as the country achieves economic liberalization and a global status change, women's lives are integrally challenged and juxtaposed in a culture of contradiction. The underlying assumption in this chapter is that like other phenomena, women's lives and challenges are in multiple layers of complexities. They stem from a culture of patriarchy, gender-based violence, lack of access to education and economic opportunities, and other obstacles. These aspects are interrelated and intersectional. The chapter will begin with a historical overview of the status of women in India, the legislative and policy initiatives geared to redressing some of the persisting inequalities backed by patriarchy, and the contributions of women's activism. Through the narrative, the goal is to focus on education and economic empowerment and the work of activists, the women's movement, and non-governmental organizations which are aimed toward ameliorating hardships and creating opportunities for women's empowerment.

India's women: patriarchy, culture, laws, and the women's movement

The title of this chapter is derived from the book *May You Be the Mother of a Hundred Sons* by Elisabeth Bumiller. Taken literally, it symbolizes patriarchy and practices that represent a preference for the male child. In this book, Bumiller presents a fascinating narrative and chronicles the tapestry of women's lives with their contradictions and accomplishments. The author affirms the belief that "the status of women deteriorated only in relatively recent times, the past two thousand years or so. Before this, some historians have theorized, there was an ancient 'golden age,' sometime around 1000 B.C., in which Indian women were considered the equals of men, or at least had a higher status than they did in the later millennia" (Bumiller 1990: 15).

In the nineteenth century, cultural revivalists and social reformers such as Raja Ram Mohun Roy and Vidyasagar ushered in a sort of Bengal renaissance that addressed some institutions embedded in patriarchy. As already discussed, while they worked at the local levels, they mobilized and were successful in having the British government pass laws to reverse the cruel practice of *Sati* in 1829. Much has been written about the practice of *Sati*, and it might provide some clues to understanding some of the underlying strands of patriarchy and discrimination and mistreatment that women continue to face in contemporary India. *Sati* conjures up images of a devoted wife who would be with her deceased husband even after death. *Sati* infers that Hindu women would voluntarily immolate themselves in the funeral pyre of their deceased husbands. At a time when women did not have the right to own property, and did not have adequate education or economic independence, widows would become burdens of their parents and in-laws, or objects of male sexual desire.

Championed by many, including leaders such as Nehru, and most notably by Mahatma Gandhi, the role of women was considered important during the nationalist movement. "Like social reformers, Gandhi perceived women as the oppressed group and opposed social customs (early marriage, dowry, purdah, etc.) that subordinated them. He envisaged a significant role for women in Indian society and advocated gender equality in legal, educational, social, and political spheres" (Patel 1998: 159). But as Patel and others have noted, Gandhi's encouragement added more women to the nationalistic political wave of independence and gave them a role in politics but did not question or address the structural causes and patriarchal underpinnings of women's subordination in India. So, even though Gandhi advocated and made it possible for women to get education and play a role in politics, they had to be done within the framework of the patriarchal society in which they were born.

In independent India, early actions of women's organizations such as the Indian Women's Association (1917) and the All-India Women's Conference (1927), or the *Akhil Hind Mahila Parishad*, included the demand for legal rights for women, ending child marriage, and creating opportunities for girls' education. Not surprisingly, their demands did not include access to education for all, especially the economically less privileged and Muslims. The communist parties also subsumed the demand for intersectional and gender equality within their overall nationalist struggle (Patel 1998: 159–160).

Nowhere is patriarchy as prominent as in ensuring the structural denial of property rights for women. The Hindu Marriage Act of 1955 banned polygamy among Hindus. The Hindu Widow's Remarriage Act 1856, the Hindu Inheritance Act, 1929, the Hindu Women's Right to Property Act, 1937, and the Hindu Succession Acts in 1956 gave some rights to women, but they were limited; women did not have full access and right to ancestral property until 2005. In retrospect, the institutions of marriage and the joint family structure were at the core of the subordinate status of women. As already mentioned, the codification of some of the laws pertaining to Hindu women and their rights to property had some impact. Likewise, the Muslim Personal Law Application Bill (1937) and the Dissolution of Muslim Marriage Bill (1938) gave Muslim women the right to inherit property and the right to divorce, respectively. Furthermore, despite progressive attitudes of nationalist leaders who recognized the role of women in society, the spheres of such freedom were clearly demarcated along gender lines that separated the boundaries of the home and the world for men and women respectively. This perspective seemed to persist even after independence. "So whereas men were free to westernize, women were not. The projection of the ideal Indian women as self-effacing was a favourite theme in nationalist discourses" (Chatterji 2009: 411–12).

Women's groups were formed as early as in the 1920s. Up until the 1970s, feminists in India focused on equality through such associations and through 'petition politics' seeking voting rights and other forms of equality. Men continued to be behind many such efforts.

Most of the activities of the Women's Indian Association and the National Council of Indian Women sought to address issues that their members faced and did not represent women at large. The All India Women's Conference had a broader base and was able to garner consensus, as was evident in the 1927 Child Marriage Bill and the subsequent passage of the Child Marriage Restraint Act. These early successes notwithstanding, the feminist momentum seemed to be co-opted by the nationalist one (Sen 2000: 15–16). In post-colonial India, the narrative of women's movements continued its focus beyond voting rights and the new nation-state assured constitutional guarantees of gender equality. Following the International Decade for Women (1975–1985), and especially since the mid-1980s, women's studies programs in academic institutions and the women's movement attempted to bring issues such as gender violence, reproductive health and choices, discrimination based on religious and social norms, and political participation to the forefront. This link between academics and activists has brought many of the challenges women face as a group to the national discourse. "Women activists and academics have worked together to redefine knowledge. Women's groups have played a vital role in the expansion of knowledge and generation and dissemination of information. Activists from women's groups and organizations are also active participants in all public forums pertaining to women's studies" (Patel 1998: 165).

Constitutional safeguards for the rights of women and minorities co-existed, and were sometimes superseded by "personal laws" which upheld discrimination based on culture and religion. The Women's Movement thus demanded for a Uniform Civil Code (UCC), which would guarantee fundamental rights over personal laws. In 1985, the Supreme Court upheld a divorced Muslim woman's (Shah Bano) right to alimony, giving precedence to UCC over Muslim personal law. As the Muslim leaders protested, the judgment made it complicated for feminists who found a women's rights issue being coopted by communal politics and especially the fundamental rightist party (BJP). There was fear among some that with its national majoritarian presence, the BJP would incorporate Hindu personal law within a UCC. The feminists remain divided on how and whether to decouple personal laws and UCC and, given the politicization of the agenda of UCC, whether to support the movement wholeheartedly.

Increasingly, there is a call for 'gender-just' legislation and policies (Sen 2000: 33–36).

Curiously, in terms of women's leadership, India is one of the few countries in the world, which has had both a *de jure* and a *de facto* woman head of state. Pratibha Patil was the first woman president of India, 2007–2012. In India's parliamentary form of government, the president is a titular and formal head of state, whereas the prime minister is the *de facto* head of government. Indira Gandhi was the first woman prime minister of India from 1966 to 1977 and then again from 1980 to 1984, when her term ended abruptly with her assassination by Sikh bodyguards, following her role in the secessionist movement in Punjab, discussed in Chapter 4.

Paradoxically, the mere rise of neither Pratibha Patil nor Indira Gandhi to the nation's highest political offices heralds the elevation of the status of women. Even though she has shown considerable leadership qualities, as daughter of Nehru, Indira Gandhi's ascent to power through the Congress Party reflects a trend of women political leaders in other developing contexts where power went to women as a kind of reflected glory from their male relatives. Mrs. Gandhi even appealed to women to "carry the responsibility of running the home" (Chatterji 2009: 412). "India, the world's largest democracy, has only 65 women representatives out of 542 members in Lok Sabha, while there are 31 female representatives in the 242 member Rajya Sabha and at present, 12.24% seats of Indian Parliament is held by women" (UN-ESCAP 2015: 56). While this is clearly a cause for concern, and because of such gaps, conventions and policies have to work in tandem with socio-cultural attitudes leading to gender based violence and challenges posed by access to education and work for women.

Women, education, and empowerment

Making education a priority is a universally shared objective. In 1990, Amartya Sen argued that women's education and economic rights were critical in every society. Preference for the male child and lack of education and health can go on to skew the sex ratio in favor of males. Because of high literacy rates, women in the state of Kerala in India also enjoy high life expectancy rates and are more successful in finding employment (Sen 1990). India's women have to give birth to children, yet they often do not have a role or authority in reproductive decision-making. Education is key to bringing a change in all this, for both the women and the men. An illiterate mother with ill health will not be able to take care of her children and raise them to become healthy contributors to the country's future labor force. An educated mother will be able to see the importance of the nutrition and education of both her daughter and son.

Empowerment is a multilayered concept which has been widely used and reused, and has become somewhat of a buzzword for decades. It is a process through which women gain greater control of resources to address inequality and establish social and economic justice. Even though it has a long history of usage, by the 1980s, some used the term 'women's empowerment' "as a more political and transformatory idea for struggles that challenged not only patriarchy, but also the mediating structures of class, race, ethnicity – and, in India, caste and religion – which determined the nature of women's position and condition in developing societies" (Batliwala 2007: 558). Batliwala shows how the term empowerment, which replaced earlier concepts such as women's welfare, has been co-opted by governments, feminist movements and organizations, and donor and development agencies alike. Within these parameters, this chapter uses the concept of empowerment as a process through which women achieve agency, primarily using access to education and economic opportunities, to address inequality and ensure economic and social justice.

In 2000, the United Nations launched the Millennium Development Goals (MDGs), setting goals and targets for development. Of the MDGs, Goals 2 and 3 were geared toward achieving universal primary education and promoting gender equality and empowerment respectively. According to the 2015 report on MDGs by the Government of India (Statistical Division; hereafter India MDG Report 2015), India has made significant progress on Goal 2, achieving universal primary education. Through this, boys and girls will get equal access to primary education. Chapter 4 of the report examines this goal and its targets, and it presents the overall success on MDG 2, achieving universal primary education for all. According to Target 5, by 2015, children will have completed their primary education. The chapter outlines the latest accomplishments, the indicators, and the policies that are in place to help achieve universal primary education. Despite a dip in enrollment caused by declining population in the age group of 0-16 years, "The overall increase in enrollment in primary education during the period 2000-01 to 2013-14 was 18.6 million while the overall increase in enrollment of boys and girls respectively was 4.6 million and 14.0 million during this period" (India MDG Report 2015: 33).

In order to examine this further, the report looks at three specific indicators – net enrollment ratio (NER) in primary education, comparing the proportion of students between Grades 1 and 5, whether those who enter Grade 1 reach Grade 5, and, finally, literacy rates of those in the age group of 15–24. NER is determined by examining the number of children in a particular age group and the actual number from among that group who are enrolling in primary schools. Here too, there was an increase in girls' enrollment compared to boys', standing at a ratio of 89.26%:87.2% (India MDG Report 2015: 34–35).

As far as data on the second indicator goes – that is, the proportion of students between Grades 1 and 5, whether those who enter Grade 1 are expected to reach Grade 5, also known as the survival rate at Grade 5 – final results are not available. Through initiatives such as the *Sarva Shiksha Abhiyan* (SSA) or Education for All, the mid-day meal programs, and creating adequate infrastructure for primary education and removing barriers for girls to access schools, there appears to be a rising trajectory to enrollment within this cohort (India MDG Report 2015: 36).

On the third and final indicator, literacy rates of 15- to 24-year-olds (also known as the youth literacy rates), the data needs to be understood in the backdrop of how literacy is defined in India. With or without formal education, anyone above the age of 7 in India who can read and write in any language is taken to be literate. The literacy rate of 15- to 24-year-olds is also called youth literacy rate and has similar criterion. Based on this, the youth literacy rate has shown a steady increase from 1991 (61.9%) to 2011 (86.14%). By 2015, the numbers were projected to be 93.8%, toward a near universal (100%) youth literacy rate. The annual increase in overall female literacy was 1.63% compared to males, 0.83% (India MDG Report 2015: 36–37). All of this bears hopeful trends for female education and literacy in India.

The Right to Education (RTE) Act came into effect in 2010. This legislation seeks to ensure that every child has equality of opportunity to receive an elementary education. A dream that the founding fathers had envisaged at the inception of the constitution took decades to fulfill. Coupled with legislative will, in fact, perhaps in order to implement the RTE, in order to make education accessible to all children regardless of socio-economic status and geographic location, other policies, initiatives, and outreach programs had to be put in place. As already mentioned, one such program, the *Sarva Shiksha Abhiyan* (SSA), was designed to assist with the universalization of elementary education. The two main aspects of this campaign were to ensure that all children had access to, and were enrolling in, primary schools and to prevent drop out, especially of those children who were forced, due to social or economic pressures, to quit school before they completed their primary school education. This initiative addressed some critical aspects of the challenge for families and children to complete primary education, and its objective, accordingly, has been to reduce the drop out rate and increase the retention rate throughout primary education. Then there was the mid-day meal scheme, which became a practical and welcome enticement for economically deprived children to attend and remain in school. It also introduced campaigns to promote awareness of the need to let girls learn and reduce the gender gap, increased community participation in educational decision-making, and promoted the idea that education is a fundamental right for every child in the country. The program also worked with schools around the country and raised awareness and capacity to collect data and information at the district level (India MDG Report 2015: 39–43).

The 2015 United Nations Report prepared by the Economic and Social Policy Commission in Asia and the Pacific (ESCAP; hereafter UN-ESCAP 2015) concludes that even though large numbers of children are still out of school and do not finish primary school, India is set to meet gender parity in education (all levels). As already pointed out, the male-female gap in literacy has narrowed quite significantly over the last few decades. Yet there are areas of concern that need to be addressed. One is in terms of creating a sustainable infrastructure through public policy priorities that would help create options as well as remove barriers to women's learning opportunities. Hence the Report calls for imminent "mandatory improvements in areas of water and sanitation, safety, teacher training and gender-sensitive curricula." The report goes on to suggest, "Over the medium term, awareness-raising campaigns to promote secondary and tertiary education of girls and women should be expanded. Access to education facilities is a significant barrier for women and girls" (UN-ESCAP 2015: 8). Getting to and from school as well as the safety of the roads are added hurdles for girls and women. The pace of female youth literacy rate in India is still slow. In 1991–2001, the percent increase in ratio of female-to-male youth literacy rate was 19.4%, whereas, in 2001–2011, it was only 13.75% (UN-ESCAP 2015: 54).

To be sure, legislation and mandates are the first steps only; they have to be supported and enhanced by policies and programs to help achieve the targets of gender equality in education in a comprehensive manner. As we have already seen, in addition to the RTE legislation implemented in 2010, programs such as the SSA have been instrumental in attaining some of the goals and targets set by the MDGs. SSA has been addressing issues such as more infrastructure development, including schools, toilet and drinking water facilities, and teacher training.

In addition to free and compulsory education mandated by law since 2010, and the policies and programs by the government at the federal and state levels to support the infrastructure and delivery of education to children of elementary and secondary levels, there remains much to be done in a nation of a billion people, many of whom are still facing huge social and economic obstacles with access to school. For decades, non-governmental organizations and alternative inclusive schools have worked in tandem and alongside government schools to provide access to education to children, especially girls from impoverished backgrounds. Other areas of empowerment of women include political and economic participation of women.

Economic empowerment of women

The aim of Goal 3 of the MDGs is to promote gender equality and empowerment of women. We have already examined some of the progress that India has achieved in this area in terms of parity in girls' and boys' education at the primary levels and above and the work that remains to be done. We have also looked at some of the policy measures and programs to ensure that the infrastructure and resources are present to facilitate retention of girls to finish their schooling. Overall, on this indicator, the United Nations reports indicate progress in terms of access to education. However, there are other areas of gender equality and empowerment that continue to be challenging.

According to the MDGs, empowerment of women will happen with improved education and equip women to make choices, which will help families and communities improve health, educational status, and overall productivity. Is this happening in India? Is increased access to education leading more women to economic empowerment? As the ESCAP Country Report indicates, "Women in India lack economic, political and social empowerment. The proportion of women working in decent jobs outside agriculture remains low; their participation in the overall labour force is also low and declining in rural areas; women in farming are constrained by lack of land ownership; and women are poorly represented in parliament" (UN-ESCAP 2015: 9).

To be sure, traditional women's work has always been a kind of enigma in India, as it is in other parts of the world, developing and developed. In order to understand the depth of the complex picture, one has to examine women's work in the informal and formal sectors, and as they intersect with social and cultural values. A recent article in the *New York Times* examined the status of women in the changing economy in India, which has, for the last decade or more, made the country a strong economic force, a close second to China. The article points out that only 27% of women in India are active in the workforce. Among the G20 countries, only Saudi Arabia has fewer women in the labor force. Belying established wisdom of the effects of education and growing economy, in India, the reverse is happening. "From 2005 to 2012, women's participation rates slid to 27 per cent from 37 percent, largely because rural women were dropping out of the workforce. Of 189 countries studied by the International Labour Organization, India ranks 17th from the bottom" (*New York Times*, January 31, 2016: 10). The *Times* article states that economists are of the opinion that there are two major factors behind the decline in women's participation in the new economy. The first is the nature of the expansion in sectors that are not attractive or conducive to female employment, such as construction. The other is the social taboo against women's work. This trend is corroborated by a World Bank report, "Republic of India: Women, Work and Employment," 2014 (Hereafter World Bank Report #ACS7935). This report provides a more detailed and fuller picture of this declining trend toward systematic economic disempowerment that is occurring in India.

The report opens with a sobering overview: "Since economic liberalization in the early 1990s, India has experienced high economic growth and made considerable progress in gender equality in areas such as primary education. However, it fared poorly on gender-parity in labor force participation (LFP). During the period between 1993–94 and 2011–12, female labor force participation rate (LFPR) remained consistently low as compared to male participation. Most alarming is the fact that female participation rate declined steadily during the same period, particularly in the rural areas" (World Bank Report #ACS7935: vi). Looking at recent National Sample Survey (NSS) data, India, 2011–2012, the report goes on to highlight the phenomenon of 'missing gender' in the workforce. Between 2004–2005 and 2011–2012, in the rural areas, about 20 million women were missing or had dropped out of the labor force (World Bank Report #ACS7935: vii). From this, two puzzles seem to surface. First is the role of education in the new economy and how it is affecting female LFPRs. The other is the overall decline in women's LFPRs in the new economy and its implications for women's role in a rising India.

Women with 'no education' in rural areas, and those with tertiary education in urban areas, had the highest LFPR. Overall the level of education for women participating in the labor force in urban areas increased between 1999–2000 and 2011–2012. There is a rise in female LFPRs between 1999–2000 and 2004–2005. But they fall for both rural and urban areas between 2004–2005 and 2009–2010. They show a slightly more positive trend thereafter. In terms of educational levels and LFPRs, the report finds "a smaller proportion of uneducated women in 2009–10 compared with 1999–00 in both rural and urban areas, and higher proportions with primary and secondary education in rural areas, and with tertiary education in urban areas. These shifts in the labor force mirror the changes in education levels during this period" (World Bank Report #ACS7935: 14). In the new economy marked by a rise of technology-based jobs, women tend to face

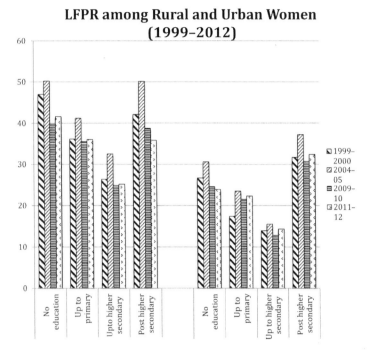

FIGURE 6.1 LFPR among rural and urban women, 1999–2012

Source: Reconstructed from data presented in World Bank Report #ACS7935 [2014], p. 78

barriers. Women with technical professional education maintained high LFPRs and, in turn, gender parity. Furthermore, there are other state-level variations as well as socio-religious customs that affect the level of female LFPRs.

Daily wages for women in the formal sector are considerably higher than in the informal sector. Looking at NSS Employment and Unemployment Survey, India, an IMF Working Paper tallies that on average, female workers in the informal sector earn Rs. 120.3, compared to Rs. 481.9 in the formal sector. Here, too, there is a gender gap. Male workers tend to earn Rs. 194.2: 632.2 in the two sectors respectively (Das et al. IMF Working Paper: 2015: 15; hereafter IMF Working Paper 2015).

To be sure, all these findings further underscore that access to education for women is critical. Even though LFPRs do not initially increase with education at the basic levels, with higher education, and especially at technical and tertiary sectors, not only does the educational gender gap narrow, but female LFPRs should also increase. These reports also indicate that the findings since the 1970s (Boserup 1970) continue to be relevant even under changing economic realities and growth patterns in contemporary India. With modernization and development, women's work in agriculture tends to suffer. For example, when machinery and tractors were introduced in agriculture, men, and not women, used them, and women were kept or even relegated to supportive or ancillary roles in the production process. As jobs in construction and manufacturing become scarce for women, they tend to gravitate back toward lower skill jobs in the informal sector, providing services and odd jobs, with little or no income stability or security.

Overall there are a number of factors that affect women's LFPRs and continue to rest on opportunities for girls' skill-based education, marriage and social norms guiding women's role in the family, socio-economic status, and workplace culture that respects women's work outside the home. The IMF working paper cited above found that marriage affects women's participation in the labor force negatively but not married men (IMF Working Paper 2015: 18). Hence, in order for growth to lead to economic empowerment for women, "India must take deliberate steps for women to participate in further growth. From policy to practical intervention, it requires action to reduce gender disparities in labor outcomes, increase women's contribution to GDP and growth, and the economic empowerment of women overall" (World Bank Report #ACS7935: xi). Creating more formal sector employment opportunities and increased spending on education and on infrastructure development will help attract more women to the labor force and help narrow the gender gap in LFPRs of men and women and realize higher economic potential (IMF Working Paper 2015: 19).

Outcomes and intersectionality: education and economic empowerment, NGOs, and gender-based violence

Clearly, the above analysis has demonstrated that beyond this debate, the fundamental issues remain whether the legal framework and state-guided reform agenda provide women with empowerment, and whether women and women's groups achieve agency for change to improve their lives. As we have already seen, education has had a liberating influence on girls and women, but the cultural intransigence, structural barriers, and infrastructure problems continue to confound the advancement and empowerment of women. Despite the progress that India has secured in granting equal access to education for girls and women, women's participation in the labor force is still lagging. The success of universal access to education is integrally linked with pragmatic policies such as SSA and the midday meal scheme, to make it a feasible reality. Other recommendations that the 2015 UN report suggest are also worth noting. They include increasing vocational education and guaranteeing land and inheritance rights for women. The amended 2005 Hindu Succession Act provided for daughters and sons to have equal access to their family property and land. However, in a country where patriarchal tradition dictates that boys and men have legitimate inheritance, where 80% of rural women work in the fields and farms, this law is not widely followed. Large numbers of women, especially in states with large farm populations such as Bihar, Madhya Pradesh, and Andhra Pradesh, continue to be deprived of their legitimate share of ownership and inheritance (*Wall Street Journal India Blog*, March 2, 2014).

Likewise, in the same year, 2005, India implemented the Mahatma Gandhi National Rural Employment Guarantee Act (MGNREGA). Did this legislation, creating the largest public employment program in India, generate higher LFPR for women? This program has provisions and features that are designed to help rural women find employment. Among other provisions, it guarantees 100 days of paid work every financial year for unskilled workers, reserves a minimum of 33% of the spots for women, and enforces gender parity in wages (IMF Working Paper 2015: 6). The "female-friendly" provisions of the MGNREGA are showing positive results for both men and women, but the higher participation rate among women is attributable to them. (IMF Working Paper 2015: 28). Overall, this report also corroborated the declining female labor force participation rates since the mid-2000s. That women work for necessity and that families would still prefer women not to work outside the home is evident in the decline in female LFPRs as family incomes rise (IMF Working Paper 2015: 13).

Evidently, economic development does not automatically help raise the status of women. Alongside, health and gender-based violence also impact the overall wellbeing and empowerment of women. Sen had warned of the 100 million girls missing due to lack of adequate healthcare and nutrition in many countries. Appropriate public policy, education, and economic empowerment are needed (Sen 1990). The NCRB data in 2014 shows that with regard to crimes against women, there has been a continuous increase in rape, kidnapping, dowry deaths, domestic violence, and other forms of violence and assault. Between 2010 and 2014, the number of rapes increased from 22,172 to 36,735. Kidnapping increased from 29,795 to 57,311. The rise in dowry deaths was comparably smaller, with 8,391 cases in 2010, compared to 9,735 in 2014. Even domestic violence, listed as cruelty by husband or close relatives, rose from 94,041 to 122,877 (NCRB Data 2014: 83). While it is possible that some of the rise is due to increased awareness and reporting, it is also true that hundreds of cases go unreported for fear of social and cultural taboos and backlash. Forms of intimidation and humiliation that women and girls have endured and continue to face in India in the form of groping and touching in public transport systems and crowded spaces as well as sexual harassment in the workplace have long been overlooked and denied. However limited and late, it is a sign of empowerment that the Indian legal system and the society in general are taking heed of such mistreatment of women.

The poor, the *Dalits*, the economically disadvantaged, and women often do not have the same access to the justice system as the wealthy, the powerful, and the advantaged. MDG3, which aims at advancing gender equality and women's empowerment, has to take note of poverty that affects women in a unique way. Impoverished women in rural and urban areas "suffer from low socio-economic status, lack of property rights, environmental degradation and limited health and educational resources. . . . Women are disproportionally affected by health problems, both directly – from exposure to pollutants, household wastes, unsafe sex and gender-based violence – and directly as caregivers" (UNFPA/CIESIN Workshop Report 2005: v). The rural, urban, poor, and women representing the Scheduled Castes (SC) or *dalit* have long been known to be subject to collective ridicule, anger, and violence in their communities. Extreme poverty sometimes leads parents to deprive their girls of education and nutrition and, worse still, to sell and traffic them to pay off debts. For the underprivileged and *dalit* women who are victims of violence, lack of access to legal actions, community taboos, and fear of reprisals stand in the way of seeking justice. Girls and women who have been trafficked or abandoned have to fend for themselves, often in abusive settings.

The 1993 passage of the 74th Amendment marked an important step in the direction of empowerment of women from Scheduled Caste (SC) and Scheduled Tribe (ST) women through Panchayati Raj institutions. While the law addressed political decentralization overall, it had advantageous impact on women. Several studies have shown that even though the outcome varies, in most cases where SC women head Gram (or village) Panchayats, there is increased reporting of crime and more gender-based policies to alleviate challenges that women and the SC population face (Mullen 2016: 76–78). In such cases, state-directed reform movements, when focused on gender empowerment, do provide agency to women and women's groups. Likewise, *dalit* women have also found ways to organize. In Uttar Pradesh, the *Dalit Mahila Samiti*, consisting of over 1,500 women, is a joint initiative by the government and feminist thinkers that has been working to empower *dalit* women since 1980s. Their major goal is to promote education and provide for economic empowerment through skills and training (Andharia 2008).

Indeed, India has a long and varied history of non-governmental organizations (NGOs) that have played a variety of roles in empowering women. Since the mid-1970s, the Self Employed Women's Association (SEWA) in Ahmedabad, with its focus on self-reliance and worker security, mostly emanating from the challenges faced by large numbers of women in the informal sector, has mobilized and organized thousands of women through cooperatives, unions, and various services. It is led by Ela Bhatt, a lawyer who was frustrated with the lack of regulations and policies to provide security to women workers in the informal sector. Law enforcement authorities would often engage in harassment to prevent such women to engage in sale of their goods from makeshift stands by the roadside in urban metropolises (Datta 2003: 351–368). Rural women who could not travel to the marketplace had to rely on middlemen to sell their crafts and goods, and they faced extortion from unscrupulous middlemen, who denied them of any profitmaking or fair prices for their goods.

There is an estimated 80,000 development NGOs in India. And (as of 2006) 32,144, NGOs were registered with the central government to receive funding from abroad. India has a long history of NGOs working in tandem with the state in creating space for self-help programs. SEWA and Annapurna Mahila Mandal were established in the 1970s. Prior to that, since the 1950s, the government had created *mahila mandals*, or women's groups. The 1987 Report of the National Commission on Women 'Shrama Shakti' focused on continued challenges that women faced, giving more impetus to self-help women's groups. Continuing that tradition, "most development NGOs in India since the 1990s have a much stronger focus on self-help approaches, and the specific targeting of women and their primary target group" (Kilby 2011: 2, 11). The impact of SEWA is far reaching, both in terms of the outreach it has managed for decades, bringing positive change in poor women's lives, and by becoming a model for NGOs working for women's empowerment across India and elsewhere. Today, SEWA is both a self-help women's cooperative and trade union and a movement. In 1975, there were 2,750 SEWA members; 400 were street vendors, and the others were garment makers, used clothing dealers, and head loaders. The SEWA cooperatives represented 15 trade groups. By 2004, in Gujarat alone, there were 470,000 members. Outside Gujarat, there were 220,000 members spread across the country, in the north, south, and east. (Chen 2006: 2–6). In the state of Gujarat, with a population of 89% Hindus and 9% Muslims, SEWA membership reflects 21% Muslims (Chen 2006: 17).

Conclusion

While the rise in women's self-help groups and NGOs, women's movements, and other forward-looking policies signal progress in the status of women, there are deep-rooted patriarchal beliefs surrounding a women's place in society that continue to challenge India, making it difficult to assess their status. In particular, as India rises, it seems that violence against women is also on the rise. December 26, 2012, marked the barbarism of a group of perpetrators who brutally gang raped a young medical student on a moving bus in Delhi. The young woman eventually succumbed to her injuries and died a tragic death. The barbarism of the incident notwithstanding, the incident unleashed a wave of protests led by women's groups and the general public and an unprecedented agility in sentencing the perpetrators.

Meanwhile, a controversial BBC documentary, *India's Daughter*, drew some of the complexities surrounding the perception of the status of women in contemporary India. Some blamed Jyoti for being out in the evening without being accompanied by a male member of her family. They invoked the traditional image of the Indian woman, who is to be subservient to the man, who is best advised not to venture outside the home. This sentiment was reinforced by one of the main perpetrators, who even went to the extent of suggesting that if Jyoti had not resisted, the brutality might have been less severe. The documentary also provided a platform and conduit to understanding the sentiment of the victim's parents. Through their narrative, another picture of India and its humanity are painted, one that elevates the position of women in contemporary India. Even though Jyoti's parents were poor, they wanted her to get the best education. She wanted to pursue a medical career; the family decided to sell their landed property to be able to support her educational expenses. The incident and the documentary demonstrated the juxtaposition of women's status in contemporary Indian society. Some suggested that the modern woman, educated and pursuing a career, often draws the angst of those who see themselves left marginalized.

This also leads to the conclusion that women in India continue to straddle the modernity of tradition with such contradictions of promise and progress alongside gender-based trauma and torture. Over and over again, the meandering issues lead to one compelling thought: will India's democratic traditions help to bring dignity to its daughters? Violence against women is not new to India or to the world, but somehow the brutality such as in this incident and the outrage that has ensued must have shaken the consciousness of a nation to help bring some good, and India's democracy has a duty to see to it that it does. In order understand how that can happen, a look at the lives of India's women is imperative, followed by the ways in which such lives can be empowered to live in dignity through democracy.

Discussion questions

1 What are some of the traditional historical and cultural practices that kept women subordinate in India?
2 From the overview presented in this chapter, do you think that the Constitution of India could have done more to improve the status of women in India?
3 India has had a woman as president and prime minister. What do you gather from this about the status of women in the country?
4 This chapter has highlighted the importance of education and economic empowerment – which do you think is more important?
5 Why do you think that, despite impressive economic growth in the country, violence against women persists and is even on the rise in India?

Further reading

Basu, A. (Ed.) (2010) *Women's Movements in the Global Era: The Power of Local Feminisms*, Boulder, CO: Westview Press.

Batliwala, S. (2014) *Engaging With Empowerment: An Intellectual and Experiential Journey*. New Delhi: Women Unlimited, an associate of Kali for Women.

Bhatt, E.R. (2006) *We Are Poor but So Many: The Story of the Self-Employed Women's Association in India*, New York: Oxford University Press.

Carr, M., Chen, M., and Jhabvala, R. (1999) *Speaking Out: Women's Economic Empowerment in South Asia*, New Delhi: Vistaar Publications.

Datta, B. (Ed.) (2010) *Nine Degrees of Justice: New Perspectives on Violence Against Women in India*, New Delhi: Zubaan, an imprint of Kali for Women.

Datta, R. and Kornberg, K. (Eds.) (2002) *Women in Developing Countries: Assessing Strategies for Empowerment*, Boulder, CO: Lynne Rienner.

Gandhi, A. (2006) *Women's Work, Health and Empowerment*, New Delhi: Aakar Books.

Jain, D. (Ed.) (1975) *Indian Women*, New Delhi: Publications Division, Ministry of Information and Broadcasting, Government of India.

Kishwar, M. and Vanita, R. (Eds.) (1984) *In Search of Answers: Indian Women's Voices From Manushi*, London: Zed Books.

Majumdar, M. and Mooij, J. (2015) *Education and Inequality in India: A Classroom View*, London and New York: Routledge.

Rose, K. (1992) *Where Women Are Leaders: The SEWA Movement in India*, New Delhi: Vistaar Publications, a division of Sage Publications, India, Pvt. Ltd.

Varma, A.P., Rehman, M.M. and Chauhan, P.S. (1996) *Women Labor in India*, Noida, India: V.V. Giri National Labor Institute.

References

Andharia, J. (2008) 'The Dalit Women's Movement in India; The Dalit Mahila Samiti', in S. Batliwala (Ed.) *Changing Their World*. Retrieved from: AIWD website: www.awid.org/sites/default/files/atoms/files/changing_their_world_-_dalit_womens_movement_in_india.pdf.

Batliwala, S. (2007) 'Taking the Power Out of Empowerment: An Experiential Account', *Development in Practice* 17(4/5): 557–565.

Boserup, E. (1970/ 2007) *Woman's Role in Economic Development*, London: EarthScan.

Bumiller, E. (1990) *May You Be the Mother of a Hundred Sons*, New York: Ballantine Books.

Chatterji, B. (2009) 'Political Development in India', in R. Chatterji (Ed.) *Politics India: State-Society Interface*, New Delhi: South Asian Publishers.

Chen, M.A. (2006) *Self Employed Women: A Profile of SEWA's Membership*, Ahmedabad: SEWA Academy. Retrieved from: http://wiego.org/publications/self-employed-women-profile-sewas-membership.

Datta, R. (2003) 'From Development to Empowerment: The Self-Employed Association in India', *International Journal of Politics, Culture, and Society* 16(3): 351–368.

International Monetary Fund (IMF) Working Paper (2015) Retrieved from: www.imf.org/external/pubs/ft/wp/2015/wp1555.pdf.

Kilby, P. (2011) *NGOs in India: The Challenges of Women's Empowerment and Accountability*, London and New York: Routledge.

Millennium Development Goals (2015) *India: Country Report*, Government of India, New Delhi: Social Statistics Division, Ministry of Statistics and Programme Implementation. Retrieved from: http://mospi.nic.in/sites/default/files/publication_reports/mdg_2july15_1.pdf.

Mullen, R. (2016) 'Panchayati Raj Institutions', in A. Kohli and P. Singh (Ed.) *Routledge Handbook of Indian Politics*, London: Routledge.

National Crimes Records Bureau, India (2014) *Crimes Against Women, Chapter 5*. New Delhi: National Crime Records Bureau, Ministry of Home Affairs. Retrieved from: http://ncrb.nic.in/StatPublications/CII/CII2014/chapters/Chapter%205.pdf.

New York Times, January 31, 2016. Retrieved from: www.nytimes.com/2016/01/31/world/asia/indian-women-labor-work-force.html.

Patel, I. (1998) 'The Contemporary Women's Movement and Women's Education in India', *International Review of Education* 44(2–3): 155-175.

Sen, A.K. (1990) "More Than 100 Million Women Are Missing." *New York Review of Books*, December 20. Retrieved from: www.nybooks.com/articles/1990/12/20/more-than-100-million-women-are-missing/.

Sen, S. (2000) 'Toward a Feminist Politics? The Hindu Women's Movement in Historical Perspective', *Policy Research Report on Gender and Development, Working Paper Series No. 9*. Washington, DC: The World Bank.

Tiwary, D. (2016) 'National Crime Records Bureau data: Slight dip in rape, crime against women', *Indian Express*. Retrieved from: http://indianex press.com/article/explained/national-crime-records-bureau-data-2015-slight-dip-in-rape-crime-against-women-3004980/.

United Nations Economic and Social Commission for Asia and the Pacific (ESCAP) (2015) *India and the MDGs: Towards a Sustainable Future for All*, on behalf of the United Nations Country Team- India, New York: United Nations. Cited as ESCAP Report 2015. http://in.one.un.org/img/uploads/India_and_the_MDGs.pdf.

United Nations Population Fund/CIESIN Workshop Report (2005) *Women's Economic Empowerment: Meeting the Needs of Impoverished Women*. Retrieved from: www.unfpa.org/sites/default/files/resource-pdf/women_economic.pdf.

UN Women, data on Violence Against Women. Retrieved from: www.unwomen. org/en/what-we-do/ending-violence-against-women/facts-and-figures.

Wall Street Journal (India) Blog. Retrieved from: http://blogs.wsj.com/india realtime/2014/03/02/the-right-to-inherit-isnt-working-for-indian-women-says-u-n-study/.

World Bank (2014) #ACS7935, India – *Women, Work and Employment*, Washington, DC: World Bank Group. Retrieved from: http://documents.world bank.org/curated/en/753861468044063804/India-Women-work-and-employment.

7

IS INDIA STILL 'AN EMERGING POWER'?

An overview of foreign relations

The cultural history of India is filled with lofty spiritual sentiments that have come down since the days of ancient civilization. While it would be misleading to suggest that India lives in
her past, several ideas stemming from that tradition have been
the cornerstones of India's culture and have certainly affected its
foreign policies.

"Ahimsa, peace and non-aggression were the hallmarks of
Indian culture. In her crowded history of over five thousand years
during which she had overthrown vast and puissant empires,
India never practiced military aggression on countries outside
her borders. . . . Centuries have gone by but the lustre of that
heritage remains undimmed" (Palkhivala 1981:47).

While such idealism has been at the heart of India's foreign policy in the early decades, the reality in which post-Independence
India has had to survive is not always set in such idealism. India
is also a land that had suffered repeated invasions, and continues
to be embroiled in regional and global conflicts, and continued

uncertainties. It has been guided by bilateral skepticism, uncertainties, and hostilities.

Chapter objectives and outline

It has been more than a decade and a half since India has been referred to as an emerging power. So it is debatable whether it can still be called an 'emerging power.' Since India's emergence as an independent state in 1950, its foreign policy and relations with global and regional powers have demonstrated a combination of and response to Nehruvian geostrategic positioning and border disputes, tempered by pragmatic unfolding of relations with its neighbors, the trajectory of the Cold War, and its own nuclear identity. It has also been affected by the terrorist attacks on U.S. landmarks on September 11, 2001, and its aftermath in South Asia, and the ripples and waves of a globalized political economy and its impact on trade and liberalization. While some of these decades-long challenges continue, India has gradually emerged as a power to be reckoned with on the global stage. However, even while such an aspiration persists, India is also a kind of ambivalent power. It is in this context that this chapter examines India's relations with external powers, mainly with Pakistan, China, and the United States. The parameters of India's relations with the former Soviet Union and other regional actors and the European Union will also be highlighted in the discussion.

Theory, philosophy, and policy: overview of India's foreign policy

Examining India's foreign policy through the theoretical lenses of realism and its later variants provides some interesting insights. India has a longer tradition with realpolitik dating centuries before Machiavelli. In the era of Emperor Chandragupta Maurya (317–293 BCE), his adviser and prime minister, Kautilya (Kanishka), offered his famous treatise, the *Arthashastra*, which systematically outlined the strategies of warfare and alliance building, and domestic welfare for citizens

(Boeshe 2003: 9–38). Like Thucydides, the central notion of Kautilya's statecraft was that of power. Centuries later, Morgenthau also championed this brand of classical realism (Morgenthau: 1948). Kenneth Waltz reinforced this image of the world by emphasizing, "Each state pursues its own interests, however defined, in ways it judges best" (Waltz 1959: 238).

The "Nonaligment Firsters" comprised leaders and diplomats from the 1950's to the 1990's, including Prime Ministers Nehru and I.K. Gujaral." India's power was more to be a "power by example," and mediating in disputes in the region, while not siding with any of the superpowers was the overall stance. In the post–Cold War came the "Broad Power Realists," such as C. Raja Mohan, who advocated for a greater role by India as its own power was increasing in a changing power balance, both globally and regionally. Finally, there are the "Hard Power Hawks," many of whom, like Bharat Karnad and Brahma Chellaney, are security scholars and researchers. Advocates of nuclear weapons and use of military force, the "Hard Power Hawks" believe in India's status as a strong military power (Schaffer and Schaffer 2016: 60–75). In terms of the structure of foreign and security policy-making, the central government plays a significant role, unlike other areas of governance, in which the states play a larger and more engaged role. However, in keeping with its democratic culture, one finds that foreign policy issues are much discussed and debated among the media and the populace. In addition to that, "... India has now had two generations of Indian strategists and foreign policy experts coping with varied experiences and creating multiple angles of vision on the same problem" (Cohen 2001: 36).

The genesis of Nehru's handiwork in foreign and strategic policies was in a combination of liberal philosophy of peaceful coexistence, nonalignment with Cold War rivals (the United States and the Soviet Union), which gave rise to the nonalignment movement (NAM), external threats from neighboring countries, and fractious domestic subversion. Born out of India's own experience with colonialism and the desire to uphold the sovereign rights of states, Nehru believed that erstwhile colonies in Africa and Asia "would end up being used as pawns in contests for power of no relevance to them. Their needs were to fight poverty, and illiteracy, and disease, and these could not be met by joining military blocs" (Chandra et al. 2000: 149).

The symbolism of NAM initially gave it some credence, mostly in terms of representation of the voice of the South at world forums like as the United Nations. That symbolism, even as it evolved amidst pragmatic concerns, is also evident in Nehru's other pillar of foreign policy, *Panch Sheel*, or the five principles of peaceful coexistence. These principles included "mutual respect for countries' territorial integrity and sovereignty, non-aggression, non-interference in each other's internal affairs, equality and mutual benefit, and peaceful coexistence" (Chandra et al. 2000: 150). The apparently idealistic *Panch Sheel* were actually grounded in the realism China's power under Chairman Mao Zedong. Both India's leadership in the NAM and *Panch Sheel* faced a litmus test in the 1962 border war with China. Unprepared for the attack, and routed by China, this was a huge blow for India. Nehru's hopes for the NAM, *Panch Sheel*, and joint leadership in the new world alongside China were shattered. There was not much support from its nonaligned partners, and India ended up requesting military assistance from the United States.

In the aftermath of the 1962 border war, especially under Indira Gandhi as prime minister since 1966, India established closer relations with the United States and the Soviet Union. Food shortages and a poor-performing economy, stymied by the wars of 1962 and 1965, prompted India to seek assistance from the United States. India, in turn, had to refrain from criticizing the U.S. bombing of Vietnam. Indira Gandhi successfully persuaded the Soviet Union to adopt a more pro-India stance, away from parity with Pakistan. In addition, she also focused on programs such as the Green Revolution to attain self-sufficiency in agriculture. The Indo-USSR Friendship Treaty marked a break from India's nonaligned stance and firmed up a strategic partnership with the Soviet Union. Between 1977 and 1980, through the Janata and Congress governments, India continued to pursue military deals with the Soviet Union. Under Rajiv Gandhi, India's foreign policy did not witness any major change or movement; the U.S. ambivalence continued, and the Soviet Union became more and more entangled in Afghanistan (Chandra et al. 2000: 170–171).

During the first Gulf War in 1990–1991, India was in a quandary with its close relationship with Iraq, and uneasiness about supporting the UN- and U.S.-led coalition. To avoid being marginalized as an important actor on the global-regional stage, it began to shift its position on several issues. These included voting to repeal the UN resolution "equating Zionism with racism" that it originally supported, followed by diplomatic recognition of Israel, and voting with the United States to condemn Libya for terrorism (Hardgrave and Kochanek 2000: 417). India also began to realize that despite support for NAM, several Arab countries, including Egypt, stood by Pakistan (Ganguly and Mukherji 2011: 25).

India's relations with regional and global powers

Nonalignment clearly did not address India's long-standing and increasingly deteriorating relations with Pakistan. In the period following the Cold War, in the context of the major changes in the global power balance, India has had to pivot and embrace structural changes in the global political economy and defense priorities.

India and Pakistan: "unending hostility" and the Kashmir issue

The dispute over Kashmir has lingered for decades and has brought the two countries to outright war in 1947, 1965, and 1999. Bilateral rivalry has been a catalyst behind the nuclear programs in both countries. Tracing the troubles in Kashmir to partition, the ruling elite in Pakistan "remain unreconciled to the status of Kashmir and entertain an irredentist claim on the disputed state. India refuses to countenance any possible territorial compromise as it fears that concessions in Kashmir could have a demonstration effect on other, ethnic secessionist movements" (Ganguly and Mukherji 2011: 36–37).

At the time of partition, keeping his democratic tenor, Nehru promised a plebiscite to the Kashmiri people to choose if they wanted to join Pakistan or to remain with India. The proposed UN-supervised plebiscite was initially welcomed by both India and Pakistan and was supported by several UN resolutions, but it never came to fruition. It seems that there is not much interest left in either country for a plebiscite. One of the issues has to do with what options the plebiscite would offer. Pakistan's hope was that the people would vote either for joining Pakistan or remaining with India. China, too, would potentially have a say after the territories it occupied after the 1962 war (Ganguly 1998: 143). Within Kashmir, the demand is for independence to be part of the plebiscite. Pakistan supported the plebiscite, but not independence. India gradually abandoned the idea of plebiscite (Wirsing 1998: 59).

The conflict that started in 1948 with Kashmir as the focal point became the source of two other open conflicts with Pakistan, in 1965 and in 1999. Soon after Nehru's death in 1964, India and Pakistan went to war again in 1965 over Kashmir. The conflict began in the disputed region innocuously at first, with some Pakistani troops crossing the cease-fire-line (CFL) and attempting to incite disturbance in the area. India sought to guard the CFL, but Pakistan continued its incursions. Armed conflict soon followed such brinkmanship (Ganguly 1998: 160, Hardgrave and Kochanek 2000: 420). In less than a month, with pressure from the United States and international community, a cease-fire was called. India was granted most of the infiltrated and disputed territory (Bajpai 2013: 117). In 1966, the Soviet Union brokered the Tashkhent Accord, creating grounds for peaceable settlement of bilateral disputes between India and Pakistan. UN peacekeepers observed the ceasefire line to prevent further outbreak of hostilities. The United States and Britain played both countries even-handedly and cut off arms supplies to both countries. "China, on the other hand, sided with Pakistan and denounced India's 'criminal aggressions,' and threatened ultimatums" (Hardgrave and Kochanek 2000: 420).

In 1971, India and Pakistan were embroiled in another conflict, but not over Kashmir per se. This was a conflict between West and East Pakistan, in which India was drawn in to support and to facilitate a movement by the East to secure independent statehood of Bangladesh, after Sheikh Mujibur Rahman, the leader of the Awami League swept the parliamentary elections in early 1971. Unwilling to accept the outcome of the election, General Yahya Khan carried on repression in the East; 10 million refugees migrated to neighboring West Bengal. After Prime Minister Indira Gandhi was refused assistance by the Nixon-Kissinger team in Washington, India signed the Treaty of Peace, Friendship, and Cooperation with the Soviet Union (Hardgrave and Kochanek 2000: 422–423). Later that year, the Indian army helped liberate Dhaka, the Pakistani army surrendered, and a new Bangladesh was born, realizing the aspirations of the subjected Bengali Muslim people. Nixon sent the nuclear-armed USS Enterprise to assist Pakistani forces. "Indians viewed the nuclear carrier steaming so close to their coastline only as Washington's missile rattling, helping further to undermine Indo-U.S. relations" (Wolpert 1991: 237).

On the diplomatic front, between 1979 and 1999, leaders such as Morarji Desai, Atal Behari Vajpayee, and I. K. Gujaral made several efforts to normalize relations with Pakistan. However, in 1999, Pakistan's encroachment into the Indian-controlled area in Kargil, although a short-lived conflict, ushered in renewed phase of mutual hostility and distrust, particularly with General Pervez Musharraf taking the reins after a military coup in Pakistan (Cohen 2001: 208). The terrorist attacks on the Indian Parliament in December 2001 further underscored this distrust in Indian quarters. Apparently, between 2004 and 2007, the two countries attempted to arrive at peaceful settlement of long standing disputes, only to be jolted by another dastardly attack by Pakistani backed insurgent group, Lashkar-e-Taiba (LeT) in Mumbai on December 26, 2008 (Ganguly and Mukherji 2011: 30–36). Jaish e Mohammed (JeM), a Pakistan-based extremist Islamic group, also sought to undermine Indian control of Kashmir and carried out violent attacks in the early 2000s. Lately, it seems JeM is focused on the Afghanistan region and has splintered into smaller units (https://web.stanford.edu/group/mappingmilitants/cgi-bin/groups/view/95). Cross-border acts of terrorism, linked to such groups, continue to fortify the distrust of India and stand in the way of open communication.

Since 2001 especially, cross-border terrorism has irked relations and continues to threaten peaceful coexistence and rapprochement. The ongoing rivalry since 1947 has caused India in terms of "blood, treasure, and in international prestige and influence" (Hardgrave and Kochanek 2000: 418–419). To overcome such distrust and mend relations, since 2009, both sides made several efforts at easing tensions and establishing normalization of relations, but to no avail. In December 2015, Prime Minister Narendra Modi made a surprise visit to Lahore and met Pakistan's prime minister, Nawaz Sharif, to further trade, to quell terrorism, and to establish more avenues for people to people interactions and other platforms of diplomatic relations. While the visit was symbolic, it remains to be seen what long-lasting effect will ensue.

India and the United States: from 'benign neglect' to 'estranged democracies' and beyond

India's relations with the United States were enmeshed with the complexities of both countries' priorities and relations with Pakistan that began with the Cold War. The U.S. military alliance with Pakistan in the early 1950s created space for a base for U-2 reconnaissance flights from Peshawar in exchange for arms, and also misgivings from India. New Delhi tried to convince Washington that Pakistan's intent was to use the weapons against India, given its hostility over Kashmir and other disputes. However, the United States saw India as an important state in its containment strategy. It readily provided India with $80 million in military assistance during the war with China in 1962. Prior to that, the United States provided considerable loans and grants for economic development, and India purchased $55 million in military equipment (Cohen 2001: 270). During the 1965 war, India reached out to, and received support from, Washington as Pakistan had violated the terms of the military alignment with the United States. However, in the 1971 conflict over Bangladesh, the Nixon administration clearly short-changed India, adding to the mistrust. "The legacy of such Cold War mistrust . . . generated dark clouds of karmic fallout that have polluted Indo-U.S. relations for over forty years" (Wolpert 1991: 248).

To be sure, the military alliance with Pakistan remained a source of deep and sustained mistrust between India and the United States. It also prompted and dragged India into an arms race. Between 1954 and 1965, Pakistan created an armored division with Patton M-48 tanks, modern F-85 jets, and naval equipment. After a brief hiatus, in 1981, 40 F-16 aircraft, upgraded M-48 tanks, artillery, and loaned warships considerably strengthened Pakistan's military arsenal (Cohen 2001: 271–273). Throughout much of the Cold War period as well as in the aftermath of the Afghan invasion, India considered the United States to be at the root of Pakistan's military build-up and intransigence on border disputes, namely on Kashmir. India thus felt compelled to build its deterrence defense arsenal.

The 1974 Peaceful Nuclear Explosion (PNE), also referred to as Pokharan I, took the United States and the rest of the world by surprise. After the Soviet invasion of Afghanistan, Washington naturally drifted closer to Islamabad and the regime of Zia-ul-Haq. There followed what has been called a 'limited rapprochement' between Reagan and Indira Gandhi, especially after her visit to Washington in 1982. Subsequently, there was some effort, but "the divergent policies of the two states and the lack of other substantial links ensured that there was no breakthrough in Indo-U.S. relations" (Ganguly and Mukherji 2011: 43). In 1985, Prime Minister Rajiv Gandhi visited the United States on the occasion of the Festival of India, but it remained a limited and ceremonial presence.

The early 1990s ushered in hope for renewed relations between the United States and India, especially on the economic front, and several opportunities opened up, with some continuing caveats. In the 1960s, PL 480 provided for agricultural and food aid totaling approximately $5 billion. But in the wake of the Bangladesh war of independence in 1971, and India's decreasing dependence on food assistance, U.S. aid to India gradually declined. With economic liberalization in 1991, several reforms opened up the markets and made it attractive for foreign investors. Some companies, such as Enron, made a $2.8 billion investment in a power project, but, overall, bureaucratic and infrastructure bottlenecks, corruption, and other challenges continue to hamstring interest by foreign firms to become more active in the market (Hardgrave and Kochanek 2000: 442–43).

After decades of "missed opportunities," economic cooperation between the two countries continues to show hopeful signs in subsequent administrations of George W. Bush and Barack Obama, and the United Progressive Alliance (UPA) government of Manmohan Singh and that of the BJP government under Narendra Modi since 2014. Between 2004 and 2008, bilateral trade increased from $30 billion to $66 billion annually. Between 2007 and 2008, India's direct investment in the United States was $4.5 billion, which increased more than 60% from 2007 (Burns 2007: 134, Feigenbaum 2010: 78).

Although India conducted its first nuclear test in 1974, dubbed "Peaceful Nuclear Explosion" (PNE), it was with its 1998 tests that it declared itself a "nuclear weapons state." Quite predictably, Pakistan followed suit by conducting its own tests, and the United States implemented economic and military sanctions through the Glenn Amendment. But, in the absence of the Cold War, and the rising potential of India's economic prowess and globalization, fortunately, U.S.-India relations did not revert back to the pendulum swing of mistrust and estrangement as in previous decades. In what can be seen as a dose of realism in India's foreign policy stance, the tests demonstrated India's, at least for its right-wing sympathizers, "assertive militaristic nationalism" (Chiriyankandath 2004: 203). It came on the heels of ongoing Chinese support toward building Pakistan's security capability, and the latter's firing of medium-range missile Ghauri, which it purchased from North Korea. The tests were also a means to publicize and demonstrate India's resolve to its own population to protect its security and territorial interests. Indeed, it gave a huge boost to enlisting positive public opinion (over 90% favorable ratings), as it also became a matter of ensuring national pride, as the National Agenda of the BJP-led government boldly announced. Citing the decades-old argument of nuclear haves and have-nots, and the threat posed by China, India continued its refusal to sign the Nuclear Non-Proliferation Treaty (NPT) and refused to sign the Comprehensive Test Ban Treaty as well (Hardgrave and Kochanek 2000: 444–445).

Despite the sanctions associated with the Glenn Amendment following the 1998 tests, high-level talks between New Delhi and Washington continued, a welcome respite from previous decades of estrangement. In 1999, President Clinton persuaded Pakistan to withdraw from Indian territory during the Kargil conflict. Subsequently, Clinton's visit to India and a return visit by Prime Minister Vajpayee suggested a strengthening of Indo-U.S. bilateral "commitment to building relations" (Chiriyankandath 2004: 207).

Furthermore, after Pokharan II in 1998, the United States accelerated its attempts to continue to persuade both India and Pakistan to accept CTBT and enter negotiations toward a Fissile Material Cut-off Treaty (FMCT). However, threats like this only led to more logjams.

The path to synergy in Indo-U.S. relations in the nuclear area was also a case of opposing policies starting with President Carter, who, after Pokharan I, cut the supply of low-enriched uranium (LEU) for the Tarapur Atomic Power Plant. President Clinton reversed a Reagan-era policy of having India depend on France for alternative supplies, and coaxed India to look to China instead. During the Bush administration, the U.S. government was more accommodating, objecting only partially to Russia's role in strengthening India's nuclear capability. In a reversal of the Clinton administration position, it decided that it would not object to "Russia supplying cryogenic engines for India's space-related Geo-Stationery Launch Vehicle (GSLV) programme, provided the related technology was not transferred" (*India-US Relations* 2003: 25). While India continued to strengthen its domestic capability to produce cryogenic engines, it also realized it was lacking in Advanced Light Water Reactors. Therefore, for its part, "India could bargain for the transfer of civil nuclear technology in areas where they can be effected by a Presidential waiver followed by Congressional approval" (*India-US Relations* 2003: 25). The groundwork for a more accommodating period of U.S.-India relations was thus achieved.

Predictably, the terror attack on September 11, 2001, played its part in ushering in a renewed sense of urgency in revisiting U.S.-India relations. Notably, "the administration did a *volte face* in the wake of the September 11 attacks" (Ganguly and Mukherji 2011: 46). Given that the training camps for Al Qaeda were in Afghanistan, the U.S. response and its impact on addressing terrorism in South Asia would surely involve India and Pakistan. Initially, the two countries worked together, and India seemed to be strengthening ties. However, it also ushered in U.S. proximity with Pakistan as it was enlisted as an ally in the war against terror. India's pleas that terror attacks in Kashmir, as well as the one on the Indian parliament that same year, were spawning from Pakistan, which, according to New Delhi, ought to be labeled a state sponsoring terrorism, fell on deaf ears. Nonetheless, after decades of wavering and misgivings, it seemed that two major democracies of the world had finally found a common raison d'être or national interest that prompted more cooperation in defense operations and work as allies, in a way that was simply elusive in previous decades (Hathaway 2003: 18–19). In a fast changing global economy, the United

States needed to leverage the favorable trends that came with liberalized and growing economies, free trade, and information technology. Other issues such as President Bush's moderate assistance during the Gujarat earthquake and Secretary Colin Powell's remarks maintaining the traditional American strategy of lumping South Asian priorities with a hyphenated India-Pakistan stance, rather than decoupling the two countries, continued to irk India (Hathaway 2003: 12–15). Strategic partnership with New Delhi would have larger and deeper significance to governance in a more cooperative sense to face common threats such as terrorism and economic challenges (Tellis 2001: 761–762). The diplomatic efforts that followed seemed to make an effort toward this end, with limited success.

In 2005, following visits by Prime Minister Singh and President Bush, respectively, the two countries formalized the U.S.-India Civil Nuclear Cooperation Initiative. As Undersecretary of State for Political Affairs Nicholas Burns noted, the United States would "de-hyphenate" its South Asia policy by working with India and Pakistan separately: "Secretary Rice also told Prime Minister Singh that the United States would break with long-standing non-proliferation orthodoxy and work to establish full civil nuclear cooperation with energy-starved India" (Burns 2007: 135). Intentional and careful negotiations led to specific progress in several strategic areas covering missile defense, civilian nuclear energy, high-technology trade, and civilian space cooperation (Ganguly and Mukherji 2011: 49). In 2006, U.S. investments in advancing India's nuclear power industry were made possible with the passage of the Hyde Act. This historic policy shift ensured a significant transformation in U.S.-India relations and India's nuclear posture. It "transformed India overnight from a target of the international non-proliferation regime to a stakeholder in it." It ensured more transparency of India's nuclear power plants, whose safeguards would now be under inspection by the International Atomic Energy Agency (IAEA) (Burns 2007: 137).

Even though this was historic progress, caveats remained, which had to be worked out. The devil, as they say, lay in the details, and, in this case, it was a dual challenge of fulfilling the requirements of bilateral agreement between India and the United States, and a multilateral one, that between India and the IAEA. Section 123 of the U.S. Atomic Energy Act required spelling out the terms of the nuclear cooperation agreement. This so-called 123 agreement took almost a year and a half and several meetings to spell out and agree on the specific details. There were many challenges, including almost seven decades of mistrust and ambivalence. As a non-NPT member, but with a nuclear program, India did not fit into any of the existing nuclear country's model; hence the U.S. side had no precedence. The negotiators from both sides tried hard and were able to agree on creative solutions to complex questions of India's autonomy on reprocessing nuclear material that required equipment, which the United States could not supply to India, under the 123 agreement.

The potential and actual success of the civil nuclear agreement could be a model for greater cooperation and joint economic ventures between the United States and India, including counterterrorism, cyber security, global health, and climate change Kaye, C.R. and Nye Jr. J.S. 2015: 32–46; cited hereafter as CFR Report No. 73, 2015 India's relationship with the United States seems to be decoupled from the latter's relationship with Pakistan, an association that took India almost seven decades to shake off. Despite India's reservations about the impact of any potential changes to the H1-B visas by the Donald Trump administration, the two countries remain united in their resolve to fight terrorism.

India and China: more than peaceful coexistence?

As with Pakistan, India's relations with China have often been entwined in regional and global geopolitical and power dynamics. India's relationship with both the Soviet Union and China began in earnest with the nonalignment perspective. Guarded realism, which was prevalent even during the nonalignment period, became more evident after the 1990s. Along with India's own economic growth and rise in global power status, there seemed to be pragmatism mixed with maturity in its foreign policy toward other global and regional powers. India continues to have to maintain "amicable ties with the same three external powers: a rapidly strengthening China, a weakened Russia, and a globally hegemonic United States" (Hagerty D.T. and Hagerty H.G. 2005: 41).

To be sure, the 1962 border war with China did shatter India's belief in nonalignment and peaceful coexistence, and, since then, India has been reticent and cautiously optimistic about opening dialog and cooperation with China. China's leaders considered China's civilization to be "older and greater than India's," and the country to be "strategically far more important than India." India, on the other hand, suspects China's intentions as those of "encircling India" and hence the close relations with Pakistan, and sabotage Indo-Soviet relations. India considered the U.S. alliance with Pakistan part of this collusion with China to encircle India (Cohen 2001: 256–57). Despite some moves in recent years to cultivate cultural ties between the two countries, for India, it seems that the scar of 1962 still continues to stand in the way of trust. Yet, it appears that despite military, technological, and economic superiority, China continues to resent India for two reasons. First is what it considers India's intransigence in holding on to the McMahon Line as the border between the two countries, a border that was decided upon by the British, without China's explicit consent. Second is India's involvement in the Tibetan dispute. By giving refuge to the Dalai Lama and a significant number of Tibetans, China suspects that India will not pass up a chance to include Tibet within its sphere of influence, should the opportunity arise. The fallout of China and the Soviet Union in 1963 and India's closeness with the Soviet Union despite a nonaligned posture obviously irked China. But it was the spread of India's influence in the region that China wanted to control. Hence it has reached out to Pakistan to create a balance of power in the region. "Pakistan is China's Israel, the largest beneficiary of Chinese aid, and a recipient of its nuclear missile technology" (Cohen 2001: 259).

Despite these difficulties, throughout the 1970s and 1980s, India and China did make some efforts toward resolving the border disputes and establish closer relations. Between 1979 and 1987, after a series of talks to address issues of mutual concern, mainly the border dispute, things seem to fall apart with China's intrusion in the Sumdorong Valley in 1986. Later, India's Prime Minister visited in 1988 and both sides agreed to make efforts toward addressing resolving bilateral issues of concern and increase scientific, technological, and cultural cooperation (Malik 1995: 317–318). In 1993, Prime Minster Narasimha Rao and Chinese Premier Li Peng signed the so-called 'peace and tranquility' treaty, and, in 1996, China's president visited India and signed another such agreement. Thus, both sides in effect agreed to, for the most part, respect the territorial status quo about Aksai Chin under Chinese control, and control of Arunachal Pradesh by India, without specifically resolving the disputes, and in effect pledging not to initiate military options against each other (Malik 1995: 318; Ganguly and Mukherji 2011: 39). Despite these and other confidence-building measures, misgivings continued between the two countries. As late as 2009–2010, China has not given up questioning the status of Arunachal Pradesh, and India continues to allege China's role in Pakistan-controlled Kashmir (Ganguly and Mukherji 2011: 41).

On balance, these overtures are yet to produce significant actual movements resulting in substantive progress. The end of the Cold War and the gradual rise of the United States as a sole global military power, coupled with the status of China and India as economic powers, have changed the dynamics of U.S.-India relations. China tried to prevent India's hegemony in South Asia and helped Pakistan with nuclear weapons and technology. "It is the adversarial nature of the Sino-Indian relationship which has driven India's and, in turn, Pakistan's nuclear weapons programme" (Malik 1995: 346). In the face of a breakdown in Indo-Pak relations, the role of China continues to be critical in India's strategic security concerns in the region.

Looking east and west, mending fences, and bending rivers: India and the world beyond the United States, China, and Pakistan

As already discussed, during the Cold War, India's friendship with the USSR was established in military and economic areas of cooperation. In recent decades, particularly after India's economic rise and the changes in the global power balance, India is well poised to pivot around the structural shifts in power in the region and beyond.

Since 2001, and especially after the fall of the Taliban government, India having a shared goal of containing Pakistan-sponsored terrorism in the region (despite Pakistan's public support of the U.S.-led war against terror), and an interest in Afghanistan's economic development, has reinvigorated its role in the reconstruction of the country. Despite structural constraints, namely the intransigent territorial and other long-standing disputes with neighbors, India can look toward Afghanistan. "In many ways, Afghanistan has become emblematic of such an ambitious course that India seems to be charting in its foreign

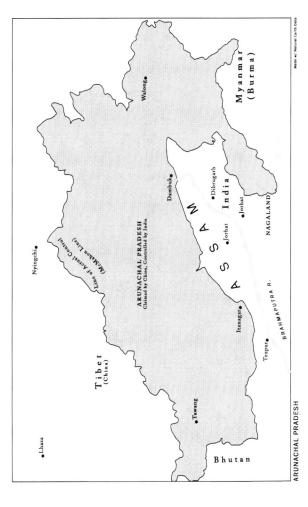

ARUNACHAL PRADESH

Note: This is a historical map and is included here for representative purposes.
The international boundaries, coastlines, denominations, and other information
shown do not necessarily imply any judgement concerning the legal status of any
territory or the endorsement or acceptance of such information. For current boundaries,
readers may refer to the Survey of India maps.

FIGURE 7.1 Map of Arunachal Pradesh

policy" (Pant 2010: 40). Guided by prudent pragmatism, slowly but surely, India is looking at Afghanistan outside of the prism of nonalignment era policy.

Why is a politically viable and economically stable Afghanistan a strategic priority for India? On the negative side, India does not want to see Afghanistan disintegrate into chaos again in the face of the resurfacing of the Taliban and the uncertain role and capacity of Pakistan to contain such resurgence. Indo-Pak relations over ongoing issues such as Kashmir and the role of Lashkar-e-Taiba (LeT), operating mainly from Pakistan, and other terror groups that are seemingly (and in some cases, verified) blessed by Pakistan and have launched attacks in India in recent years are also of concern. On the more positive side, as mentioned above, it is in India's interest to have a stable Afghanistan. Following up on its continued support for the pre-Taliban Northern Alliance and subsequently the Karzai government, India signed several bilateral initiatives to support infrastructure projects such as the Zaranj-Delaram Road, and agreements to facilitate smoother trade, education, aviation, and cultural and media relations (Pant 2010: 40–53).

Looking eastward, following Nehruvian foreign policy interests, even as India aspired to become a leader in Asia, it was uncomfortable joining ASEAN, as it saw the group as an outpost of American security interests in Asia, and the member states, at the behest of Washington. Since 1979, notably coinciding with the Soviet entry into Afghanistan, a gradual move away from this nonchalance is evident, rooted perceptibly on its nonaligned posture, to a more active interest on the part of India to become associated with ASEAN. Finally, in 1995, India became a member of the ASEAN Regional Forum (ARF); and has since become more actively engaged in establishing closer relations with countries in Southeast Asia. Through this, India has "steadily increased its presence in Southeast Asia and has sought to foster important commercial and military ties with a range of states in the region extending from Vietnam to Singapore" (Ganguly and Mukherji 2011: 53).

In addition to hostilities with Pakistan, China, and others already discussed, India's role in her immediate vicinity needed some attention. Not all of it was easy for India to resolve. For example, in the decades-long civil war in Sri Lanka, India remained challenged by the Tamil militants. After the 1987 accord, which empowered India to attempt a "cessation of hostilities," the Indian army failed to resist the Tamil fighters, and had to retire in 1990, after a significant loss of army personnel (Hagerty and Hagerty 2005: 33–34). Since the 1980s, from a strategy of bilateral dealings, presumably whereby it could exert more leverage with a weaker state in the region, India became more actively engaged in the South Asian Association for Regional Cooperation (SAARC). Designed to promote economic growth and social and cultural exchanges and advancement, SAARC has not been very effective or initiated drastic results but has provided a multilateral forum for the states in the region. SAARC is not empowered to address bilateral disputes; hence, long-standing and newer issues affecting India's relations with specific countries could not be addressed through it.

Apparently, economic interests remain a primary focus of the Modi strategy, as is evident in its willingness to open doors with Bangladesh. A vital part of the newly achieved transit deal with Bangladesh makes room for the transport of goods through Indian territories to reach to Nepal and Bhutan. Likewise, India gained similar goods transit access to Myanmar through Bangladesh. Some of the other aspects of resolving river waters and land disputes between Bangladesh and India had begun in earnest during the previous government of Manmohan Singh. In a show of nonpartisan political deftness, Modi was able to overcome the resistance of the opposition parties, which under the leadership of the Congress and the BJP, had in the past, provided roadblocks, as the land agreement meant that India stood to lose some ground, as the original agreement carved out by Indira Gandhi in 1974 read. Even though some issues remain, notably with West Bengal's resistance to the distribution of Teesta waters, the progress made toward establishing economic connections and the inclusion of a multilateral approach to resolving some of the water-related issues are hopeful signs in Indo-Bangladeshi relations (Schaffer and Schaffer 2016: 272–78). Modi has continued this strategy with other neighbors, such as Sri Lanka and Nepal, extending opportunities for sharing economic successes. With Nepal, it started with promise but has met with some setback with the blocking of fuel carrying trucks along the border. While India denies any official blockade, an unhappy Nepal has turned to China, adding to the complexity of the issue and complicating India's next move.

Contemporary India's so-called 'Look East' policy, combined with its greater engagement with South Asian countries since the last two decades, includes a wider perimeter, including countries in the region and Southeast Asia, East Asia, and even reaching out to Australia and New Zealand. It also falls within India's realpolitik based foreign policy that is guided by aspirations of a regional power as well as to strengthen its economic prospects. Its increased participation in ASEAN, East Asia Summit, and the Asia-Europe Meeting (ASEM) covers a wide variety of areas of trade, tourism, and other mutual exchanges, and it is a significant source of economic and financial integration. Within a decade or so after the active engagement policy was introduced in the mid-1990s, the region became one of India's largest trade partners, a significant source of foreign direct investment (FDI) (Sikri 2009: 131–132).

The Modi government is also exploring closer ties with the European Union (EU). In the post-Brexit scenario, this could open the possibilities of negotiating past bottlenecks with visas for Indian workers and tariffs. Germany, in particular, has indicated willingness to discuss EU trade deals with India (Delcker 2017). Prior to Brexit, India and the EU had been working on differences in perception between developed and developing countries about market access and free trade. An area of particular interest for EU is skills for labor market. While the EU attracts worldwide migrant labor, "[i]n 2013, EU contributed to less than 1 per cent of the migrant stock in India and accounted for less than 7 per cent of India's global stock of emigrants" (Chanda and Gupta 2015: xvii). Given the EU's aging labor force and shortage in specific skill areas, several prospects remain for greater EU-India collaboration. Professional visas, the promotion of an integrated labor market in the EU with uniform immigration regulations for foreign workers, and agreed-upon recognized worker qualifications with more flexibility within EU countries and India's available skilled labor force – there is room for cooperation (Chanda 2015: 221–224). "For India, the EU is an indispensable partner and the time is propitious for India and the EU to forge new partnerships reflecting the full potential of the possibilities" (Ram 2002: 11). If this was the perception more than a decade ago, the prospects of renewed EU-India partnership are even brighter today. Alongside, India could strategically enhance the prospects for bilateral foreign and economic relations with the UK in a post-Brexit Europe as well.

Conclusion

As the above analysis demonstrates, the election of Narendra Modi and the BJP's solo mandate in 2014 have given a boost to the new India. Generally speaking, the BJP demonstrates an affinity with the Hawks perspective. In somewhat of a departure from that line with his *Vasudhaivam kutumbakam* perspective, which embraces the world as family guest, Modi is demonstrating his unique brand of foreign policy, which is a mix of populism and 'cultural nationalism.' It is clear that India does not want to remain indifferent or independent toward its neighbors any longer. "India's long term ambition to become a 'great power' will be assessed by the international community in terms of its strategic capacity to deal with instability in its own backyard" (Pant 2010: 59). India will also have to "assure the United States it sees little interest in destabilizing a Pakistan that is caught in a political vortex of its own making"(Ganguly and Howenstein: 2009: 138). In the first two years in office, Modi has reached out to Pakistan through a rather hasty and informal visit with Pakistan's Prime Minister Nawaz Sharif. He has also visited the United States, a country that he was barred from entering until his election as prime minister, already more than once since taking office in 2014. The first time, he warmed up to the Indian diaspora, and the second was in March 2016, when he attended a nuclear summit in Washington, DC. The 2005 U.S.-India civil nuclear agreement allows India to align "its domestic laws with global nonproliferation regimes it seeks to enter, such as the Nuclear Suppliers Group and the Missile Technology Control Regime" (CFR Report No. 73, 2015: 35). In addition to assuring the United States of India's readiness on this journey, Prime Minister Modi has reached out to archrival Pakistan, as well as China, Japan, and Russia (Schaffer and Schaffer 2016: 79).

To be sure, "India wants to be a regional leader whose economic success benefits the whole neighborhood, and it is prepared to listen to its neighbors' views in the process. Maintaining India's preeminence is still the goal, but with more honey than vinegar" (Schaffer and Schaffer 2016: 291). Territorial and water disputes with its neighbors persist, as is evident in Kashmir and demarcating the Sino-Indian border. Even if limited, the success of a multilateral agreement such as the Indus Water Treaty signed in 1960 shows that by outliving three wars in 1965, 1971, and 1999, third-party involvement can bring positive outcomes, even if not wholehearted cooperation (Bajpai 2013: 119–122). Alongside, India needs to sustain economic growth if it wants to achieve its global power status. "An India that can grow at the 10 percent rates China has experienced over the past three decades will transform itself faster as a power on the world stage" (CFR Report No.73, 2015: 32).

Kashmir remains "a war of attrition, which India cannot manage to win and Pakistan cannot afford to lose" (Mitra and Schottli 2007: 26). On balance, Prime Minister Modi's policies and strategies so far resemble prudent pragmatism, and they go on to underscore that India is taking steps to open doors with its neighbors and promote its aspirations of becoming a recognized and stable power in the region. It remains to be seen what this will mean in the long run.

Discussion questions

1 What is the impact of the Kashmir issue in India's major power status – does it help or hurt India's image as a democratic power?
2 Discuss the prospects and challenges of U.S.-India relations.
3 Is India still an emerging power? Argue fully.
4 How can India and Pakistan establish more cooperative bilateral relations?
5 What are the prospects of closer Sino-Indian relations?
6 Discuss the strengths and challenges of India's foreign policy perspectives that define its power in the contemporary world.

Further reading

Bajpai, K.P., Basit, S. and Krishnappa, V. (Eds.) (2014) *India's Grand Strategy: History, Theory, Cases*, New Delhi and London: Routledge.

Bajpai, K.P. and Shukul, H.C. (Eds.) (1995) *Interpreting World Politics*, New Delhi: Sage Publications.

Chari, P.R. (Ed.) (2016) [2009] *Indo-US Nuclear Deal: Seeking Synergy in Bilateralism*, New Delhi and London: Routledge.

Chellaney, B. (1993) *Nuclear Proliferation: The U.S.–Indian Conflict*, New Delhi: Orient Longman.

Datta, R. (1994) *Why Alliances Endure: The United States–Pakistan Alliance 1954–1971*, New Delhi: South Asia Books.

Ganguly, S. (2016) *Deadly Impasse: Indo-Pakistani Relations at the Dawn of a New Century*, Cambridge: Cambridge University Press.

Ganguly, S. (1986) *The Origins of War in Kashmir*, Boulder, CO: Westview Press.

Karnad, B. (2002) *Nuclear Weapons and Indian Security: The Realist Foundations of Strategy*, New Delhi: Macmillan.

Lu, Yang, (2017) *China–India Relations in the Contemporary World: Dynamics of National Interest and Identity*, London and New York: Routledge.

Perkovich, G. (1999) *India's Nuclear Bomb: The Impact on Global Proliferation*, Berkeley: University of California Press.

Sidhu, W.P.S. (1997) *Enhancing Indo–US Strategic Cooperation*, Adelphi Paper 313, London: Oxford University Press for the International Institute for Strategic Studies.

Thomas, R.G.C. and Gupta, A. (Ed.) (2000) *India's Nuclear Security*, Boulder, CO: Lynne Rienner.

References

Bajpai, K. (2013) 'India's Regional Disputes', in W.P.S. Sidhu, P.B. Mehta, and B. Jones (Ed.) *Shaping the Emerging World: India and the Multilateral Order*, Washington, DC: Brookings Institution Press.

Boesche, R. (2003) 'Kautilya's Arthasastra on War and Diplomacy in Ancient India', *The Journal of Military History* 67(1): 9–38.

Burns, R.N. (2007) 'America's Strategic Opportunity With India: The New U.S. – India Partnership', *Foreign Affairs* 86(6): 131–146. Retrieved from: www.jstor.org/stable/20032513.

Chanda, R. (2015) 'The Way Forward to a Strategic Engagement', in Chanda, R. and Gupta, P. (Ed.) *India-EU People Mobility*, New Delhi: Cambridge University Press.

Chanda, R. and Gupta, P. (Ed.) (2015) *India-EU People Mobility*, New Delhi: Cambridge University Press.

Chandra, B., Mukherjee, M. and Mukherjee, A. (2000) *India After Independence: 1947–2000*, New Delhi: Penguin Books.

Chiriyankandath, J. (2004) 'Realigning India: Indian Foreign Policy After the Cold War', *The Round Table* 93(374): 199–211.

Cohen, S. (2001) *India: Emerging Power*, Washington, DC: Brookings Institution Press.

Delcker, J. (2017) *Germany Pushes for Post-Brexit EU Trade Deals With India*. Retrieved from: www.politico.eu/article/eu-india-trade-germany-pushes-for-post-brexit-deal/.

Feigenbaum, E.A. (2010) 'India's Rise, America's Interest: The Fate of the U.S. Indian Partnership', *Foreign Affairs* 89(2): 76–91. Retrieved from: www.jstor.org/stable/20699852.

Ganguly, S. (1998) *The Crisis in Kashmir: Portents of War, Hopes for Peace*, Cambridge, UK: Cambridge University Press and Washington, DC: Woodrow Wilson Center Press.

Ganguly, S. and Howenstein, N. (2009) 'India-Pakistan Rivalry in Afghanistan', *Journal of International Affairs* 63(1): 127–140.

Ganguly, S. and Mukherji, R. (2011) *India Since 1980*, New York: Cambridge University Press.

Hagerty, D.T. and Hagerty, H.G. (2005) 'India's Foreign Relations', in D.T. Hagerty (Ed.) *South Asia in World Politics*, Lanham, MD: Rowman and Littlefield Publishers.

Hardgrave Jr., R.L. and Kochanek, S.A. (2000) *India: Government and Politics in a Developing Nation*, Austin, TX: Harcourt College Publishers.

Hathaway, R. (2003) 'The US-India Courtship: From Clinton to Bush', in S. Ganguly (Ed.) *India as an Emerging Power*, London: Fran Cass.

India-US Relations: Promoting Synergy (2003) Report of an Independent Core Group, New Delhi: Institute of Peace and Conflict Studies.

Kaye, C.R. and Nye Jr., J.S. (2015) 'Working With a Rising India: A Joint Venture for the New Century', *Independent Task Force Report No. 73*. New York: Council on Foreign Relations. [Cited as CFR Report No. 73, 2015].

Malik, J.M. (1995) 'China-India Relations in the Post-Soviet Era: The Continuing Rivalry', *The China Quarterly* 142: 317–355. Retrieved from: www.jstor.org/stable/655419.

Mitra, S.K. and Schottli, J. (2007) 'The New Dynamics of Indian Foreign Policy and Its Ambiguities', *Irish Studies in International Affairs* 18: 19–34.

Morgenthau, H.J. (1973) [1948] *Politics Among Nations: The Struggle for Power and Peace*, New York: Alfred A. Knopf.

Palkhivala, N.A. (1981) *India's Priceless Heritage*, Bombay: Bharatiya Vidya Bhavan.

Pant, H.V. (2010) 'India's Challenge in Afghanistan: With Power Comes Responsibility', *Contemporary Readings in Law and Social Justice* 2(1): 36–67.

Ram, A.N. (2002) 'India and the European Union in the New Millennium', in R.K. Jain (Ed.) *India and the European Union in the 21st Century*, New Delhi: Radiant.

Schaffer, T.C. and Schaffer, H.B. (2016) *India at the Global High Table: The Quest for Regional Primacy and Strategic Autonomy*, Washington, DC: Brookings Institution Press.

Sikri, R. (2009) 'India's "Look East" Policy', *Asia-Pacific Review*, 16(1): 131–145.

Tellis, A. (2001) *India's Emerging Nuclear Posture: Between Recessed Deterrent and Ready Arsenal*, Santa Monica, CA: RAND.

Waltz, K.N. (1959) *Man, the State and War*, New York: Columbia University Press.

Wirsing, R.G. (1998) *India, Pakistan, and the Kashmir Dispute*, New York: St. Martin's Press.

Wolpert, S. (1991) *India*, Berkeley, CA: University of California Press.

8

TOWARD 'A BETTER WORLD'

Impact of India's soft power

Prologue

The bus travelled through what were distinctly Muslim, Jewish, Hindu, and Christian neighborhoods. There were places of worship, sites to bury the dead, and markets that specialized in festival accessories pertaining to the rituals of various ethnic and religious groups, all co-existing in a city that obviously was running out of physical space to accommodate all these different ethnicities, but remained elastic when it came to having space in its heart for people representing a wide variety of beliefs and practices.

Then the bus dropped us off at Chittaranjan Avenue in the central part of Kolkata. From there we took a walking tour of the city; we literally lived the 'cultural confluence.' We walked through a narrow lane, which is also known as the Bow Barracks. This area was where most families were of Anglo Indian origin. Very few of them were still in the city; many had migrated to Australia, Canada, and the UK since independence. The buildings were old and dilapidated; elderly people enjoyed the winter sun on their balconies; children ran around the buildings; some played roadside cricket. Anglo Indian families lived on Buddhist Temple Street, where we learned that Kripasharan Mahasthavir had built a Buddhist temple to revive the religion in Bengal.

A few months later, during a routine taxi ride from the commuter train station in suburban New Jersey, the driver told me that he loved Bollywood films; they were very popular in Morocco, where he is from. His favorite Bollywood star was Yusuf Khan, he said. Having had my introduction to Bollywood movies in the late 1970s, I told him I had not heard about Khan. "You must have, he is very famous. Sure you must have heard about Dilip Kumar!" I was embarrassed with my lack of information about Bollywood stars but also happy to know about the widespread global appeal and popularity of Bollywood films.

The tour among the old and the new in the city was symbolic of the new India, which cherishes its past but has also embarked on this modernization and liberalization with new energy. It, and the conversation I had with the taxi driver, formed the prelude to these questions: How does this new India accommodate the past and the present? How does it correspond and communicate its identity with the rest of the world in this age of globalization? Do Bollywood films portray the reality that is India?

– Author's Note, January 2014

Chapter objectives and outline

Having looked at India's resilient democracy, unprecedented economic boom, and the fissures within the fabric of Indian society, the challenges of gender inequality, and military strength and foreign relations, this concluding chapter, which also serves as the conclusion of the book, will focus on the rich tradition of continuity and change amidst diversity that India can harness in terms of becoming recognized for technological innovation, cultural enrichment, and economic interaction. As N. R. Narayana Murthy (2009) argues, India can use its inherent talent to address those issues that remain as hamstrings to making India the powerhouse that it has the potential to become. The chapter will therefore assess India's soft power, innovation, and the place it has made for itself on the global stage. Home of the world's largest film industry, the impact of Bollywood both on India's society and on defining India abroad will also be discussed. The goal is to understand the aspects of India's soft power and reflect on and present a concluding overview of contemporary India's ongoing challenges and strengths.

Each of the chapters in this book has covered an aspect of India's uniqueness and its power in the face of many challenges, be it of historical richness, democratic governance amidst dissidence, economic boom, military security, socio-economic inequality, and gender empowerment. Before embarking on discussing the elements of soft power in India, a brief overview of the concept itself will help us contextualize India's potential in wielding it. The chapter does not argue whether soft power can be a substitute for hard power; instead, it makes the case for a broader sense of development priorities and, ultimately, a reliance on India's democratic attributes as a source of sustainable strength.

Power and soft power

In the field of political science, power is said to be the capacity to influence others. Robert Dahl highlighted the relational aspect of power. "*A* has power over *B* to the extent that he can get *B* to do something that *B* would not otherwise do" (Dahl 1957: 202–203). As we have seen in Chapter 7, realists and neo-realists have argued in favor of the importance of 'hard power' or defense and military strength, and a nation's interest defined in terms of power (Morgenthau 1948; Waltz 1959, 1979, and others). Most realists and neo-realists believe that military and economic power constitutes this strength. Traditionally, military threats and economic sanctions have served the coercive elements of power, whereas economic incentives have offered 'carrots.'

There is a third view that was introduced by Joseph Nye (1990), implying "soft power." There are two major aspects of Nye's "soft power." One is the notion of "co-optive power." Essentially, it implies that a powerful nation is able to mold or bring into the fold other nations to acquiesce to its perspective or policy position. "Co-optive power can rest on the attraction of one's ideas or on the ability to set the political agenda in a way that shapes the preferences the others express" (Nye 1990: 31). In other words, it is able to 'co-opt' other nations. Such ability to influence others stems from the stature of a nation in terms of culture, ideology, and regime norms. "Soft power is therefore the ability to modify other states' preferences because of their perception of you" (Blarel 2012: 28). The second aspect of soft power is that embedded within it is the notion of 'influence.' It is not how much tangible power a state has but how it is able to influence others. "Traditionally, power in world politics was always seen in terms of military or economic power. Yet, the U.S. lost the Vietnam War, the Soviet Union was defeated in Afghanistan, and – even after becoming the world's sole superpower – the U.S. has been discovering in recent years in Iraq, the wisdom of Talleyrand's old adage: 'The one thing you cannot do with a bayonet is to sit on it'" (Tharoor 2008: 35). Simply put, no matter how much absolute military and economic power a nation-state has, its ability to influence its allies and adversaries depends on something more, something intangible. In that sense, it is not a new notion. Dahl had emphasized that power as the ability to influence a change in the behavior of others. In short, it appears that states need hard and soft power and will succeed to the extent they are able to balance the two effectively.

Elements of India's soft power

Like most nation-states, the story of India's emergence and contemporary status outlined in this book is a tale that began with a quest for hard power. India's is also a tale of soft power. Despite Nehru's idealism and lofty rhetoric of peaceful co-existence, a fundamental aspect of the foreign policy he espoused since the early days of independence was as much a recognition of India's great historical heritage and culture as much as its need for and dependence on military power. As we saw in Chapters 4 and 5, India inherited hostilities since independence with the unresolved status of Kashmir and border issues with Pakistan and China. After four wars with Pakistan and some near misses, and a humiliating defeat in the hands of China in 1962, India can hardly ignore hard power. Yet, India also boasts of its rich culture and heritage. How does India do it? Does it help to enhance India's 'co-optive power'?

The literature on soft power is emerging and clearly shows some areas of strength for India and others that remain as challenges. Shashi Tharoor talks about four debates in contemporary India. The first, he characterizes as 'bread versus freedom.' The second is the debate between 'centralization and federalism,' followed by 'pluralism versus fundamentalism,' and 'globalization versus self-reliance.' Previous chapters of this book have discussed these ongoing debates and how they are shaping priorities in a fast changing and growing India, coupled with institutions that continue to either stymie or add to the heritage of India. To the above, Tharoor adds the 'guns versus ghee' debate, alluding to military power as opposed to economic growth. "It is difficult to deny that without adequate defence a country cannot develop freely. Yet, it is equally impossible to deny that without development there will not be a country worth defending" (Tharoor 2008: 33). Here, Tharoor appears to focus on human development. Chapter 5 referred to human development, an issue posited against strictly economic development that calls for attention to expansion of equity in education, income, health, and environment. While it is true that human development is a necessary aspect of development, it is not necessarily 'soft power.' In fact, Tharoor is making the case that due to India's spotty record on spreading the benefits of development equitably (India has one of the highest number of billionaires in Asia, but also 260 million people who live below the poverty line), India should not vie for a spot as a global leader in terms of economic development, which to him, is still 'incomplete.' Instead, he argues that "if there is one attribute of independent India to which increasing attention should now be paid around the globe, it is not economics or military or nuclear strength, but the quality that India is already displaying in ample measure today. And that is our soft power" (Tharoor: 2008: 35).

It is, however, not easy, as Blarel (2012: 28) argues, to identify soft power. Attempting to identify the elements of soft power of the United States, Joseph Nye concluded that there are skeptics who object to the use of the concept, mostly "because governments are not in full control of the attraction. Much of American soft power has been produced by Hollywood, Harvard, Microsoft and Michael

Jordan. But the fact that civil society is the origin of such soft power does not disprove its existence. In a liberal society, government cannot and should not control the culture" (Nye 2004: 17). In Nye's example, the soft power emanated from films, education, technology, and sports. India has had a historically rich tradition of education, but contemporary India has yet to fully harness its assets in education, sports, and other areas. In addition, as we have already seen, Nye also continues that soft power implies others' perceptions about a country, and culture is an important aspect of it. This calls for a look at India's contributions to soft power coming through cultural attributes such as films (Bollywood). In addition, like Tharoor, Maya Chaddha has emphasized that India's 'civilizational experience' and its diaspora carry important banners of the country's soft power. Finally, Chaddha also adds India's democracy as an element of soft power (Chaddha 2014: 215). We will conclude the chapter with a discussion of India's democratic attributes and their impact on both soft and hard power.

In June 2016, during his visit to the United States, Prime Minister Narendra Modi made a presentation to the Joint House of Congress. In his address, he identified some parallels between the two countries, which interestingly touched upon elements of both hard and soft power. In terms of hard power, he talked about U.S.-India civil military nuclear pact as well as economic cooperation that led to the green revolution in India and the latter's commitment to solar energy. His remarks were unmistakably underlined with a reference to the soft power that influenced and strengthened the partnership of the two countries.

> Engagement between our democracies has been visible in the manner in which our thinkers impacted one another, and shaped the course of our societies. Thoreau's idea of civil disobedience influenced our political thoughts. And, similarly the call by the great sage of India Swami Vivekananda to embrace humanity was most famously delivered in Chicago. Gandhi's non-violence inspired the heroism of Martin Luther King. . . . The genius of Dr. B.R. Ambedkar was nurtured in the years he spent at the Columbia University a century ago. (excerpt from Narendra Modi speech, *Indian Express*, June 10, 2016)

Lest his previous reference to religious tolerance of Vivekananda and Gandhi paint a picture of India's past laurels, Modi was quick to add in that same speech, what is critical to contemporary India, and in every way, aspects of hard power.

> Fast forward to today. Our S&T collaboration continues to helps us in cracking the age-old problems in the fields of public health, education, food, and agriculture. Ties of commerce and investment are flourishing. We trade more with the U.S. than with any other nation. . . . Defence purchases have moved from almost zero to ten billion dollars in less than a decade. . . . Civil Nuclear Cooperation . . . is a reality. (excerpt from Narendra Modi speech, *Indian Express*, June 10, 2016)

Here, Prime Minister Modi is clearly hailing India's economic, commercial, scientific, and defense-related achievements, albeit in partnership with the United States. This juxtaposition of hard and soft power raises the question of their relative importance in India. Tharoor (2008) says that scholars are divided on the importance of hard and soft power in India and what the country should be focusing on. India's appeal to the world in terms of soft power is legendary, but India does have an image problem. Tharoor outlines several aspects of India's soft power, which will unravel in the next section, along with other elements, and how and whether India is able to use these to exert soft power.

Bollywood and beyond

For decades, Bollywood has served as a main vehicle through which India exports its soft power. A recent narrative recounts a film from the early 1950s called *Awara* (meaning 'vagabond' in Hindi), which was so popular in China that most Chinese adults are known to recognize its title song, "Awara hoon . . . main" ("I am a vagabond"). It is said that even Chairman Mao Zedong considered it to be one of his favorite movies. 3.6 billion people watched 1,100 films that Bollywood made in 2003, compared to 2.6 billion who watched the 600 Hollywood films (Khanna 2007: 257–258).

By way of filling gaps in modern hectic and polarized, conflict-ridden lives, the Bollywood story lines provide a respite, depicting a Cinderella story of dream fulfillment, the victory of good over evil, or removing class barriers (*Awara*, 1951), a woman's indomitable spirit (*Mother India*, 1957), or a feast of drama, post-colonial patriotic spirit, and music (as in the Oscar-nominated *Lagaan*, 2001). Through the event sequence in the film where peasants bring down the mighty British in a game of cricket, *Lagaan* also stirred a feeling of national-istic pride, decades after they had left the shores of India. Some of the films carrying story lines and settings in India that have been transfor-mational – such as *Monsoon Wedding* (2001), the Oscar-winning *Slum-dog Millionaire*, or *The Best Exotic Marigold Hotel* (2011) and its sequel *The Second Best Exotic Hotel Marigold* (2015) – are not Bollywood productions but have played the role of conveying India's soft power effectively. The *Hotel Marigold* films – with a mix of humor and the star power of Western actors such as Judi Dench, Maggie Smith, and others – have successfully conveyed a powerful message. Albeit fiction, they have a broad appeal, and especially among retirees with India as a destination, who may travel to India to receive affordable surgery but end up forming human connections that blur divisions of race, caste, and sexual preference. Given the rise among some westerners to choose India as a destination location for elective surgeries, in this case, fiction is part fact, to be sure.

But do Bollywood films and the westernized versions of India through the films mentioned above reflect India's cultural authen-ticity? Are Western interpretations and Hollywood appropriating authentic Indian storytelling through such hybridized films? One such claim was rather direct and clear: "Bombay cinema is my cinema. I know what it's all about. . . . I don't like those Johnny-come-lately ignorant Westerners and media people advising me about it" (Samant 2005: 86, cited in Athique 2008: 299). And this was prefaced with a more spe-cific reference to one such film, *Bride and Prejudice*: "All this preaching by the Western media about what I should appreciate from my own popular culture. One Bride and Prejudice (Gurinder Chadha 2004) comes along aimed at white ignorant audiences, and they lap it up because everything Indian is the flavour of the season" (Samant 2005:

84, cited in Athique 2008: 299). Given that Sapna Samant is a trustee of the Asia Film Festival Aotearoa, this view might have more resonance than merely a critical one.

Evidently, the impact of Bollywood worldwide has not been uniform and has undergone a transformation in recent years. Along with globalization, 'Bollywoodization' is spreading too, beyond the UK, the United States, and countries in the Middle East. One example of how recent rebranding of Bollywood films is becoming inextricably linked with India's soft power is evident in Australia. According to one assessment, "whilst a mainstream audience for Indian movies remained putative during 2003–2005, the profile of Indian films had undeniably been heightened within the intertextual and transnational media sphere operating across Australian society" (Athique 2008: 308). Without historical connections that India has had with countries such as the UK, its ties and impact of Bollywood has also been different. India's rising stature as a powerful economy, with its IT industry and a viable competitive model to China's, is transforming the perception with which the country is viewed by the outside world: an important aspect of soft power: "[A] new picture of India is emerging in the pages of English-language news and business glossies, replacing its previous role as spokesman for the 'traditional' societies of the Third World with a new role as a dynamic, modernizing, capitalist society amenable to incorporation into the New World Order" (Athique 2008: 308).

Bollywood's influence has also trickled into music, and the larger popular cultural artifacts and media also constitute elements of soft power in this regard. Before looking at the global influence of Bollywood music, we have to keep in mind that classical music and dance legends such as Ravi Shankar (Sitar), Uday Shankar (Dance), Zakir Hussain (Tabla or percussion instrument), and others have successfully brought Indian music and culture to the world stage. Even though not widespread in popular appeal, the writings, lyrics, and melody of Tagore's songs have helped spread the message of universal brotherhood and internationalism. In 1913, for his contribution to literature and his collection of poems, *Gitanjali*, Tagore received the Nobel Prize for literature, making him the first non-European and first Asian to get the recognition. William Rothenstein, the artist who was host to Tagore during his 1912 visit to England, and the poet W.B. Yeats were foremost among those who introduced Tagore to the West. They were both enthralled with the mysticism and beauty of the human spirit that resonated with them through Tagore's writing. In that, and his numerous poems, short stories, novels, dance dramas and music, Tagore's universalism is deeply felt and appreciated across cultures. "To Yeats, Tagore represented the wisdom and dignity of the East, and justified the faith that he had placed on the strength and vitality of Asian philosophy. For Tagore, Yeats was a vibrant symbol of the creative energy of the West" (Hurwitz 1964: 55). Despite a Nobel Prize and a huge following among the Bengali diaspora, constituting those in West Bengal as well as Bangladesh, Tagore's legacy in the West is sporadic at best. Noted filmmaker Satyajit Ray, who also hailed from Bengal, has made many films outside the Bollywood genre to the critical acclaim of film circles all over the world that continue to be discussed in film and culture programs for the cinematography. His adaptation of Tagore's *Home and the World* was a critically acclaimed film, but there is hardly much evidence of its impact on the popular imagination in the West. Hence, music and culture of India do resonate with the outside world, albeit without mass appeal. For example, even though Ravi Shankar's name may not be a household one in the world outside India, George Harrison, a major voice among the *Beatles*, is, and he made sitar a familiar instrument to the Western audience. India's gift to the conducting world through Zubin Mehta is also an element of narrating the story of soft power in terms of agency.

To be sure, the impact of Bollywood music is audibly and visibly clear in contemporary India and abroad. This is not a new phenomenon, and it needs to be contextualized. In the 1970s, some popular Hindi films focused on the 'youth culture' through outreach to themes and music with western influence. Songs from films such as *Hare Rama Hare Krishna* (1971) clearly fit this genre and became popular. Between the 1970s and 1990s, the music industry itself went through several changes, new companies were formed, and distribution and copyright were affected the liberalization of the economy (Booth 2011: 216). Even after changes in the 1970s and 1980s, when non-film music seemed to be on the rise, for most of its history, India's popular music industry has had to walk in tandem with Bollywood, as the latter is a powerful vehicle with wide outreach: "[T]he globalization of mediated culture – the widespread Indian access to satellite television and global music styles and the current worldwide distribution of Hindi films – are economic and cultural factors that reconfigured the market for Hindi films and songs in a range of ways" (Booth 2011: 220). In this context, the Bollywood brand is a successful, commercial industry, which, by dint of the number of films and ticket sales annually, has become the world's largest film producer. Because its market is primarily India, where ticket prices are much lower, it does not bring in as much revenue as Hollywood films do. "But recently, the economic performance of Bollywood has risen rapidly. In 2006, Bollywood was acknowledged by investors as one of India's central growth industries and in the process of becoming a future global giant" with all indicators pointing to Bollywood being "well on its way to becoming integrated with the global economy" (Lorenzen, M. and Taube, F. A. 2008: 287).

India's diaspora and soft power

Any discussion about diaspora in the current climate of anti-immigrant sentiments prevalent in Europe, the United States, and elsewhere needs to take into account the identity politics that seems to overshadow the cultural confluence that surrounds globalization and the role of the diaspora in bringing about cultural cosmopolitanism. Soft power seems to have benefited from globalization and free trade. With flow of goods also comes flow of people and culture and ideas. Recent verdicts such as with Brexit and the election of Donald Trump as the U.S. president bear testimony to this rising brand of economic nationalism and its hostility to mass immigration, albeit allegedly from open borders with Europe. An apostle of integration with EU and the virtues of globalization, former prime minister Tony Blair has identified the source of the ideological angst as follows: "The right attacks immigrants while the left rails at bankers, but the spirit of insurgency, the venting of anger at those in power and the addiction to simple, demagogic answers to complex problems are the same for both extremes. Underlying it all is a shared hostility to globalization" (Blair, June 24, 2016).

Indeed, this does not ring the death knell to globalization per se or soft power altogether, but it does put a dent in it and makes it more complicated, especially when it comes to the impact of the diaspora on soft culture. When it comes to immigration from India, it has several different origins that corresponded to different phases and strands. In colonial India, European companies took Indian laborers to work in Caribbean countries, where they gradually got assimilated. With the end of the colonial era, many of them continued to maintain 'emotional ties' to India, especially in the context of India's rising power and global status. (Chaddha 2014: 227). Indians have been migrating to the United States since the nineteenth century, and they increased in the early part of the twentieth century. "The increasing trend was, however, restricted by the Congressional exclusion laws of 1917 and 1923" (Kanjilal 2000: 5). In 1946, the legislation was reformed, allowing an increase in the number of Asian Indian immigrants in the United States. By and large, since the 1970s, Indian migration to the United States, Canada, and England began to rise, and the oil boom attracted many to the Middle East. The first wave consisted of mostly professionals, who were followed by small-business owners, taxicab drivers, and others. Even though they form only about 1% of the overall population, Indian-Americans constitute one of the fastest growing immigrant groups in the United States (Chaddha 2014: 228).

The Indian diaspora, however, was not reckoned as a significant source of soft power until about the 1990s. During the 1971 Bangladesh War, the Nixon-Kissinger team displayed hostile and misogynistic attitude toward the leadership of Indira Gandhi and overall disdain for India; they even portrayed Indians as savages (Hymans 2009: 247–48). Even though relations between New Delhi and Washington continued to be ambivalent until the early 2000s, India's soft power did appeal to other sections of society and culture in America. From Dr. Martin Luther King's adoption of Gandhi's civil disobedience and nonviolent passive resistance strategies in the civil rights movement to the Beatles guitarist George Harrison's benefit concert for Bangladesh, "by the 1970s India had accumulated a sizable amount of attractive soft power with the rising youthful forces in American culture" (Hymans 2009: 250). A large number of India's best and brightest students come to the United States for higher education every year, and they establish a link to influence U.S. policy-making through bipartisan congressional caucus as well as lending support to political parties in their native India (Chiriyankandath 2004: 207).

Since the 1980s and 1990s, there appears to be an intergenerational effort among the Indian-American diaspora toward spreading Indian culture abroad. To take one example, in the metropolitan New York–New Jersey area, as well as other parts of the United States, there are several cultural groups and drama, music, and dance schools that offer lessons and shows. One school, *Kalamandir*, specializes in the dance form of *Katthak*, which represents India's rich history of Hindu, Persian, and Mughal cultural amalgamation, as discussed in Chapter 2, and it aligns them with a contemporary flair (www.kalamandirdanceco.com/?page_id=370). Along with *Katthak*, this company has integrated with other styles. It integrates classical Indian dance styles with Capoeira, Flamenco, Modern, and Ballet dance forms (www.brinda guha.com/#!kalamandir/c1o5m). Likewise, *Nritya Creations* promotes multidisciplinary dance, including classical Indian styles, contemporary fusion, and Bollywood. Both these schools draw Western and non-Western students, beyond the South Asian diaspora. Pandit Sanjoy Banerjee, an accomplished north Indian classical vocalist who trained in the Kirana Gharana, teaches at Chhandayan Center in the United States and teaches in Bangladesh, the UK, Australia, and Germany (http://tabla.org/).

While a large number of the Indian diaspora is in the sciences, healthcare, finance, business, education, and the IT industry, in the past two decades there has also been a diversification in that more Indian-Americans are entering fields such as politics, arts, entertainment, media, and other "fields that were inaccessible to the first generation of Indians in America" (Chaddha 2014: 229). Indian immigrants and Indian Americans have accomplished high-level recognition in a wide variety of fields. They include Nobel Prize–winning economist Amartya Sen, also the recipient of numerous distinguished awards and accolades including the National Humanist Medal (2011); Pulitzer Prize–winning authors such as Dr. Siddhartha Mukherjee, Jhumpa Lahiri, and others; high-profile public officials and company executives such as U.S. Ambassador to the UN Nikki Haley, former California State Attorney General and currently U.S. Senator Kamala Harris, former U.S. Surgeon General Dr. Vivek Murthy, Pepsico CEO Indra Nooyi, Sun Microsystems' Vinod Khosla, Google CEO Sundar Pichai, co-founder of Juniper Networks Pradeep Sindhu, and many others – representing a wide variety of fields and areas and numerous start-up companies in Silicon Valley and other parts of the United States.

Meanwhile, the Indian-American lobby has also gradually consolidated its role in affecting pro-India policy. This activism has been instrumental in laying the groundwork for the 2006 bipartisan U.S.-India civil-military nuclear deal. "With India expected to purchase weapons systems worth $100 billion for long term defence plans (2012–2027), many major U.S. corporations have thought it prudent to support the India lobby and contribute money to it. They are hoping that the nuclear deal will open the path to other lucrative deals, including building more nuclear power plants in India from which they can profit for years to come" (Chaddha 2014: 233–233). Thus, even though within the limits of soft power, the diaspora is able to enhance business prospects and hard power of both countries.

Beyond soft power: the state, democracy, growth, and more

In many ways, India is a work in progress, a democracy at work. Some of the aspects of India's soft power – its culture, music, art, and food – have made, and continue to make, their mark on the world stage. If, however, one is to rely on India's stature based on soft power, it may not be far-fetched to surmise that India in the minds of the outsider still resides in the realm that we have traditionally seen – a respect for its historical past, art, and culture. Undoubtedly, India's democracy is the experiment that makes it unique. Mainstreaming India, although in the process, is still an uphill task. Through its hard and soft power, economic potential, and economic prospects, India stands tall. But there are intransigent challenges as well. Balancing them will take both soft and hard power. Edward Luce identifies four broad challenges that the country faces. These relate to the areas of poverty and gainful employment, the environment, HIV-AIDS, and liberal democracy (Luce 2007: 335–354). Taken together, these cover economic and political dimensions of India's governance challenges that were outlined in Chapters 3, 4, 5, and 6.

India's economic growth trajectory is nothing short of impressive. The country seems to have withstood the downturn of the 2008 global recession. However, much of the growth in recent decades has been reliant on the service sector. Even though jobs are being created, farm and non-farm employment needs to grow. The problem of rural poverty is related to small farmers lacking the ability to afford mechanization of agriculture and to a lack of proper infrastructure. Absence of adequate infrastructure such as passable roads has a catapulting effect on challenging access to health centers and schools (Luce 2007: 337). Then there is the inequality in the outcome of economic development. Incomes around the top 20% of the population have increased remarkably. For workers who are in the informal sector and those doing 'unskilled' work has been slow. The impact of wage discrepancy is also reflected in the very low rise in per capita expenditure for poor households in both rural and urban areas and for 'unskilled' workers (Drèze and Sen 2013: 29).

Managing the country's air and water quality should be a matter of urgency for the government. There needs to be consistent or intentional vision driving such effort. Major water bodies continue to be people's main source of water to drink, bathe in, wash clothes, and immerse clay idols after festivals. In 2015, the government has launched the 'Namami Gange' program, a five-year plan with 1,000 projects to address pollution and to modernize the banks of the River Ganga, which flows through various states in northern and eastern India. "More than 1,500 million litres of raw sewage is discharged into the river every day. Add to that 500 million litres of industrial waste from 700 highly polluting industries and thousands of tonnes of non-biodegradable solid waste that are dumped into the river daily" (*The Economic Times* 2016, referenced under 'Namani Gange' Project Launch).

As already alluded to in Chapter 5, India's lack of public health care is close to being a crisis. Providing public health is indeed a challenge. Public health is a comprehensive task and includes "immunization, sanitation, public hygiene, waste disposal, disease surveillance, vector control, health education, food safety regulation" (Drèze and Sen 2013: 179). While it might not be advisable to provide funding for preventing HIV-AIDS at the expense of providing other basic health needs, unless India unless India addresses the impact of the spread of AIDS, its healthcare system could be challenged by the magnitude of the epidemic (Luce 2007: 344). With resolve and public consciousness, improvements can be made, making the state responsive to people's basic human development needs and rights. Some successful examples are the state of Tamil Nadu, where people have demanded and made public services available, and programs such as National Rural Health Mission (NRHM), which has delivered vaccinations and promoted other amenities that helped reduce infant mortality (Drèze and Sen 2013: 168–180).

Disparity in development is another area where changes are critical. In India's villages, only about half of the homes have electricity (Luce 2007: 342). People who do not have electricity, as in rural homes or urban pavements where many people live in makeshift homes, tend to use dried cow dung cakes (Gobar Upla/Ghute) as fuel. In urban areas, in the winter months, people who live on the sidewalks in makeshift shelters often burn scraps of wood, plastic, leaves, and whatever they can find to keep warm, without any thought about the fumes. Despite the government's efforts in 2007–2008 to include electrification, irrigation, housing, and other rural development plans through the *Bharat Nirman* (Building India) program, they did not yield to satisfactory levels of agricultural development or improving the plight of farmers in many states. This has led to farmer 'distress' and suicides in several states (Ganguly and Mukherji 2011: 95–97).

By and large, through the 'dangerous decades,' India has encountered balkanization, made some mistakes, conceded to some sectarian demands, and dissipated others using force. Even though millions of people are below the poverty line, barring some groups that still challenge the governance structures that disenfranchise them, poverty has not radicalized people en masse to engage in large-scale terrorism. Our discussion has also shown that India's secularism remains both unique and incomplete. It has been challenged in recent decades and continues to evolve.

It appears therefore that India is balancing a combination of soft and hard power: "India's soft power no longer resides in the Nehruvian traditions of socialism, scientific temper, and rejection of military power. In the post–Cold War era, its soft power draws on the acquisition of sophisticated weapons and weapons systems, the ability to project power beyond India, and the productivity of its newly inaugurated market economy" (Chaddha 2014: 235). The long-standing dispute in Kashmir needs to be resolved using all resources, including third-party negotiation and more communication and confidence building measures with Pakistan. Such measures ought to go beyond people-to-people interaction and include conventional and nuclear confidence-building measures (Parthasarathy 2004: 439). China is an important actor in the region as well as in the world, and India needs to continue to engage with China, particularly with the latter's presence in disputed regions bordering Kashmir and Arunachal Pradesh. Through its soft power, economic potential, and economic prospects, India stands tall. But as already mentioned, there are intransigent challenges as well. Where does India stand in the balance?

Conclusion

The concluding thoughts on India's soft power also serve as conclusions one can draw about the various aspects of contemporary India discussed in this book. As already stated, the argument in this chapter is not about India's hard versus soft power. India's stature among world powers as well as its neighbors is on an upward trajectory. India's leadership is well poised to continue its vision for strengthening such partnerships for trade and energy cooperation, and continue its economic progress. As already mentioned, it is up to the leadership as well as the electorate to ensure more equitable development. Such equity ought to cover class, caste, gender, ethnic-religious, as well as regional bases. Deep seated cultural norms and patriarchy still stand in the way of women's empowerment. Addressing gender-based violence is critical for the country's health and economic stature. Through it all, India remains an exciting experiment, a confluence of tradition and modernity, democracy and development, and challenges and opportunities.

A recent public service video campaign aligns some of the contemporary challenges and prospects that India is facing. It uses technology, gender imagery, economic and soft power in the government's 'Swacch Bharat' campaign, aimed at cleaning up litter, garbage, and dirt that seems to stubbornly adorn sidewalks and roadways. It uses a video with voices of popular Bollywood stars to bring the message home. The not so subtle video shows how those who do not respect their surroundings and keep the shops and roadsides free of litter and garbage, will not be welcoming Goddess Lakshmi, a symbol of prosperity. In a country that believes in pro-business growth, where the new India has generated a new culture of entrepreneurship, where the state has undertaken a more flexible approach to political economy, this image of Lakshmi is significant. Three decades ago, Lloyd and Susanne Rudolph had reminded us that Lakshmi "invokes an Indian world view, one that orients and recognizes how many Indians, although not necessarily intellectuals, think about political economy. Lakshmi, the goddess of wealth, is a figure out of the popular pantheon" (Rudolph and Rudolph 1987: 393). Beyond the symbolism, the Rudolphs prompted us to think about political economy in a way that it is meaningful to the individual as well as the collectivity. In other words, if people are able to connect their immediate economic circumstances to the progress at the macro level, they become agency for that progress. Leaving aside the question about using the image of a Hindu Goddess in a secular country, the ad campaign seems to have made the connection of the individual prosperity to collective good, in a material sense. In an age where social media and individual ownership go a long way, these strategies might work, and might even bring in longer-term cultural change.

Ultimately, one hopes that the democratic ethos and the country's watchdog media will, as they have in the past, channel people's aspirations as well as make the government accountable. India is uniquely poised to bring a balance of state services without enforcement of mandatory policies that infringe on individual rights. One example is the recent initiative that uses technology to reach millions of people in terms of distributing subsidies and services. This is through the 'Aadhar' identification system, which seeks to eliminate fraud and authenticate identities in a cost-effective way. The role of the state in such initiatives was vetted through the democratic process. Change by force does not suit democratic India. As already seen, behind the successes of public services in Tamil Nadu and literacy programs in Kerala, for example, lies democratic discourse. The people's consciousness went a long way to bring about positive changes in public policy.

This book celebrates India's commitment to military security and economic growth. It also discusses the challenges contemporary India is riddled with. In the final analysis, India is best served when it can use its democratic institutions and processes to seek cohesion and give voices to its uniquely and vastly diverse population. Institutions such as the party and the press could ensure that the country is not hamstrung or held hostage to religious fundamentalism, misogyny, caste-based discrimination, and other scourges of bigotry that are enemies of liberal democracy. An inclusive society, which respects religious freedom and gives women and marginalized groups the agency to promote policies to benefit all, is a matter of both onus and ownership. As India soars and muddles through, it is the onus of the people and policy-makers to make India's development and democracy work for all, so that they can all share ownership of its future. In the ultimate analysis, India's commitment to freedom, as it has done in the past, will set it free from bondage, ignorance, poverty, and strife. In that sense, what Tagore had dreamed more than a century ago, is very much relevant for contemporary India, to establish a country "[w]here the mind is without fear and the head is held high."

Discussion questions

1 What is 'soft power,' and what is its importance in international relations?
2 Does India have 'soft power'? What are its focal points, strengths, and weaknesses?
3 Argue the case for and against soft power and its relevance in the emergence of India as a great power.
4 Should India focus only on economic and military power? Discuss the different views for and against this question.
5 If you were asked to identify one aspect of contemporary India that you can take away after reading this book, what would it be?

Further reading

Adeney, K. and Wyatt, A. (2010) *Contemporary India*, New York: Palgrave Macmillan.

Bald, V. (2013) *Bengali Harlem and the Lost Histories of South Asian America*, Cambridge, MA: Harvard University Press.

Bose, S. (2013) *Transforming India: Challenges to the World's Largest Democracy*, Cambridge, MA: Harvard University Press.

Corbridge, S., Harriss, J. and Jeffrey, C. (2013) *India Today: Economy, Politics and Society*, Cambridge, UK: Polity Press.

Doniger, W. and Nussbaum, M.C. (Ed.) (2015) *Pluralism and Democracy in India*, Oxford/New York: Oxford University Press.

Giridharadas, A. (2011) *India Calling: An Intimate Portrait of a Nation's Making*, New York: Times Books, Henry Holt & Company.

Jayal, N.G. (1999) *Democracy and the State: Welfare, Secularism and Development in Contemporary India*, New Delhi: Oxford University Press.

Karnad, B. (2015) *Why India Is Not a Great Power (Yet)*, Oxford: Oxford University Press.

Taber, M.A. and Batra, S. (Ed.) (1996) *Social Strains of Globalization in India: Case Examples*, New Delhi: New Concepts.

Tharoor, S. (2007) *The Elephant, the Tiger, and the Cell Phone: Reflections on India, the Emerging 21st Century Power*, New York: Arcade Publishing.

Tully, M. (2007) *India's Unending Journey: Finding Balance in a Time of Change*, London: Rider.

References

Athique, A. (2008) 'The "Crossover" Audience: Mediated Multiculturalism and the Indian Film', *Continuum: Journal of Media and Cultural Studies* 22(3): 299–311.

Blair, T. (2016) 'Brexit's Stunning Coup', *New York Times*, June 24. Retrieved from: www.nytimes.com/2016/06/26/opinion/tony-blair-brexits-stunning-coup.html?smprod=nytcore-ipad&smid=nytcore-ipad-share&_r=0.

Blarel, N. (2012) 'India's Soft Power: From Potential to Reality'? IDEAS Special Report, London School of Economics. Retrieved from: www.lse.ac.uk/IDEAS/publications/reports/pdf/SR010/blarel.pdf.

Booth, G.D. (2011) 'Preliminary Thoughts on Hindi Popular Music and Film Production: India's "Culture Industry(ies)", 1970–2000', Working Notes, *South Asian Popular Culture* 9(2): 215–221.

Chandayan School of Music, New York. Retrieved from: http://tabla.org/.

Chaddha, M. (2014) *Why India Matters*, Boulder, CO: Lynne Rienner Publishers Inc.

Chiriyankandath, J. (2004) 'Realigning India: Indian Foreign Policy After the Cold War', *The Round Table* 93(374): 199–211.

Dahl, R.A. (1957) *The Concept of Power*. Retrieved from: www.unc.edu/~fbaum/teaching/articles/Dahl_Power_1957.pdf.

Drèze, J. and Sen, A. (2013) *An Uncertain Glory: India and Its Contradictions*, Princeton & Oxford: Princeton University Press.

Ganguly, S. and Mukherji, R. (2011) *India Since 1980*, New York: Cambridge University Press.

Hurwitz, H.M. (1964) 'Yeats and Tagore', *Comparative Literature* 16(1). Retrieved from: www.jstor.org/stable/1769883?seq=1#page_scan_tab_contents.

Hymans, J.E.C. (2009) 'India's Soft Power and Vulnerability', *India Review* 8(3): 234–265.

Kalamandir Dance School and Company, New Jersey and New York. Retrieved from: www.kalamandirdanceco.com/?page_id=370; www.brindaguha.com/#!kalamandir/c1o5m.

Kanjilal, T. (2000) *Indian Americans: Participation in the American Domestic Political Process*, Calcutta: A. Kanjilal.

Khanna, T. (2007) *Billions of Entrepreneurs: How China and India are Reshaping Their Futures – and Yours*, Boston, MA: Harvard Business School Press.

Lorenzen, M. and Taube, F.A. (2008) 'Breakout From Bollywood? The Roles of Social Networks and Regulation in the Evolution of Indian Film Industry', *Journal of International Management* 14: 286–299.

Luce, E. (2007) *In Spite of the Gods: The Strange Rise of Modern India*, New York: Doubleday.

Modi, N. (2016) 'Speech at US House of Congress', *Indian Express*. Retrieved from: http://indianexpress.com/article/india/india-news-india/prime-minister-narendra-modi-us-congress-speech-2842046/.

Morgenthau, H.J. (1973) [1948] *Politics Among Nations: The Struggle for Power and Peace*, New York: Alfred A. Knopf.

'Namami Gange' Project Launch (2016) *The Economic Times*, July 6. Retrieved from:http://economictimes.indiatimes.com/articleshow/53080510.cms?utm_source=contentofinterest&utm_medium=text&utm_campaign=cppst.

Nritya Creations Academy of Dance, New Jersey. Retrieved from: https://nrityacreations.com/.

Nye Jr., J.S. (1990) *Bound to Lead: The Changing Nature of American Power*, New York: Basic Books.

Nye, Jr. J.S. (2004) *Soft Power: The Means to Success in World Politics*, New York: Public Affairs.

Rudolph, L.I. and Rudolph, S.H. (1987) *In Pursuit of Lakshmi: The Political Economy of the Indian State*, Chicago: University of Chicago Press.

Samant, S. (2005) 'Appropriating Bombay Cinema: Why the Western World gets Bollywood So Wrong', Metro, Winter, cited in A. Athique (2008) 'The "Crossover" Audience: Mediated Multiculturalism and the Indian Film', *Continuum: Journal of Media and Cultural Studies* 22(3): 299–311.

Tagore, R. (2013) *Gitanjali*, Kolkata: Sahitya Samsad.

Tharoor, S. (2008) 'India's Soft Power', *India International Center Quarterly* 35(1): 32–45.

PHOTO 11   Rickshaw. Photo: R. Veit

PHOTO 12 Shopping mall. Photo: A. Mazumdar

PHOTO 13 Educating girls. Photo: G. T. Woolston

PHOTO 14 Street sign. Photo: A. Mazumdar

PHOTO 15 Woman carrying firewood. Photo: A. Mazumdar

PHOTO 16 India is great. Photo: R. Veit

PHOTO 17   India preparing for Republic Day. Photo: R. Datta

PHOTO 18 The Ganges River. Photo: A. Mazumdar

PHOTO 19   The Nano Car. Photo: R. Datta

PHOTO 20   Contemporary India's window to the world: Mumbai Airport. Photo: A. Mazumdar

BIBLIOGRAPHY

Ahluwalia, M.S. (1995) *First Raj Krishna Memorial Lecture: Economic Reforms for the Nineties*. Retrieved from: http://planningcommission.gov.in/aboutus/speech/spemsa/msa033.pdf.

Athique, A. (2008) 'The "Crossover" Audience: Mediated Multiculturalism and the Indian Film', *Continuum: Journal of Media and Cultural Studies* 22(3): 299–311.

Bajpai, K. (2013) 'India's Regional Disputes', in W.P.S. Sidhu, P.B. Mehta, and B. Jones (Eds.) *Shaping the Emerging World: India and the Multilateral Order*, Washington, DC: Brookings Institution Press.

Banerjee, S. (2010) 'Radical and Violent Political Movement', in P.R. Brass (Ed.) *Routledge Handbook of South Asian Politics*, London: Routledge.

Basu, P. (2009) 'Religious Cleavage, Politics, and Communalism', in R. Chatterji (Ed.) *Politics India: State-Society Interface*, New Delhi: South Asian Publishers.

Batliwala, S. (2007) 'Taking the Power Out of Empowerment: As Experiential Account', *Development in Practice* 17(4/5): 557–565.

Béteille, A. (1969) *Castes: Old and New*, Bombay: Asia Publishing House.

Bhagwati, J. (1993) *India in Transition*, Oxford: Clarendon Press.

Bhagwati, J. and Panagariya, A. (2013) *Why Growth Matters*, New York: Public Affairs, a Council on Foreign Relations Book.

Blair, T. (2016) 'Brexit's Stunning Coup', *New York Times*, June 24. Retrieved from: www.nytimes.com/2016/06/26/opinion/tony-blair-brexits-stunning-coup.html?smprod=nytcore-ipad&smid=nytcore-ipad-share&_r=0.

Blarel, N. (2012) 'India's Soft Power: From Potential to Reality'? IDEAS Special Report, London School of Economics. Retrieved from: www.lse.ac.uk/IDEAS/publications/reports/pdf/SR010/blarel.pdf.

Boesche, R. (2003) 'Kautilya's Arthasastra on War and Diplomacy in Ancient India', *The Journal of Military History* 67(1): 9–38.

Bose, S. and Jalal, A. (1998) *Modern South Asia*, New Delhi: Oxford University Press.

Boserup, E. (1970/ 2007) *Woman's Role in Economic Development*, London: EarthScan.

Booth, G.D. (2011) 'Preliminary Thoughts on Hindi Popular Music and Film Production: India's "Culture Industry(ies)", 1970–2000', Working Notes, *South Asian Popular Culture* 9(2): 215–221.

Brass, P.R. (1968) 'Coalition Politics in North India', *American Political Science Review* 62(4): 1174–1191.

Brass, P.R. (1988) 'The Punjab Crisis and the Unity of India', in A. Kohli (ed.) *India's Democracy: An Analysis of Changing State-Society Relations*, Princeton, NJ: Princeton University Press.

Bumiller, E. (1990) *May You Be the Mother of a Hundred Sons*, New York: Ballantine Books.

Burke, J. (2016) 'Protests to Continue at Indian University After Student Leader's Arrest', *The Guardian*, February 15. Retrieved from: www.the guardian.com/world/2016/feb/15/jawaharlal-nehru-university-kan haiya-kumar-student-arrest-india.

Burns, R.N. (2007) 'America's Strategic Opportunity With India: The New U.S. – India Partnership', *Foreign Affairs* 86(6): 131–146. Retrieved from: www.jstor.org/stable/20032513.

Chacko, P. and Mayer, P. (2014) 'The Modi *lahar* (wave) in the 2014 Indian National Election: A Critical Realignment?' *Australian Journal of Political Science* 49(3): 518–528. Retrieved from: *Political Science Complete*, EBSCO-host (accessed May 5, 2016).

Chaddha, M. (2014) *Why India Matters*, Boulder CO: Lynne Rienner Publishers Inc.

Chanda, R. (2015) 'The Way Forward to a Strategic Engagement', in R. Chanda and P. Gupta (Eds.) *India-EU People Mobility*, New Delhi: Cambridge University Press.

Chanda, R. and Gupta, P. (Ed.) (2015) *India-EU People Mobility*, New Delhi: Cambridge University Press.

Chandra, B., Mukherjee, M. and Mukherjee, A. (2000) *India After Independence: 1947–2000*, New Delhi: Penguin Books.

Chatterji, B. (2009) 'Women and Politics in India', in R. Chatterji (Ed.) *Politics India: State-Society Interface*, New Delhi: South Asian Publishers.

Chatterji, R. (2009) 'Political Development in India', in R. Chatterji (Ed.) *Politics India: State-Society Interface*, New Delhi: South Asian Publishers.

Chen, M.A. (2006) *Self Employed Women: A Profile of SEWA's Membership*, Ahmedabad: SEWA Academy. Retrieved from: http://wiego.org/publications/self-employed-women-profile-sewas-membership.

Chibber, P. and Verma, R. (2014) 'The BJP's "Modi Wave": An Ideological Consolidation of the Right', *Economic and Political Weekly* 49(39): 50–56. [Web document appears as pages 1–7].

Chiriyankandath, J. (2004) 'Realigning India: Indian Foreign Policy After the Cold War', *The Round Table* 93(374): 199–211.

Cohen, S. (2001) *India: Emerging Power*, Washington, DC: Brookings Institution Press.

Coleridge, S.T. (1834) *The Rime of the Ancient Mariner*. Retrieved from: www. poetryfoundation.org/poems-and-poets/poems/detail/43997.

Dahl, R.A. (1957) *The Concept of Power*. Retrieved from: www.unc. edu/~fbaum/teaching/articles/Dahl_Power_1957.pdf.

Dahl, R. (Undated) 'Democracy', *Encyclopædia Britannica*. Retrieved from: www.britannica.com/topic/democracy.

Dandavate, M. (1997) Foreword in Bhattacharya, S. compiled, *Subhas Chandra Bose: Pioneer of Planning*, New Delhi: Planning Commission. Retrieved from: http://planningcommission.nic.in/reports/publications/pub_scbosh.pdf.

`Das, G. (2002) [2000] *India Unbound*, New Delhi: Penguin Books.

Das, S. (2001) *Kashmir and Sindh: Nation-Building, Ethnicity and Religious Politics in South Asia*, Kolkata: K P Bagchi and Company.

Das, S., Jain-Chandra, S., Kochar, K. and Kumar, N. (2015), 'Women Workers in India: Why So Few Among So Many'? *IMF Working Paper*, Washington, DC: International Monetary Fund. Retrieved from: www.imf.org/ external/pubs/ft/wp/2015/wp1555.pdf (Also listed under Web Sources as International Monetary Fund (IMF) Working Paper, 2015).

Datta, R. (2003) 'From Development to Empowerment: The Self-Employed Association in India', *International Journal of Politics, Culture, and Society* 16(3): 351–368.

Delcker, J. (2017) *Germany Pushes for Post-Brexit EU Trade Deals With India*. Retrieved from: www.politico.eu/article/eu-india-trade-germany-pushes-for-post-brexit-deal/.

Dodwell, H.H. (1963) *The Cambridge History of India, Volume V*, New Delhi: S.S. Chand.

Dumont, L. (1980) *Homo Hierarchus: The Caste System in India and Its Implications*, Chicago: University of Chicago Press.

Drèze, J. and Sen, A. (2013) *An Uncertain Glory: India and Its Contradictions*, Princeton and Oxford: Princeton University Press.

Embree, A.T. (2003) 'Religion', in S. Ganguly and N. DeVota (Ed.) *Understanding Contemporary India*, Boulder: Lynne Rienner.

Feigenbaum, E.A. (2010) 'India's Rise, America's Interest: The Fate of the U.S. Indian Partnership', *Foreign Affairs* 89(2): 76–91. Retrieved from: www.jstor.org/stable/20699852.

Frankel, F.R. (2006) *India's Political Economy 1947–2004*, New Delhi: Oxford University Press.

Ganguly, S. (1998) *The Crisis in Kashmir: Portents of War, Hopes for Peace*, Cambridge, UK: Cambridge University Press and Washington, DC: Woodrow Wilson Center Press.

Ganguly, S. and Howenstein, N. (2009) 'India-Pakistan Rivalry in Afghanistan', *Journal of International Affairs* 63(1): 127–140.

Ganguly, S. and Mukherji, R. (2011) *India Since 1980*, New York: Cambridge University Press.

Guha, R. (2007) *India After Gandhi*, New York: Harper Collins.

Gupta, D. (2005) 'Caste and Politics: Identity Over System', *Annual Review of Anthropology* 34: 409–427.

Hagerty, D.T. and Hagerty, H.G. (2005) 'India's Foreign Relations', in D.T. Hagerty (Ed.) *South Asia in World Politics*, Lanham, MD: Rowman and Littlefield Publishers.

Hardgrave Jr., R.L. (1998) 'The Representation of Sati: Four Eighteenth Century Etchings by Baltazard Solvyns', *Bengal Past and Present* 117: 57–80. Retrieved from: www.laits.utexas.edu/solvyns-project/Satiart. rft.html.

Hardgrave Jr., R.L. and Kochanek, S.A. (2000) *India: Government and Politics in a Developing Nation*, Austin, TX: Harcourt College Publishers.

Harris, G. (2015) 'Holding Your Breath in India', *New York Times*. Retrieved from: www.nytimes.com/2015/05/31/opinion/sunday/holding-your-breath-in-india.html.

Harrison, S. (1960) *India: The Most Dangerous Decades*, Princeton, NJ: Princeton University Press.

Harriss, J. (2010) 'Political Change, Political Structure, and the Indian State Since Independence', in P. R. Brass (Ed.) *Routledge Handbook of South Asian Politics*, London: Routledge.

Hathaway R. (2003) 'The US-India Courtship: From Clinton to Bush', in S. Ganguly (Ed.) *India as an Emerging Power*, London: Fran Cass.

Hunter, W.W. (1966) *The Indian Empire: Its People, History, and Products*, New York: AMS Press.

Huntington, S. (1968) *Political Order in Changing Societies*, New Haven: Yale University Press.

Hurwitz, H.M. (1964) 'Yeats and Tagore', *Comparative Literature* 16(1). Retrieved from: www.jstor.org/stable/1769883?seq=1#page_scan_tab_contents.

Hymans, J.E.C. (2009) 'India's Soft Power and Vulnerability', *India Review* 8(3): 234–265.

India-US Relations: Promoting Synergy (2003) Report of an Independent Core Group, New Delhi: Institute of Peace and Conflict Studies.

Iyer, P.V. (2016) 'Bank Insecurities', *Indian Express*, February 9. Retrieved from: http://indianexpress.com/article/opinion/columns/rbi-bad-debts-psb-npabank-insecurities/.

Kanjilal, T. (2000) *Indian Americans: Participation in the American Domestic Political Process*, Calcutta: A. Kanjilal.

Kaye, C.R., Nye Jr., J.S. and Ayres, A. (2015) 'Working With a Rising India: A Joint Venture for the New Century', *Independent Task Force Report No. 73*. New York: Council on Foreign Relations. [Cited as CFR Report No. 73, 2015.]

Khan, N. (2012) quoted in "Bollywood's Expanding Reach," BBC. Retrieved from: www.bbc.com/news/world-asia-india-17920845.

Khanna, T. (2007) *Billions of Entrepreneurs: How China and India are Reshaping Their Futures – And Yours*, Boston, MA: Harvard Business School Press.

Khilnani, S. (1999) *The Idea of India*, New York: Farrar, Straus, and Giroux.

Kilby, P. (2011) *NGOs in India: The Challenges of Women's Empowerment and Accountability*, London and New York: Routledge.

Kohli. A. (Ed.) (1988) *India's Democracy: An Analysis of Changing State-Society Relations*, Princeton, NJ: Princeton University Press.

Kohli. A. (1990) *Democracy and Dissent: India's Growing Crisis of Governability*, Cambridge, UK: Cambridge University Press.

Kohli, A. (2004) *State-Directed Development: Political Power and Industrialization in the Global Periphery*, Cambridge, UK: Cambridge University Press.

Kohli, A. (2006) 'Politics of Economic Growth in India, 1980–2005: Part I: The 1980's', *Economic and Political Weekly* 41(13): 1251–1259. Retrieved from: www.jstor.org/stable/4418028.

Kohli, A. and Singh, P. (Ed.) (2013) *Routledge Handbook of Indian Politics*, London and New York: Routledge.

Kothari, R. (1964) 'The Congress System in India', *Asian Survey* 4(12): 1161–1173. Retrieved from: http://as.ucpress.edu/content/4/12/1161.

Kothari, R. (1967) 'India's Political Transition', *Economic and Political Weekly* 2(33/35): 1489–1497. Retrieved from: www.jstor.org/stable/24477855.

Lamb, B.P. (1975) *India: A World in Transition*, New York: Praeger.

Lipset, S.M. (1994) 'The Social Requisites of Democracy Revisited: 1993 Presidential Address', *American Sociological Review* 59(1): 1–22. Retrieved from: ProQuest Central.

Lorenzen, M. and Taube, F.A. (2008) 'Breakout From Bollywood? The Roles of Social Networks and Regulation in the Evolution of Indian Film Industry', *Journal of International Management* 14: 286–299.

Luce, E. (2007) *In Spite of the Gods: The Strange Rise of Modern India*, New York: Doubleday.

Majumdar, R.C., Raychaudhuri, H.C. and Datta, K. (1978) *An Advanced History of India*, New Delhi: Palgrave Macmillan.

Malik, J.M. (1995) 'China-India Relations in the Post-Soviet Era: The Continuing Rivalry', *The China Quarterly* No. 142: 317–355. Retrieved from: www.jstor.org/stable/655419.

Mani, L. (1986) 'Production of an Official Discourse on "Sati" in Early Nineteenth Century Bengal', *Economic and Political Weekly* 21(17): WS32–WS40. Retrieved from: www.jstor.org/stable/4375595.

Manor, J. (1988) 'Parties and Party System', in A. Kohli (Ed.) *India's Democracy: An Analysis of Changing State-Society Relations*, Princeton, NJ: Princeton University Press.

Mansingh, S. (2006) *Historical Dictionary of India*, Lanham, MD: Scarecrow Press Inc., a subsidiary of Rowman Littlefield.

Mehta, P.B. (2003) *The Burden of Democracy*, New Delhi: Penguin Books.

Mitra, S.K. and Schottli, J. (2007) 'The New Dynamics of Indian Foreign Policy and Its Ambiguities', *Irish Studies in International Affairs* 18: 19–34.

Morgenthau, H.J. (1973) [1948] *Politics Among Nations: The Struggle for Power and Peace*, New York: Alfred A. Knopf.

Morris-Jones, W.H. (1966) 'Dominance and Dissent', *Government and Opposition: A Quarterly of Comparative Politics*, March, 451–466.

Moore, B. (1966) *Social Origins of Dictatorship and Democracy*, Boston: Beacon Press.

Mullen, R. (2016) 'Panchayati Raj Institutions', in A. Kohli and P. Singh (Ed.) *Routledge Handbook of Indian Politics*, London and New York: Routledge.

Nagaraj, R. (2016) 'India's Economic Development', in A. Kohli and P. Singh (Ed.) *Routledge Handbook of Indian Politics*, London and New York: Routledge.

Naipaul, V.S. (1990) *India: A Million Mutinies Now*, New York: Viking.

Narayana Murthy, N.R. (2009) *A Better India: A Better World*, New Delhi: Allen Lane/Penguin Books.

Nayyar, D. (1998) 'Economic Development and Political Democracy: Interaction of Economics and Politics in Independent India', *Economic and Political Weekly* 33(49) (December 5–11). Retrieved from: www.jstor.org/stable/4407443.

Nehru, J. (1947) Speech delivered in the Constituent Assembly, New Delhi, August 14, 1947, on the eve of the attainment of Independence. Retrieved from: www.wwnorton.com/college/english/nael/20century/topic_1/jaw nehru.htm.

Nehru, J. (2004) [1946] *The Discovery of India*, New Delhi: Viking/Penguin.

Norton, J.H.K. (2005) *India and South Asia*, Dubuke, IA: McGraw-Hill/Dushkin.

Nye Jr., J.S. (1990) *Bound to Lead: The Changing Nature of American Power*, New York: Basic Books.

Nye, Jr. J.S. (2004) *Soft Power: The Means to Success in World Politics*, New York: Public Affairs.

Oberst, R.C., Malik, Y.K., Kennedy, C.H., Kapur, A., Lawoti, M., Rahman, S. and Ahmad, A. (2014) *Government and Politics in South Asia*, Boulder: Westview Press.

Palkhivala, N.A. (1981) *India's Priceless Heritage*, Bombay: Bharatiya Vidya Bhavan.

Palshikar, S. (2016) 'Regional and State Parties', in A. Kohli and P. Singh (Ed.) *Routledge Handbook of Indian Politics*, London: Routledge.

Panagariya, A. (2008) *India: The Emerging Giant*, New York: Oxford University Press.

Pant, H.V. (2010) 'India's Challenge in Afghanistan: With Power Comes Responsibility', *Contemporary Readings in Law and Social Justice* 2(1): 36–67.

Parthasarathy, G. (2004) 'India-Pakistan Relations: Ways Forward', in R. Thakur and O. Wiggen (Eds.) *South Asia in the World: Problem Solving Perspectives on Security, Sustainable Development, and Good Governance*, Tokyo: United Nations University Press.

Patel, I. (1998) 'The Contemporary Women's Movement and Women's Education in India', *International Review of Education* 44(2–3): 155-175.

Patnaik, P. (1979) 'Industrial Development in India Since Independence', *Social Scientist* 7(11): 3–19.

Ram, A.N. (2002) 'India and the European Union in the New Millennium', in R.K. Jain (Ed.) *India and the European Union in the 21st Century*, New Delhi: Radiant.

Rehman, G. (2012), 'India Worst G20 Country for Women', Trustlaw survey report, November 30. Retrieved from: www.trustwomenconf.com/news/i/?id=7952bd09-c89a-4e28-8864-9eebdf76e7d0. Full Poll Report, "India Advances but Many Women Are Still Trapped in Dark Ages". Retrieved from: http://news.trust.org//spotlight/G20-Countries-the-worst-and-best-for-women/.

Rice, C. (2000) 'Promoting the National Interest', *Foreign Affairs* 79(1): 45–62.

Rudolph, L.I. and Rudolph, S.H. (1987) *In Pursuit of Lakshmi: The Political Economy of the Indian State*, Chicago: University of Chicago Press.

Rushdie, S. (2006) [1981] *Midnight's Children*, New York: Random House.

Samant, S. (2005) 'Appropriating Bombay Cinema: Why the Western World Gets Bollywood So Wrong', Metro, Winter, cited in A. Athique (2008) 'The "Crossover" Audience: Mediated Multiculturalism and the Indian Film', *Continuum: Journal of Media and Cultural Studies* 22(3): 299–311.

Schaffer, T.C. and Schaffer, H.B. (2016) *India at the Global High Table: The Quest for Regional Primacy and Strategic Autonomy*, Washington, DC: Brookings Institution Press.

Schumpeter, J. (1950) *Capitalism, Socialism, and Democracy*, New York: Harper and Row, cited in S.M. Lipset (1994) 'The Social Requisites of Democracy Revisited: 1993 Presidential Address', *American Sociological Review* 59(1): 1–22.

Sen, A. (1999) 'Democracy as a Universal Value', *Journal of Democracy* 10(3): 3–17.

Sen, A.K. (1990) 'More Than 100 Million Women Are Missing', *New York Review of Books*, December 20. Retrieved from: www.nybooks.com/articles/1990/12/20/more-than-100-million-women-are-missing/.

Sen, S. (2000) 'Toward a Feminist Politics? The Hindu Women's Movement in Historical Perspective', *Policy Research Report on Gender and Development, Working Paper Series No. 9*. Washington, DC: The World Bank.

Sen, A. (2005) *The Argumentative Indian*, New York: Farrar, Straus and Giroux.

Sen, A. (2007) 'Imperial Illusions', *The New Republic*, December 31. Retrieved from: https://newrepublic.com/article/61784/imperial-illusions.

Shah, G. (2001) 'Dalit Politics: Has It Reached an Impasse?', in N.G. Jayal and S. Pai (Ed.) *Democratic Governance in India: Challenges of Poverty, Development, and Identity*, New Delhi: Sage.

Sharma, C.K. (2011) 'A Discursive Dominance Theory of Economic Reform Sustainability: The Case of India', *India Review* 1(2): 126-184.

Sharma, S. (2003) 'Indian Politics', in S. Ganguly and N. DeVota (Ed.) *Understanding Contemporary India*, Boulder, CO: Lynne Rienner.

Sikri, R. (2009) 'India's "Look East" Policy', *Asia-Pacific Review* 16(1): 131–145.

Singh, R.S.V. (2015) 'Muslim Population Growth Slows', *The Hindu* [Census 2011, Religion Data], August 25. Retrieved from: www.thehindu.com/news/national/census-2011-data-on-population-by-religious-communities/article7579161.ece.

Singhal, D.P. [1972] (1993) *India and the World Civilization*, Calcutta: Rupa.

Sridharan, E. (2003) 'Coalitions and Party Strategies in India's Parliamentary Federation', *The Journal of Federalism* 33(4): 135–142.

Srinivas, M.N. (1966) *Social Change in Modern India*, Berkeley and Los Angeles: University of California Press.

Tagore, R. (1919), Public letter to Lord Chelmsford, Viceroy of India, published by *The Statesman (June 3, 1919)*, and in the *Modern Review (July 1919)*. Retrieved from: www.indiaofthepast.org/contribute-memories/read-contributions/major-events-pre-1950/320-tagore-and-the-jallianwala-bagh-massacre-1919.

Tagore, R. (2013) *Gitanjali*, Kolkata: Sahitya Samsad.

Tellis, A. (2001) *India's Emerging Nuclear Posture: Between Recessed Deterrent and Ready Arsenal*, Santa Monica, CA: RAND.

Thakur, R. (1995) *The Government and Politics of India*, New York: St. Martin's Press.

Thapar, R. (2013) 'The Secular Mode for India', *Social Scientist* 41(11–12): 3–10. Retrieved from: www.jstor.org/stable/23610452.

Tharoor, S. (2008) "India's Soft Power", *India International Center Quarterly* 35(1): 32–45.

Tharoor, S. (2016) *An Era of Darkness: The British Empire in India*, New Delhi: Aleph.

Tummala, K.K. (2004) 'The 2004 General Election in India and Its After-math', *Asian Journal of Political Science* 12(2): 31–58. Retrieved from: *Political Science Complete*, EBSCO*host*.

Varshney, A. (2003) *Ethnic Conflict and Civic Life: Hindus and Muslim in India*, New Haven: Yale University Press.

Varshney, A. (2007) 'India's Democratic Challenge', *Foreign Affairs*, March/April. Retrieved from: www.foreignaffairs.com/articles/india/2007-03-01/indias-democratic-challenge.

Waltz, K.N. (1959) *Man, the State and War*, New York: Columbia University Press.

Waltz, K.N. (1979) *Theory of International Politics*, New York: McGraw-Hill.

Weiner, M. (1977) 'The 1977 Parliamentary Elections in India', *Asian Survey* 17(7): 619–626.

Wilkinson, S. I. (2004) *Votes and Violence: Ethnic Riots in India*, New York: Cambridge University Press.

Wirsing, R.G. (1998) *India, Pakistan, and the Kashmir Dispute*, New York: St. Martin's Press.

Wolpert, S. (1991) *India*, Berkeley, CA: University of California Press.

Web Sites and Data Sources:

Andharia, J. (2008) 'The Dalit Women's Movement in India; The Dalit Mahila Samiti', in S. Batliwala (Ed.) *Changing Their World*. Retrieved from AIWD website: www.awid.org/sites/default/files/atoms/files/changing_their_world_-_dalit_womens_movement_in_india.pdf.

Census Data India (2001) *Religion*. Retrieved from: http://censusindia.gov.in/Census_And_You/religion.aspx.

Census Data India (2001) *Language*. Retrieved from: http://censusindia.gov.in/Census_And_You/religion.aspx.

Census Data India (2011) *Religion*. Retrieved from: www.census2011.co.in/religion.php.

Census Data India (2011) *Provisional Population Totals*. Retrieved from: www.censusofindia.gov.in/2011-prov_results_paper1_india.html.

Chandayan School of Music, New York. Retrieved from: http://tabla.org/.

The Constitution of India. Retrieved from: https://india.gov.in/my-government/constitution-india.

Right to Education Act, article in *The Hindu*. Retrieved from: www.thehindu.com/news/national/education-is-a-fundamental-right-now/article337111.ece.

Election Commission of India, Full Statistical Reports. Retrieved from: http://eci.nic.in/eci_main1/ElectionStatistics.aspx.

Election Data from Interparliamentary Union. Retrieved from: www.ipu.org/parline-e/reports/2145_arc.htm.

Election Results for 2014. Retrieved from: http://indiatoday.intoday.in/elections/2014/alliance/nda.html.

India Today – for 1996 election results; Subramaniam, A. (1996). *India Today, Walking a Tightrope*, June 15. Retrieved from: http://indiatoday.intoday.in/story/bjp-govt-falls-president-summons-united-front-leader-devegowda-to-form-new-govt/1/281325.html.

International Monetary Fund (IMF) Working Paper (2015) Retrieved from: www.imf.org/external/pubs/ft/wp/2015/wp1555.pdf.

Jawaharlal Nehru's Speech delivered in the Constituent Assembly, New Delhi, August 14, 1947, on the eve of the attainment of Independence. Retrieved from:www.wwnorton.com/college/english/nael/20century/topic_1/jawnehru.htm.

Kalamandir Dance School and Company, New Jersey and New York. Retrieved from: www.kalamandirdanceco.com/?page_id=370; www.brindaguha.com/#!kalamandir/c1o5m.

Mapping Militant Groups. Retrieved from: https://web.stanford.edu/group/mappingmilitants/cgi-bin/groups/view/95.

Millennium Development Goals (2015) *India: Country Report*, Government of India, New Delhi: Social Statistics Division, Ministry of Statistics and Programme Implementation, [Cited in this volume as India MDG Report 2015]. Retrieved from: http://mospi.nic.in/sites/default/files/publication_reports/mdg_2july15_1.pdf.

Modi, N. (2016) 'Speech at US House of Congress', *Indian Express*. Retrieved from: http://indianexpress.com/article/india/india-news-india/prime-minister-narendra-modi-us-congress-speech-2842046/.

'Namami Gange' Project Launch (2016) *The Economic Times*, July 6. Retrieved from: http://economictimes.indiatimes.com/articleshow/53080510.cms?utm_source=contentofinterest&utm_medium=text&utm_campaign=cppst.

National Crimes Records Bureau, India (2014) *Crimes Against Women, Chapter 5*. New Delhi: National Crime Records Bureau, Ministry of Home Affairs. Retrieved from: http://ncrb.nic.in/StatPublications/CII/CII2014/chapters/Chapter%205.pdf.

National Planning Commission Data on Economic Growth in India – At a Glance. Retrieved from: http://planningcommission.nic.in/data/datatable/data_2312/DatabookDec2014%2018.pdf.

New York Times, January 31, 2016. Retrieved from: www.nytimes.com/2016/01/31/world/asia/indian-women-labor-work-force.html.

News Report Fuel Fire Online Sale. Retrieved from: www.cbsnews.com/news/why-cow-dung-patties-are-selling-like-hot-cakes-online-in-india/.

Nritya Creations Academy of Dance, New Jersey. Retrieved from: https://nrityacreations.com/.

Pratibha Patil Biography. Retrieved from: www.britannica.com/biography/Pratibha-Patil.

Prime Minister Modi and Sharif Visit (2015) *The New York Times*. Retrieved from: www.nytimes.com/2015/12/26/world/asia/narendra-modi-nawaz-sharif-india-pakistan.html?_r=0.

Rainbow Program, Loreto Day School, Sealdah, and a human rights education model. Retrieved from: www.hurights.or.jp/archives/human_rights_edu cation_in_asian_schools/section2/2005/03/human-rights-education-in-school-loreto-sealdah.html.

'Sati' – Notes and Information, National Archives, UK. Retrieved from: (www.nationalarchives.gov.uk/education/empire/usefulnotes/g2cs4s1u.htm.

Trustlaw Report on Crimes Against Women in India (2013) Retrieved from: http://news.trust.org/item/20130423132636-8whug/?source=spotlight.

United Nations Economic and Social Commission for Asia and the Pacific (ESCAP) (2015) *India and the MDGs: Towards a Sustainable Future for All*, on behalf of the United Nations Country Team-India, New York: United Nations. Cited as ESCAP Report (2015). Retrieved from: http://in.one.un.org/img/uploads/India_and_the_MDGs.pdf.

UN Women, data on Violence Against Women. Retrieved from: www.unwomen.org/en/what-we-do/ending-violence-against-women/facts-and-figures.

Wall Street Journal (India) Blog. Retrieved from: http://blogs.wsj.com/indiarealtime/2014/03/02/the-right-to-inherit-isnt-working-for-indian-women-says-u-n-study/.

World Bank Data (World Development Indicators) on Rural Population in India. Retrieved from:http://data.worldbank.org/indicator/SP.RUR.TOTL.ZS?locations=IN.

World Bank (2014), #ACS7935, *India – Women, Work and employment*. Washington, DC: World Bank Group: 78. Retrieved from: http://documents.worldbank.org/curated/en/753861468044063804/India-Women-work-and-employment.

INDEX